SEXUAL EXCITEMENT
Dynamics of Erotic Life

Also by the Author

Sex and Gender, Volume I: *On the Development of Masculinity and Femininity*
Splitting: *A Case of Female Masculinity*
Sex and Gender, Volume II: *The Transsexual Experiment*
Perversion: *The Erotic Form of Hatred*

SEXUAL

EXCITEMENT

Dynamics of Erotic Life

Robert J. Stoller, M.D.

PANTHEON BOOKS
New York

All rights reserved under International and Pan-American Copyright Con-
ventions. Published in the United States by Pantheon Books, a division of
Random House, Inc., New York, and simultaneously in Canada by Random
House of Canada Limited, Toronto.

Library of Congress Cataloging in Publication Data

Stoller, Robert J.
  Sexual excitement.

  Includes index.
  1. Sex (Psychology) 2. Hostility (Psychology)
3. Women—Sexual behavior. 4. Sex symbolism. I. Title.
BF692.S79   155.3′1   78–20426
ISBN 0–394–49778–3

Since this copyright page cannot accommodate all acknowledgments, they
are to be found on the following pages.

Manufactured in the United States of America

First Edition

I wish to acknowledge and thank the following for permission to use portions of my previously published material:

The American Medical Association: For "Sexual Excitement," by Robert J. Stoller, M.D., from *Archives of General Psychiatry* 33 (1976) 899–909. Copyright © 1970 by the American Medical Association.

The American Psychoanalytic Association: For "Primary Femininity," by Robert J. Stoller, M.D., from *Journal of the American Psychoanalytic Association* 24 (1976): 59–78. Copyright © 1976 by the American Psychoanalytic Association.

"Femininity in Females," by Robert J. Stoller, M.D., in *Women in Context: Development and Stresses,* ed. M. Horner, M. Kirkpatrick, et al. (New York: Plenum Publishing Corporation, in press).

Grateful acknowledgment is also made to the following for permission to reprint previously published material:

Basic Books, Inc., Publishers: Excerpts from "Human Sexuality: Research and Treatment Frontiers" by Richard Green, in *The American Handbook of Psychiatry,* 2nd ed., vol. 6, ed. Sylvano Arieti. Copyright © 1975 by Basic Books, Inc.

Basic Books, Inc., Publishers, and Routledge & Kegan Paul Ltd.: Excerpts from *An Object-Relations Theory of the Personality* by W. R. D. Fairbairn. Copyright 1952 by William Ronald Dodds Fairbairn.

Farrar, Straus & Giroux, Inc.: Excerpts from *Masochism in Modern Man,* by Theodor Reik. Copyright 1941 by Theodor Reik. Renewal Copyright © 1969 by Theodor Reik, Margaret H. Beigel and Gertrud M. Kurth.

Heinz Lichtenstein, M.D.: Excerpts from "Identity and Sexuality," *Journal of the American Psychoanalytic Association* 9 (1961): 179–260.

The Menninger Foundation: Excerpt from "On Moods and Introjects" by R. R. Greenson, *Bulletin of the Menninger Clinic* 18 (1954): 10. Copyright 1954, The Menninger Foundation. Excerpt from "A Short History of the British School of Object Relations and Ego Psychology" by A. M. Mendez and H. J. Fine, *Bulletin of the Menninger Clinic* 40 (1976): 358. Copyright © 1976, The Menninger Foundation. Excerpt from "What Splits in 'Splitting'?" by P. W. Pruyser, *Bulletin of the Menninger Clinic* 39 (1975): 19–19. Copyright © 1975, The Menninger Foundation.

The New Yorker: Quotation from Marcel Duchamp from the article "Not Seen and/or Less Seen" by Calvin Tomkins, *The New Yorker,* February 6, 1965.

W. W. Norton & Co., Inc., and The Hogarth Press Ltd.: Excerpts from *The Language of Psychoanalysis* by J. LaPlanche and J.-B. Pontalis, trans. by Donald Nicolson-Smith, 1974.

Philosophical Library, Inc.: Excerpts from *Being and Nothingness* by Jean-Paul Sartre. Copyright © 1956 by the Philosophical Library, Inc.

Psychoanalytic Quarterly: Excerpts from "An Unusual Fantasy in a Twin with an Inquiry into the Nature of Fantasy" by E. D. Joseph, *Psychoanalytic Quarterly,* 28 (1959): 189–90.

Simon & Schuster: Excerpts from *My Secret Garden* by Nancy Friday (New York: Trident Press). Copyright © 1973 by Nancy Friday.

Contents

Acknowledgments

Drs. M. F. Basch, K. M. Colby, and W. W. Meissner have generously offered their ideas concerning fundamental problems of psychoanalytic theory and then allowed me to publish them herein. In addition, Dr. Colby has, for untold hours and with benign patience, enthusiasm, humor, and erudition, guided me into the problems and nonanalytic literature concerning the nature and function of consciousness, thinking, motives, intention, and awareness. I would never otherwise have advanced so effectively to the core of my confusion on these issues, or been as alerted also to seeing that confusion in the center of most psychoanalytic thought.

As before, Jean Strouse, with firm intelligence and kindness, has led my writing to greater clarity and preciseness and cooled down some of the extravagances.

Finally, once again I express my debt and gratitude to my secretary, Thelma Guffan, for defending the space in which I work.

Introduction

This is a study of sexual excitement. It is the fifth book—perhaps more accurately, the fifth chapter in one work—on masculinity and femininity (gender identity), carrying forward ideas examined in my last book, *Perversion*. As many have noted since Freud said it decades ago, it is so difficult to draw a line between excitement one can call "perverse" and normal excitement that the word "normal" loses definition. The woman to be described in these pages exemplifies that observation, for her life has not been one of disorder and pathology nor her sexual experiences outside the range expected in our society. Only her fantasy life sounds odd, and even that impression weakens in the light of the kinds of daydreams in which most people indulge. This is not to say she is not unique or was not unhappy. She certainly had plenty of experience with anxiety and sadness; and since she caused most of it herself, she was a good candidate for analysis.

One day when she was well into her treatment, she mentioned an erotic daydream in which she was being raped by a horse while a group of silent men watched, the performance controlled by a sadistic Director. I gradually learned that this was by far the dominant scenario for her sexual excitement; by the end of our work together, we knew rather well when and how it was created. Her analysis tests an idea: she condensed into a favorite script the story of her erotic life. This led to a broader hypothesis, laid out long ago by Freud,[1] that people in general have a paradigmatic erotic scenario—played in a daydream, or in choice of pornography, or in object choice, or simply in actions (such as styles of intercourse)—the understanding of which will enable us to understand the person. I shall try to show that the function of daydreams is to state a problem that has been disguised and then to solve it, the problem and the solution being the poles between which excitement flows.

A task necessary for the success of her treatment and for understanding her erotism was to find why, out of all the stories she could have used, she invented this one; why did this plot, and not others, excite her? And since we are trying to understand sexual excitement better, we can also ask why her fantasy would not suit others as it did her.

In this book, I shall tease out, from the immeasurable tangle that makes up an analysis, the theme of her sexual excitement. I shall try to show how her prototypic erotic daydream was invented and rewritten until it took on the form necessary for her adult sexual life. I shall also describe how the analytic process dissolved the fantasy by softening the demands that underlay it.

Masculinity and femininity make a roomy subject; one can ramble therein for decades, doing research without suffering the claustrophobia that leads to careful experiments, proper statistics, and other demands of a scientific conscience. For a while, my focus was on people with chromosomal, hormonal, and anatomic abnormalities of maleness and femaleness. Then came a stage of seeing as many people as possible with any sort of gender disorder, often without biologic defect. Of course, one cannot just observe patients as if one's office were a museum; I become involved with and then treat them and their families. At that point, fascinating syndromes turn into people with motivations; the biologist contracts.

But studying adults has its limitations, even with psychoanalysis. Because the adult patient, as any analyst knows, points to childhood, I began to look more and more at children and their families. Preferring to use analysis (though I believe other therapies are effective), and having no great skill in dealing with other people's children, nowadays when studying gender disorders I treat one of the parents while colleagues treat the child and, if possible, the other parent.

Some patients were perverse. However, I was not interested in perversions per se but only in aberrations that illuminated gender identity issues. Still, one can work for just so long with perverse people before beginning to wonder about the structure of perversions.

In brief, I found that hostility—the urge to harm one's sexual object —was a central dynamic in the sexual excitement I called "perverse." There is not much challenge in looking for hostility—it is so blatant— in some of the perversions, such as sadomasochism, so I tried to test the hypothesis more vigorously with cases in which hostility was not at the surface. In the perversion called exhibitionism, for example, you will find, if you get to talk with an exhibitionist, that his purpose in displaying his genitals is not to seduce a woman into making love with him but rather to shock her. If she is upset—is embarrassed, becomes angry, runs away—and especially if she calls the police, he has, he feels, absolute proof that his genitals are important. When you learn that he is likely to exhibit himself following a humiliation earlier in the day, you will be alert to the hostile components he experiences in his excitement. For him, this sexual act serves as a kind of rape—a forced intrusion (at least, that is how he fantasizes it) into the woman's sensibilities and delicacy. If he cannot believe that he has harmed her, the act has failed for him. (He is mortified by the woman who is amused, not shocked, at his show.) Therefore, we find that the exhibitionist displays himself to strange women, not to his wife, who could hardly feel assaulted by a view so ordinary. To show his wife his genitals would be to risk further humiliation, for he knows she would never respond dramatically to the sight, with outrage or a sense of being invaded.

His idea—his fantasy—of what is going on includes, then, the following features. He has done something hostile to a woman; he has been the active force, not the passive victim as he was earlier in the day when someone humiliated him. He has converted this trauma to a triumph, capped by his success in becoming sexually excited. In choosing a stranger as the object of his performance, he has protected himself from experiencing her as fully human. In other words, he has reduced her to a fetish. This idea that he is powerful, a dominating male who causes fear as he subdues a woman by the mere sight of his genitals, is, then, an illusion he has brought into the real world. He seems to be running great risks: he may be caught and arrested, his family and job put in jeopardy. But the true danger that perversion is to protect him from—that he is insignificant, unmanly—is not out there on the street but within him and therefore inescapable. It is so fundamental a threat that he is willing to run the lesser risk, that of being caught.

The search for the dynamics of perversion occupied me for a while. When I was no longer sure who was perverse and who not, that truism led me to study sexual excitement—not just in the perverse, but sexual excitement in general. And so this book, a main purpose of which is to show that the same factors, though in differing degrees and with different scripts, are present in excitements labeled perverse and in those considered normal.

Some of my thoughts on the dynamics of excitement started years ago (before I shifted from an ordinary analytic practice to one primarily involved with gender disorders), especially with the analysis of the woman—Belle—on whom this book is focused. In the years since her analysis ended, my ideas have become clearer. They are tentative and need testing, especially by other analyses, but they are, I hope, a useful start. A weakness in the development of these ideas is my leaving latent the theme of affection, tenderness, and love. Instead, perhaps blinded by the obvious, I have stressed the role of hostility in those people (most people, I think) who can become excited only if they have wounded—crippled—their capacity to love. What might have been—the ability to be intimate, friendly, generous, steadfast, and tender, and yet passionate

—is not considered herein. Still, my description makes sense only if we know we are considering an aberration: too many people have perverted their erotism.

Please concentrate on this; Genet has it right:

> Though it was at my heart's bidding that I chose the universe wherein I delight, I have at least the power of finding in it the many meanings I wish to find: *there is a close relationship between flowers and convicts.* The fragility and delicacy of the former are of the same nature as the brutal insensitivity of the latter. (My excitement is the oscillation from one to the other.) Should I have to portray a convict—or a criminal— I shall so bedeck him with flowers that, as he disappears beneath them, he will himself become a flower, a gigantic and new one. Toward what is known as evil, I lovingly pursued an adventure which led me to prison.[2]

Most of us, most of the time, feel of one piece. We do not notice the seams, though artists and analysts—by nature and profession—are more alert than many others (except, perhaps, psychotics) to the fact that the whole cloth is nonetheless made up of well-joined parts. Although some speak of ego, id, and superego, of inner objects, or of object representations, I want to underline what analysts since Freud and Melanie Klein have endlessly shown: that our mental life is experienced in the form of fantasies. These fantasies are present as scripts —stories—whose content and function can be determined. And I want to emphasize that what we call thinking or experiencing or knowing, whether it be conscious, preconscious, or unconscious, is a tightly compacted but nonetheless separable—analyzable—weave of fantasies. What we consciously think or feel is actually the algebraic summing of many simultaneous fantasies.

This position puts me on the side of those theorists who feel that psychoanalysis deals with meaning, not energy, and who insist that psychic energy and its resultant, psychic structure, are only metaphors, that meaning alone is the constant essence of mental function. Sex is not cathexis.

In accordance with this emphasis on meaning, I shall often talk of scripts, scenarios, scenes, daydreams, and fantasies. The connotations of these words overlap,[3] so let me indicate how they will be used. The generic is fantasy, the private meaning we give to each element of mental life. A fantasy can be conscious, preconscious (available to consciousness if desired), or unconscious (out of consciousness and not retrievable just by willing it there).[4] A script or scenario is a story line —a plot—complete with roles assigned to characters and a stream of action. When a script is conscious, it is, if private, either a spontaneous, unwilled emergence or a daydream. If published, the daydream takes such forms as novels, nonfiction, plays, films, music, or paintings. Unconscious scripts can be deciphered by means of psychoanalysis, unearthed from their hiding places in character structure, neurotic symptoms, sexual behavior, posture, clothing—in any behavior.[5,6]

In my analytic practice and writing, I stress, as do all analysts, the recovery of unconscious or subliminal fantasies. But I try also to describe psychic function in ordinary rather than in technical language. The temptation to use the vocabulary of theory is great, because it seems more scientific than everyday speech. It is historically connected to Freud's great discoveries of unconscious thought, intrapsychic conflict, defense, and symptom formation and contrasts with the raucous, exuberant, unscholarly thinking of some who write about scripts and interpersonal transactions. Still, the language and study of scripts can yield knowledge not acquired with our more intellectualized thinking.

In his clinical work, the analyst deals with meaning, but when he wonders where meaning comes from, he considers historical, cultural, economic, parental, and other external sources; conditioning (though he does not call it that) or other related forces that impinge directly to modify the brain and peripheral nervous systems; and physiologic anlagen ("drives," "instincts"). These then take form in meaning: intrapsychic states of information-processing experienced as fantasies. From Freud on, analysts have tried to mesh these four factors into a general theory of psychology; that effort has been the business of metapsychology, but it has so far, I think, had no great success.

And so I have not reviewed the analytic literature on theory concerning the major subjects discussed in this book, such as sadomasochism, exhibitionism, or dissociationism—the belief that consciousness is not unitary, a study that antedates psychoanalysis. To do so would blur the focus on clinical matters. More important, I disagree with the emphasis in analytic theory on using undefined terms (such as "psychic energy") in constructing explanations. I cannot bring myself to such talk as "exhibitionism is the cathexis of the self (self-representation, etc.) with narcissistic libido." That seems such an awkward way to say that in exhibitionism one is strongly concentrated on oneself, hardly a stunning insight even when decked out with "cathexis" (especially because, at the rock bottom of theory, cathexis *is* narcissism). We should not use our analytic vocabulary to cover weaknesses we almost sense in our data or concepts.[7] I prefer to let clinical material be the major voice.

Cautions concerning writing style. First, I try to make myself visible to the reader, both in the way I am as a therapist and as I am when thinking about psychoanalytic theory. This can distract you from the argument and to my idiosyncrasies. I do this, despite the obvious risks, for a research reason. As in my earlier books, I am still concerned about whether psychoanalysis is a science and whether and how one can do psychoanalytic research. Most analysts believe analysis is a science. I do not, so long as one essential is missing that is found in the disciplines accepted by others as sciences: to the extent that our data are accessible to no one else, our conclusions are not subject to confirmation. This does not mean that analysts cannot make discoveries, for scientific method is only one way to do that. But it does mean that the process of confirmation in analysis is ramshackle.

Second, there is no way to calibrate the primary research instrument of psychoanalysis, the analyst, so the audience has no reliable way to judge the accuracy of our work.[8] I worry that we cannot be taken seriously if we do not reveal ourselves more clearly. To do so, however, may lead to messy reporting (and confuse the readers, whose own fantasies may make them feel they are peeking in on forbidden scenes). No one but the analyst can know how much the uncertain process of fixing and editing the data renders this reporting enterprise a fiction. In regard to research, says David Shakow, "Love, cherish and respect the therapist—but for heaven's sake don't trust him."[9] Artists lie to tell the truth, and scientists tell the truth to lie.

The problem of reporting accurately on how one collected one's data as well as the problem of the true form the data took before being subjected to the cosmetics of editing is now acknowledged in the hard sciences. Historians and philosophers of science show us how often great discoveries *preceded* careful data-collecting; how the process of data-collecting can be slanted to guarantee a needed discovery; and how —in really sticky situations—people (Newton, for instance) fake their data. Our only defense against the rascals, including the inspired ones, is persistent application of the scientific method, which strives (as its practitioners sometimes fail to do) for incorruptible techniques of confirmation.

If only we could let the raw data stand free, even on shaky legs. But this throws a strain on the researcher as writer, for publication is a part of research, not an after-product; the moment I think about, let alone write about, what happened, data become opinions. Certainly in psychoanalytic reports, style becomes content.

Third, picturing the readers of this book as being both psychoanalysts and nonanalysts, I need to keep the different backgrounds in mind. At times, therefore, ideas or findings obvious to an analyst will be earnestly discussed rather than taken for granted. On another page, I shall wrestle with a subject that fascinates analysts but may seem esoteric or trivial to others. (Usually, that is dealt with by burying it at the book's end.)

A few words about recording the data: I took shorthand notes (rather than tape-recording) to show the movement of the hour, writing exact quotations only for dreams or remarks by either of us that I thought, for whatever reason, were interesting enough to need literal transcription. These notes were the basis for the longer reports dictated onto tape each day. From these, years later, this study was built. (The manuscript in each draft and proof has been read and corrected by Belle, who has found it an interesting experience now she is no longer a patient.)

Subjective states of sexuality fall into two categories: gender identity and erotic desire. Inside us, the categories are merged, of course. But to ground the argument of this book, I shall separate the two in the first chapters, laying out hypotheses about their origins and dynamics. After a chapter on sexual excitement and another on gender identity, we can turn to the particular, the analysis of Belle, a rather normal woman by the standards of our society, who allowed me to know the script that underlay her sexual excitement.

In this way, I hope to suggest the dimensions of an area of behavior not yet systematically studied: *erotics.*

PART 1
Hypotheses
on Sexuality

1

Sexual Excitement

IT HAS SURPRISED ME recently to find almost no professional literature discussing why a person becomes sexually excited. There are, of course, innumerable studies that have to do with that tantalizingly vague word "sexuality": studies on the biology of reproduction, masculinity and femininity, gender roles, exotic beliefs, mythology, sexuality in the arts, legal issues, civil rights, definitions, diagnoses, aberrations, psychodynamics, changing treatment techniques, contraception, abortion, lifestyles, transsexual operations, free-ranging and experimental animal behavior, *motoro,* pornography, shifts in age of menarche and loss of virginity, masturbatory rates, research methodology, bride prices, exogamy, incest in monkeys and man, transducers, seducers, couvade, genetics, endocrinology, existentialism, and religion. Statistical studies of the external genitals, foreplay, afterplay, accompanying activity, duration, size, speed, distance, metric weight, and nautical miles. Venereal disease, apertures, pregnancy, berdaches, morals, marriage customs, subincision, medical ethics, sexism, racism, feminism, communism, and priapism. Sikkim, Sweden, Polynesia, Melanesia, Micronesia, Indonesia, and all the tribes of Africa and Araby. Buttocks, balls, breasts, blood supplies, nervous supplies, hypothalamic supplies, gross national product, pheromones, implants, plateaus, biting, squeezing, rubbing, swinging. Nude and clothed, here and there, outlets and inlets, large and small, up and down, in and out. But not sexual excitement. Strange.

There is another problem: even the term "sexual excitement" is inexact. "Sexual" has so many uses that we scarcely comprehend even the outer limits of what someone else indicates with the word; does he or she refer to "male" and "female," or "masculinity" and "femininity," or "erotism," or "intercourse," or "sensual, nonerotic pleasure," or "life-force"? Similarly, "excitement" suggests not quite an affect but rather what may color an affect. "Excitement" unmodified by fuller description can indicate a wanted or an unwanted quality. It is a present state that carries within itself a future expectation. But what pleasure is anticipated, what danger awaited; what risks may arise and what hopes of avoiding them are built into one's subliminal awareness? Does "sexual excitement" not refer to the period of anticipation before an act; and to the sensual build-up during an act; and to the genital sensations alone; and to nongenital sensations alone; and also to a total-body erotic involvement? To me, "excitement" implies anticipation in which one alternates with extreme rapidity between expectation of danger and just about equal expectation of avoidance of danger, and in some cases, such as in erotism, of replacing danger with pleasure. And certainly excitement is a mental state, that is, a perceived complex sensation that one senses is the product of fantasy (past experience remembered and reinvented to serve a need).

With customs changing and sex a subject of open discourse, we may turn up practical reasons for a more precise vocabulary; but until now, our language has only perpetuated a blurring of related yet different sensual, emotional states. "Lust" means thick, mindless excitement; "erotism" implies "capacity for" more than "presence of"; "desire," "urge," "appetite," "longing," "craving," "wanting," "coveting," and "need" are a bit vague and can refer to states in which the body's anatomy and physiology are not yet fully engaged; "attraction" is too low-keyed; "voluptuousness" is too round and turgid to fit most circumstances; "lasciviousness" and "prurience" too fancy-dirty; "concupiscence" and "carnality" too biblical; "libido" too vague; "sexy" too cute; "horny" is good but slangy and useful only for an anticipatory state; "hot" is real but too provocative for scientific propriety; "lechery" is too snickering; "passion" or—even more swooning—"ecstasy" too operatic or, like "fervor," "amorousness," and "ardor," too literary; "tumescence" too objective and anatomic; "stimulation" connotes cause more than resultant feelings; "response" is too objective. "Arousal" is close; the new slang expression "turned on" is perhaps even closer. But I only note our awkwardness; I have not invented the indicated vocabulary.

It would help discourse if we could be clearer about this interesting activity. (Considering how appalling existence is for most humans, we in our society are lucky to be able to wring our hands over flawed sexual pleasure.) My concern with preciseness comes, not from love of pedantry, but rather from the hope that we can communicate more clearly and learn more about the nature of these different states of subjective experience. For instance, the excitement of an impotent voyeur is different from that of a fetishistic cross-dresser who gets an erection while fondling women's clothes, or from the trembling, diffuse but intense, nongenital body excitement of a woman daydreaming a sadistic attack. These states differ physiologically, and in the fantasies that accompany them, in the daydreams that for years anticipated them, and in the earlier events in life that for each of these people made an erotic experience out of what is nonerotic for another. But when "sexual excitement" is used for all without also a full description of the subjective experience, not enough is communicated. In fact, most of the time the term unwittingly obscures our understanding of what goes on mentally.

This chapter serves to review my ideas of what mental common denominators, regardless of culture or era, energize sexual excitement —and only sexual excitement. Not gratification; the two are decidedly not the same. And I shall not take up such qualities as beauty, virginity, gracefulness, perfection of physical appearance, conformity to a society's professed ideals of character or anatomy, or other attributes that may be laudable, noble, or saintly but that by no means necessarily induce excitement. In fact, such attributes, when sensed unambivalently as worthy, generally dampen sexual excitement unless one is excited at the idea of sullying them. The epitome of this sad situation is that for most people, just those qualities in another that produce a feeling of love work against being able to lust.

I am unable, from published reports, to simulate a theory of the origins of sexual excitement. Even in the psychoanalytic literature, where there are extended discussions about the origins and dynamics of other affects, no theory of sexual excitement is propounded. It is time to try. The following attempt is at best incomplete; in significant parts it may be wrong. But it can serve as a start, against which to place other data and hypotheses. (In order not to obscure the weaknesses in my argument, I shall not translate the ideas into psychoanalytic language.)

In setting forth this theory, I leave as background two givens: physiologic mechanisms, and the chronic, institutionalized "character structure" of a society as implied in the concept of culture. (The latter, for our present purpose, need be drawn on only when its presence is causing mental activity in an individual.) In other words, this theory attempts only to delineate mental factors at work in the individual. Because these ideas come out of my work of the last twenty or so years, they may be distorted from the start. If this research had begun as a study of sexual excitement, it might have been slanted differently; instead it is the product, across the years, of the two intertwined areas of sexuality I have studied: the development of masculinity and femininity (gender identity), and the dynamics of perversion. As time passed, the first led to the second, and both then brought me to this third: the study of sexual excitement.

My theory is as follows: In the absence of special physiologic factors (such as a sudden androgen increase in either sex), and putting aside the obvious effects that result from direct stimulation of erotic body parts, it is hostility*—the desire, overt or hidden, to harm another person—that generates and enhances sexual excitement. The absence of hostility leads to sexual indifference and boredom. The hostility of erotism is an attempt, repeated over and over, to undo childhood traumas and frustrations that threatened the development of one's masculinity or femininity. The same dynamics, though in different mixes and degrees, are found in almost everyone, those labeled perverse and those not so labeled.

That, baldly, is the theory; the rest of this book will elaborate on these ideas.

I came to these hypotheses as I sought—and failed to find, as many others (including Freud) also had failed—a line on the continuum of sexual behavior that could separate "normal" from "perverse." Looking at the manifestations of sexual excitement or the enticements to it that are accepted by society at large—as revealed in such communications as the entertainment media, advertising, books, jokes and cartoons, newspapers and journals, and pornography for the masses—I felt that either the mechanisms to be described were not restricted to the perversions or that most people are perverse (as others of more cynical bent have long been saying). How you want to put it is your choice; the evidence for either statement is the same.

The following, then, are the mental factors present in perversions that I believe contribute to sexual excitement in general: hostility, mystery, risk, illusion, revenge, reversal of trauma or frustration to triumph, safety factors, and dehumanization (fetishization). And all of these are stitched together into a whole—the surge of sexual excitement —by secrets. (Two unpleasant thoughts: First, when one tabulates the factors that produce sexual excitement, exuberance—pure joyous pleasure—is for most people at the bottom of the list, rarely found outside fiction. Second, I would guess that only in the rare people who can indefinitely contain sexual excitement and love within the same relationship do hostility and secrecy play insignificant parts in producing excitement.)

Excitement—any, not just sexual—is a dialectic, a rapid oscillation

*I prefer the word "hostility" to "power," for it has a crisper connotation of harm and suffering.

between two possibilities (and their affects). One we tell ourselves has a positive, the other a negative outcome: pleasure/pain, relief/trauma, success/failure, danger/safety. Between the two lies risk. The synthesis is the creative product: daydream, pornography, painting, symphony, religious ritual, drama.[1]

Let us take fetishization as the key process in the creation of erotic excitement. We might best begin by calling it *dehumanization;* the fetish stands for a human (not just, as is sometimes said, for a missing penis). A sexually exciting fetish, we know, may be an inanimate object, a living but not human object, a part of a human body (in rare cases even of one's own), an attribute of a human (this is a bit less sure, since we cannot hold an attribute in hand), or even a whole human not perceived as himself or herself but rather as an abstraction, such as a representative of a group rather than a person in his or her own right ("all women are bitches"; "all men are pigs"). The word "dehumanization" does not signify that the human attributes are completely removed, but just that they are reduced, letting the fetish still remind its owner of the original human connection, now repressed. As a result, the same move (like a seesaw) that dehumanizes the human endows the fetish with a human quality.

Why do people do this to those they might love? In the first place, dehumanization is a throwback to the earliest stages of one's development before the world becomes "humanized." The infant, most of us assume (who is to know?), does not at first comprehend a class of objects around it as being humans; only gradually do attributes congeal into the complex abstraction of a separate, whole being who is like itself. When that awareness begins, its development is not arrested by reality but instead expands, especially in childhood fantasy, to include nonhumans: animals, plants, inanimate things. Anthropomorphizing is ubiquitous and, in this form, nonpathologic in small children; that is, such animism occurs without being motivated by intrapsychic pain and the need to resolve conflict.

But this capacity for humanization is not absolute. It varies from time to time in a person's life, and from person to person as well. It is scarcely there in the severely retarded or the autistic, is badly awry in schizoid people or psychopaths, and is as rare in saints as in sinners. But in most of us who develop the capacity to know another as human and similar to ourselves, it is vulnerable to regression. If my theory is right, only those who can perceive people as people are able to be perverse, for that perception, obviously, is needed in order to perform the act of dehumanization. A child, virtually defenseless against those who threaten or actually harm it, can invent fantasies and restore the balance, or even make the attacker suffer in the fantasy what the child has had to suffer in reality. *Revenge.* What purer form can it take than to inflict on one's attacker the same trauma or frustration one has been forced to suffer? The torture of one's object in fantasy becomes even more exquisite if one degrades him or her into nonhumanness or to the status of part-object. In that way, one torments the fantasized victim by letting him or her continue to exist but robbed of human—that is, valuable—qualities (as children believe is done to them when they are traumatized); pure obliteration would not be enough. For a child feels that those who inflict pain on it do so in part to crush one or another of its human attributes.

To fetishize, one must also deal with the excremental. The anatomic closeness of the reproductive and excretory systems, the overlapping of intense sensations between the two, and the tension between dirtiness and cleanliness created by toilet training erotize urination and defecation and give erotics an excremental cast. It is therefore all too easy to deal with a sexual object as if he/she/it were fully or in its sexual parts an eliminatory organ, or were a product to be unconsciously retained or discharged or both at once. Some people do their fetishizing by forming a cleaned-up object; the dirty details of reality are left out of their scripts: pinup girls are airbrushed to remove blemishes; one closes one's eyes to dandruff, a snotty nose, poor taste in underwear, skin lesions, or smells.

On the other hand, some people need the excremental: to use language they consider filthy, to defecate or urinate on or be defecated or urinated on by their partners, to lick or be licked on the anus, to choose people they consider fecal (e.g., black, Jewish, poor, uneducated, prostituted).

The creation of a fetish, then, is made up of several processes (fantasies). (1) A person who has harmed one is to be punished with a similar trauma. (2) The object is stripped of its humanity.* (3) A nonhuman object (inanimate, animal, or part-aspect of a human like a breast or penis) is endowed with the humanness stolen from the person on whom one is to be revenged. In this way the human is dehumanized and the nonhuman humanized. (4) The fetish is chosen because it has some quality that resembles the loved, needed, traumatizing object.

Fetishization, therefore, is an act of cruelty. The completed, complicated mechanism (fantasy) is attached to—"put into"—the (mental representation of the) nonhuman object, upgrading it to a humanoid

---

*This is easier to do with breasts, buttocks, legs, and penises than with faces. We reside in our faces; it takes more work to annihilate the person in the face. But we can judge another's total personality by the shape of her breasts, his muscles, their skin color.

toward which one need not feel hatred. It is now a fetish, while the human who is being punished is consciously no longer so important, not seen fully any more as the person he or she is. Thus, *frustration and trauma are converted to triumph,* and, in fantasy, the victim of childhood is revenged: no more a victim but the erotically successful victor.[2]

A woman patient, for whom, since childhood, fear of humiliation had colored every move she made, said that her finest moment in intercourse is not her orgasm but earlier, just before her partner comes, when she knows that now he can no longer control himself. Late in analysis, she caught for the first time her awareness that she did with her body whatever was needed to guarantee that her lover would always ejaculate prematurely.

A useful way to differentiate acts we call perverse from those we would simply consider sexual is the degree of—the need for—fetishization present. The trouble with fetishizing others is that it dehumanizes oneself. Khan describes this clearly in describing "the pervert":

The pervert himself cannot surrender to the experience and retains a split-off, dissociated manipulative ego-control of the situation. This is both his achievement and failure in the *intimate* situation. It is this failure that supplies the compulsion to repeat the process again and again. The nearest that the pervert can come to experiencing surrender is through visual, tactile and sensory identifications with the other object in the intimate situation in a state of surrender. Hence, though the pervert arranges and motivates the idealization of instinct which the technique of intimacy aims to fulfill, he himself remains outside the experiential climax. Hence, instead of instinctual gratification or object-cathexis, the pervert remains a deprived person whose only satisfaction has been of pleasurable discharge and intensified ego-interest. In this subjectivity the pervert is *un homme manqué.*[3]

The following fantasies, each by a different woman, taken (by turning pages at random; there are dozens more like these) from a book on women's sexual fantasies, exemplify this dehumanization and its utility for vengeful reversal of trauma; men as a class are the fetish. I do not believe these fantasies are exotic, but rather that they are like those of countless women.

I'm very brave and aggressive in my fantasies. In fact, I take the lead. My fantasies are always about young men. . . . I think the reason that I imagine that the man is always fifteen or twenty years younger than I am is that it makes him less frightening to me. In fact, he's always someone who is a virgin, close to it. Somebody who doesn't really know what it—the bedroom, you understand—is all about. So it's up to me to teach him, and nothing he's going to do can surprise or worry me. He's just a boy. . . . Fantasies get worn out; somehow they finally lose their erotic charge. So you have to make up new ones. [A long description follows of how she outplays him in a game of strip poker, teases him into sexual excitement, ties him hand and foot to the bed, and proceeds to work him over.]

Sometimes when I masturbate there is this lovely person, who is, of course, my lover, and he gathers together a bunch of darling gentlemen who want very much to fuck me. . . . seems there are always these guys in my fantasies just dying to get at me. . . .

I imagine a variety of things when I masturbate. Sometimes it's that a man has come to the door selling something and I invite him in. While he stands there displaying his Fuller brushes or whatever, I begin to caress myself. He watches, obviously aroused, and finding it harder and harder to continue his sales spiel. Then I remove my clothes and begin to masturbate, all the while watching his efforts to control himself. He's in a real state, and of course I'm very cool—in one sense, but I'm also getting very worked up. . . . Sometimes I change the plot: I make no attempt to entice or encourage the man. But once in the house, he is unable to withstand my quite formidable charms and he rapes me, right there in the living room. . . .[4]

Though tormenting men is not the only manifest theme in these published daydreams, it is a dominant one. And even with no information on the women who describe these fantasies, the theme of reversing frustration and trauma is easy to see.

What may be the other most popular erotic theme for women in our culture is the masochistic one. Here the triumph in suffering is not manifest (though it can be revealed, as we shall see).

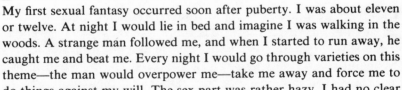

My first sexual fantasy occurred soon after puberty. I was about eleven or twelve. At night I would lie in bed and imagine I was walking in the woods. A strange man followed me, and when I started to run away, he caught me and beat me. Every night I would go through varieties on this theme—the man would overpower me—take me away and force me to do things against my will. The sex part was rather hazy. I had no clear ideas on that at that age. By thinking about this before going to sleep, I could make myself dream about it, too. Later the fantasy changed to me being taken away to the East and sold as a slave. There were an infinite number of possibilities to the story, as I was bought and sold by a number of men in succession. Very occasionally I still fantasize about this. My fantasies obviously fall into the "being on exhibition" category in the humiliation sense rather than one of showing off.[5]

The power struggle is found in men also.

A male patient described what may be a common factor in the excitement of those who like to watch others masturbate. Believing his own masturbation was dirty and a sign of weakness, he experienced his greatest excitement from being allowed to watch a woman become abandoned in her masturbation; it let him briefly feel superior.

Kate Millett, who aptly encapsulated these issues of power as "sexual politics," begins her book with a quotation from Henry Miller that represents the anatomic sloshing about decisive in pornography for many men:

> I would ask her to prepare the bath for me. She would pretend to demur but she would do it just the same. One day, while I was seated in the tub soaping myself, I noticed that she had forgotten the towels. "Ida," I called, "bring me some towels!" She walked into the bathroom and handed me them. She had on a silk bathrobe and a pair of silk hose. As she stooped over the tub to put the towels on the rack her bathrobe slid open. I slid to my knees and buried my head in her muff. It happened so quickly that she didn't have time to rebel or even to pretend to rebel. In a moment I had her in the tub, stockings and all. I slipped the bathrobe off and threw it on the floor. I left the stockings on—it made her more lascivious looking, more the Cranach type. I lay back and pulled her on top of me. She was just like a bitch in heat, biting me all over, panting, gasping, wriggling like a worm on the hook. As we were drying ourselves, she bent over and began nibbling at my prick. I sat on the edge of the tub and she kneeled at my feet gobbling it. After a while I made her stand up, bend over; then I let her have it from the rear. She had a small juicy cunt, which fitted me like a glove. I bit the nape of her neck, the lobes of her ears, the sensitive spot on her shoulder, and as I pulled away I left the mark of my teeth on her beautiful white ass. Not a word spoken.[6]

It would be interesting to hear Ida's version of this exchange.

Probably only an analyst is in a position to get enough information to move below the surface of such daydreams, for one can presume that few people, on first telling, give all the details of an erotic fantasy, much less the motives—conscious or unconscious—for choosing those details. But as treatment progresses and understanding accumulates, some details blurry to the patient's imaginary eye gradually become clearer or the story line changes so that certain elements are emphasized and others drop away.

I get the impression also from popular sex-enlightenment magazines that such fantasies are not extraordinary. (Some people may have an increment of excitement when pornography is decked out in scientific costume.) Although editors may rewrite erotic fantasies sent in by readers and perhaps even invent a few, we can presume that, when doing this, they know their public's mind and that the letters—genuine or not—touch the fantasies of subscribers. So, although the following comes to us from just such a suspect source, the content will not strike most of us as rare:

I have one regular customer—twice a week—who pays me to let him enact a rape. It's the only way he can get it on. Usually the scene goes like this. I am dressed in very sedate clothes, in the way he thinks a librarian looks, tweed skirt, white blouse, slip and "sensible" shoes. My hair is done up in a bun and I wear glasses. I am sitting in my room reading a book when he knocks, and when I answer the door he pretends to be a salesman who I let in. Once inside the door, he pulls out a gun (actually a plastic model) and forces me back into the center of the room near the bed. I plead with him not to kill me and tell him that he can take anything he wants, just not to hurt me.

The more I beg, the more he gets excited, and, in a low voice he tells me to shut up. Then he snatches off my glasses and tells me to let down my hair. I start to sob but slowly, very slowly take out the bobby pins which are holding my hair up.

Finally my hair, which is actually very long, falls down over my face and shoulders while I continue to beg him not to hurt me. "Now, take off your blouse," he says, his voice getting louder. When I refuse he shoves the gun to my face, and I slowly—still crying—unbutton the blouse and take it off. Then the skirt and the slip, each time protesting and each time having him threaten me with his gun.

By this time all I have on is a bra and a garter belt, stockings and shoes. No panties, and he always says, "Ha, I always knew your type played with yourselves in secret." But my only response is to cry and try to hide my body. Then he pushes me back on the bed, and with the gun pointed at the back of my head, he takes off the bra hooks and turns me over. As the bra falls off, I can see that he has a full erection bulging in his pants.

As I slowly take off my clothes, he unzips his fly. I scream, but as my mouth is open, he grabs my head and forces his penis in my mouth and at the same time keeps the gun pointed at my temple. I begin to suck him off, but after a few seconds, he pushes me back on the bed and climbs on. I try to fight him off me, rolling him off, closing my legs, pushing at his face, crying. Gradually, though, he overpowers me, pins my arms down, and forces his way inside. As he begins to move in and out, my expressions of fear and horror change to increasing joy and by the time he comes—never very long—I am pretending to have an orgasm, pressing him closer, thrashing around the bed moaning.

After several times of doing this scene, he told me that he was terrified that he would really rape someone and that doing this with a prostitute was the only way he could reduce the compulsion. I was the only one, he said, that he found could act the part to his own satisfaction.

Since then we've varied the routine. Sometimes I come to the door as a housewife in a peignoir, sometimes as a little girl. Once he even forced me off the street with a knife. That time I was really scared and that was the only time I really did have an orgasm since he never let the knife go the whole time.

And I'm not the only hooker who has johns like this. Several of my friends go through different acts, but all simulate a rape in one way or another. If we weren't around, these guys would just be out there really raping people and maybe even killing women.[7]

Freud points to the importance of sadomasochism, with its components of danger and humiliation, in erotic life in four papers allied to the subject of sexual excitement: "A Special Type of Choice of Object Made by Men,"[8] "On the Universal Tendency to Debasement in the Sphere of Love"[9] "The Taboo of Virginity,"[10] and "A Child Is Being Beaten."[11] In the second of these papers, the title itself indicates how people need debased, inferior love objects. With the word "tendency," he raises the still debated question how frequently this mechanism is present. He seems to feel it is always there: "The curb put upon love by civilization involves a universal tendency to debase sexual objects." He also points up the well-known fact that "an obstacle is required in order to heighten libido; and when natural resistances to satisfaction have been insufficient men have at all times erected conventional ones so as to be able to enjoy love."[12]

Let me add that it is not inevitable, even if "universal," that people debase their sexual objects. To the extent that, in its earliest relationships to its parents, a child feels it is debased, it will, in creating its sexual excitement throughout life, reverse this process of debasement in fantasy so that the sexual objects are now—in disguised or open form —its victims. One of my theses, for which this book is an illustration, is that the exact details of the script underlying the excitement are meant to reproduce and repair the precise traumas and frustrations— debasements—of childhood; and so we can expect to find hidden in the script the history of a person's psychic life.[13]

We can now go on to other mechanisms that I believe help produce sexual excitement, keeping in mind the thesis that the excitement is the proximate result of fantasies—conscious and unconscious—best understood if we look on the process as the unfolding of a scenario written and continually refined throughout one's life. So far I have said that this script is created to undo frustration, trauma, and intrapsychic conflict, thus extending into the ordinary world a central psychoanalytic thesis that these painful experiences are at the root of perversions.

And let me now note without elaboration, but nonetheless as a necessary part of the argument, that data have been collected and theory elaborated by analysts from Freud on to indicate that castration anxiety, penis envy, the fantasy of the phallic woman, and actual body damage contribute to sexual maldevelopment, particularly fetishism.[14] A review of these matters is omitted so that I can focus on how fantasy deals with *hostility*—that which one feels is aimed at oneself and the retaliatory hatred one then directs onto others—to create excitement.

Because of the difference in power, the child cannot defend itself well against those in the real world it perceives as attackers (usually parents) and therefore comforts itself with fantasy, especially with consciously told stories—daydreams. The daydream functions to preserve the sense of self, of existing, as a male or female; to restore the balance of power between child and attacker; and to get revenge. Thus from the start, we are in the midst of interchanges of hostility. (In certain circumstances "hostility" is better rendered as "anger," "rage," "power," "cruelty," "violation," or "hatred," all of which imply desire to cause damage.) But others would not appreciate the selfishness, the ruthlessness, with which they are treated in our daydreams, and our consciences must also be fooled. Secrets, from others and from ourselves, do that job.

One of the reasons sexual excitement has been difficult to study is the *secrecy* that accompanies it. This secrecy functions in two different ways. First, for most people—even the irreligious—sex is sin, and not just because of society's rules but because our consciences know how "bad" these forbidden desires are. So erotic pleasure is preserved by secrets. These are secrets operating between ourselves and the outside world.

Second, and more important for this study, secrecy is built into the sexual scripts, the story lines people use consciously and preconsciously for ensuring their excitement. Secrets in this category operate as barriers between one part of oneself and another part, serving especially to provoke or heighten excitement—not, as in the first case, to protect an already present capacity for excitement.

Perhaps other analysts share my experience that patients seldom fully report the key script—daydream, sexual or otherwise—until well into the analysis, and then only if a deep sense of trust in the analyst has developed. Instead, we get a summary from which are omitted the details that would most reveal what the patient feels is his or her true nature. And so not only are secrets preserved, but the manner in which the secret is preserved is also a secret. The motives may be unconscious and the product of infantile experiences. But whatever the unconscious roots, at the final point of delivery—at the edge of speech—that elusive devil "free will" is at work; one consciously decides not to speak. In other words, we are in the presence of a secret: a piece of information consciously withheld in order that one may gain an advantage (or not lose an advantage, or not suffer a disadvantage).*

What relationship do secrets and secretiveness have to sexual excitement? I have just noted two kinds of secrets related to erotic behavior. The first, the less important for our present purpose, is the need to keep secrets from others. When this is the case, the secret is usually used less to enhance sexual excitement than to keep it safe. The second, close to the heart of excitement, is the game in which we pretend to keep secrets from ourselves. We shall look shortly at the ways in which people create the scripts of daydreams by ignoring what they know—one part of themselves treats the knowledge as if it were a secret that another part must not acknowledge knowing. In these situations, what one knows is not repressed, denied, or otherwise made the object of pressure to take it or keep it in part or in whole out of consciousness.[15] Instead, the tension comes from the illusion of secretiveness, wherein one treats oneself quite knowingly as if one were someone else from whom a secret must be kept. When these uses of secrets are combined, we at times have a third means of enhancing excitement: one carries the secret beyond one's mind and into the real world, where the risk of the secret being discovered can heighten the excitement immensely. An example is the transvestite who puts on women's clothes and goes out in public, frightened but intensely excited. Or: Belle knows from her masturbatory pleasure that she enjoys mild anal stimulation. She wants her lovers to do this, but if they do so knowing it excites her, then she has only intense discomfort; only as long as it is her secret can it be erotic.

When, at a particular moment, a patient is keeping a secret from me, I feel puzzled. That feeling is different from the kind aroused when a

*Even in the more complicated situation when a slip comes out of one's mouth, a secret is present, not a repressed element. But a slip is different from a well-kept secret, which is under full conscious control; with a slip, a part of oneself—conscience—wants the secret revealed (as is also the case with shame). Example: A man, trying to be faithful to his wife while his eyes survey the bosomy depths of the woman with whom he is talking, turns to go, saying, "I think I'll get a breast of flesh air" (R. R. Greenson's anecdote). The mechanism that makes his tongue trip so cleverly may be out of consciousness, but the struggle certainly is not. Example: An employee, ticked off by the boss for a minor piece of irresponsibility, apologizes, adding, "It just was a lack of poor planning." And compare these two ways of dealing with secrets with blocking, wherein access to speech is denied by repression, not conscious will or conscious conflict. With slips and blocks, scripts collide.

resistance is coming from sources unconscious to the patient. In this latter case, my empathy is unimpaired and rouses me to search inside myself to find what is happening in the patient. But when a patient is consciously holding back, the process of communication between us is inharmonious. Then, as an act of will—no longer empathy—I must remember that this sort of puzzlement may signal a secret. With Belle, this experience meant that she was acting out a script she had brought in at the hour's start but would have no pleasure from unless she knew it was a secret; for instance, "I am wearing this blouse because in it I am a sprouting adolescent, sexual and innocent: my doctor will now be a kindly, fatherly initiator of this girl—me—into sex."

Men's fear of femininity—defensive masculinity—is kept a secret but is not wholly unconscious. The tough young man who beats up a homosexual is not without conscious knowledge of his fear that he is not masculine enough. The man who drinks for courage is aware that he feels himself to be weak; the idea is not unconscious. People who need pornography know they are perverse; they are quite conscious of their specific needs when they choose the pornography that excites them and disregard the rest. The process is secretive, not unconscious, though the roots of the excitement are unconscious.[16]

Now let us take up other components of the excitement. First _mystery_, which, though not synonymous with secrecy, has features in common with it.* How is mystery built into the script so as to contribute to excitement? Fashion is a good example, since it is universal in humans. It seems that in all societies, something is done to change the appearance of the nude body, to make it appear less as it is, in order to heighten its appeal. Even in societies where everyone is nude, there are occasions when some body part is disguised. Often coverings, tattoos, scarification, paints, cosmetics, or hair arrangements serve aesthetic but nonerotic functions of religious ritual or taboo. But sometimes these effects are created in order to stir up sexual excitement. If this is true where clothing is not a major part of life, how many more tricks are possible in societies like ours where, whatever other functions fashion may have, clothes may also be designed to produce tantalizing mixtures of hiding and revealing, of disguising, distorting, promising, and refusing? And when these conflicting feelings are present in the sum, the susceptible observer senses that vibration, that oscillation, called excitement.

*Mystery is a product of secrecy. An unknown expands into a mystery when the person mystified believes a Will—God's, Woman's, Nature's, the Universe's, Fate's—has been at work to move the unknown toward divinity. Mystery is a chiller, a thriller that we choose to imagine exists, a dramatization always worth at least one capital letter. Mystery is opera, excitement pumped into mundane ignorance. In this way the frights of infancy are re-experienced with a hysterical veneer: trauma is converted to art.

In sexual relationships, real or imagined, pathologies reciprocate or the business ends; in our society, men's training in forbidden looking meshes with women's knowledge of themselves as people who are to allow what they are to forbid. A woman who is not a patient gives the following story:

> Since childhood, she knew her vocation was to be a nun. The choice was unforced and easily made, and so in her teens she began her training. Although her siblings married and had children, and though she got great pleasure from children, she felt fulfilled in caring for those of others. She would have liked to have children of her own but feels she has not been deprived because, with nephews and nieces and in the nature of her work for the Church, she has gratified her mothering impulses. Her wish to mother was not associated with sexual desire; although she comprehended humanity's sexual excitement, she never once in her life experienced it herself—until a few years ago. At that time, when she was in her forties, her order changed from traditional garb to shorter skirts that revealed her legs. From the first time she put on such a garment to the present, she has been afflicted with persistent, conscious sexual excitement when in public in a short skirt. She smiles ruefully as she describes this and says that at least she now has the benefit of knowing something about suffering and can use her suffering as a gift to God.

In this sort of voyeuristic and exhibitionistic interplay (present everywhere in our society), the mystery being managed emanates from sexual anatomy: primary and secondary sex characteristics. (I shall not review the massive psychoanalytic literature on the fateful consequences of the anatomic differences between the sexes, of which these exchanges are the social manifestation.) The point is not simply that in the past a person was frightened by mystery but that, paradoxically, *he or she is now making sure the mystery is maintained.* Although there must not be too much danger (the risk must not be too high), if the appearance (façade) of mystery does not persist, excitement will fade. (Yet this playing with mystery only gives the illusion that the mystery is innocuous, for in the depths the danger persists. The mystery of that other person's body is never solved. One has merely fooled oneself, by being the author of one's own daydream, into believing one controls the risks. For many people, each meeting with a not yet fetishized object—for some, each episode of excitement—is a confrontation, a return to danger.)

It is important for the excitement that the mystery be a possession one's object—a tantalizing woman, a bullying man—will not willingly give up. The excitement, then, depends on a belief that one is forcibly uncovering what is not rightfully one's own (stealing secrets). Should the gestalt shift from mysterious to familiar, the purpose of one's hostility is lost; when a view of flesh is freely given, it cannot then be stolen. A whole industry—photographs of nude women—is based on this dynamic, and one can expect that with little left visually to be uncovered, the editors must be nervously searching for a breakthrough.

I presume at present—meaning this next idea is even more tentative —that the management of mystery plays a greater part in sexual excitement for males than for females. Most societies have set it up so that a male body holds less mystery for girls and women than a female body does for boys and men; males do not have to learn to sit just right or guard against revealing a glimpse of nipple. Not only are boys and men not supposed to see female breasts and genitals, but in a female body they must confront, without hope of possessing or comprehending, the vast reproductive interior with its unimaginable dimensions and power. (These issues are familiar to analysts under the rubric of "castration anxiety.")

Buried in excitement may be another awareness, that of contrast. Between the known and the unknown, the familiar and the mysterious, the overt and the hidden (these pairs are not quite synonymous), there can be a dynamic of pseudo-risk (controlled surprise) that drives the process to the level sensed as excitement. The vibration between the male's desires to merge with and separate from mother may also underlie excitement and be a fundament for an awareness of contrast. Boys must learn, accept, and be proud that they are not physically similar to their mothers; the anatomic contrasts between mothers and sons may contribute to the greater emphasis placed on women's anatomy in men's erotic imagination. Perhaps if the contrast is too great— beyond our control—we just get frightened, and if it is too little, bored. (I am not yet clear enough about this factor of contrast to decide if it is generally the case, and if so, what are the exceptions. Also, better data are needed than I now have to show how, at different levels of scripting, in what appears on the surface to be excitement generated by similarity —homosexual excitement, for example—contrast is nonetheless present.)

It seems, then, that the oscillation making up the excitement in mystery is between knowing and not knowing, seeing and not seeing, safety and danger. The secret here is the one that must be hidden from oneself yet—paradoxically—still be conscious:[17] the knowledge that the story is contrived, the daydream manufactured, the pornography a myth, the prostitute a paid actress, the spouse or lover a player in one's theater. One part of oneself must know this script is illusion and thus under control, while another, saying it does not know this secret, convinces the genitals that the story is real—and the reality of tumescence momentarily makes the story convincing. But when excitement subsides, the secret is out; illusion ends, and truth may bring disgust, lethargy, or estrangement from oneself, sometimes romanticized into *post coitum triste*.

To carry these ideas along, let us change the word "danger" now to "risk." *Risk* implies danger for which the chance of successful outcome can be estimated (again that quality of oscillation implied in "excitement").[18] The problem, when constructing an erotic daydream, is how to maintain a sense of risk in the story—the delicious shudder—while at the same time minimizing true risk. So one writes in *safety factors* that reduce danger to the *illusion* of danger. In grossest form, this is done by picturing events in which one would never dare become involved in reality. The perversion masochism especially exemplifies this illusion of risk. Masochists choose cautiously who is to inflict their pain, how it is to be done, which parts of the body are to be stimulated. Most important of all, the script is played out so that the masochist has control of the action, when the business starts and stops and what and how much is done. Most women who dress up in response to fantasies of being raped would be shocked if actually assaulted.

It follows that these mechanisms (risk, illusion, mystery) will be present in the choice not only of objects one uses in making daydreams but also of those one picks in the real world. Of course, real people are not always fully manipulable, so one must choose with care and even then pay attention to the game of risks, lest it get out of hand. Picking those we shall love or be excited by is not just a matter of chemistry and thunderbolts.

The daughter of a powerful, brutal, exciting, handsome, professionally brilliant but failed man and a distant, withdrawn woman who did not shield her from her fascinating father's rages, the patient—an unmarried twenty-year-old student—was excited only by those men who were handsome, with bodies tall and hard; masculine, in that their style was heterosexual, potent, intense, and focused on sex; intelligent; educated; financially well off; professionally successful; and concentrated on her regardless of their other girlfriends—in other words, the dream man of many American women. However, she came to see (and in the process lost her obsession with such men) that before each affair she had established that the man had almost invisible but fatal flaws. Despite notable achievements, all had an undercurrent of despair: because they had compromised their own standards of professional performance; because according to their own morality they were harming someone else in turning to her; because they were unable to express openly the love they felt for her; and, crucial for her excitement, because they exhibited their knowledge that they were suffering. She could pick one out across the room even before being introduced.

Early in treatment, she was only aware that there was this uncanny feeling when "I just look at this man [for the first time] and get excited," the surface awareness that condenses and disguises so much of what goes on in people's minds during intense emotional experiences. Her excitement was not erotic at that great moment but was rather an alert, sharp, forceful anticipation. Still, we learned in time, the checklist had unconsciously been scanned right then: the attributes summed; the hairline, irreparable crack of weakness appraised (perhaps just a moment's fluster interrupting his poise); and her own strengths matched up so that the risks inherent in his phallicness were already in that first instant recognized to be less than her capacity to defeat him. Her father had been beyond her control, and this had been so awful that when, during adolescence, she learned to use intelligence, strength, poise, and good looks, she discovered a means to undo endlessly the trauma that had, nonetheless, to be unendingly undone. Her sexual excitement depended on her picking men who seemed strong enough to be dangerous—the illusion of risk —but her unconscious planning guaranteed that she chose those she would outplay.

In judging risk, we must not use our own criteria. What we might consider too risky may not be for someone else, as when we think the masochist risks harming himself—that is, his self, not his body—on exposure to pain. Real risks, such as those to life, limb, social status, success, freedom, honor, or profession, may be built into sexual behavior, but I think close scrutiny reveals that in the algebra of danger, the reality risks—for example, the exhibitionist's likelihood of being caught —are not the risks one must avoid. In the case of the exhibitionist, as we have seen, the risk is that women will find him unmanly, and the very fact that he stirs up a fuss and may be arrested is not only not a risk to his tranquillity but becomes strong proof that he really has a penis that detonates others' fear. In the matter of sexual excitement, the dangers to be faced are intrapsychic, and the risks to be run are also controlled so as to deal ultimately with the inner world. If outer reality is engaged, it is chosen because it fits proportions that fantasy demands. Obviously, then, the secret we keep from ourselves is that the risk is only the illusion of risk; we compartmentalize, but are quite conscious in knowing that we have invented our own daydream.

Dr. Gilbert Herdt tells me of a tribe with whom he lived in New Guinea in which the men have the greatest horror of women's menstrual blood. Yet at a high point of religious ritual, they smear themselves with red substances—berries, mud—that are said to be (consubstantiation or trans-?) the same as menses. The result is—the purpose is—ritual-induced, not erotic, excitement. But what are its dynamics?

Quite like those for all other excitements. In the erotic daydream, the truth that we know is to be hidden and the falsity defended (in religious circles, to the death): excitement is possible—anxiety is defeated—because the risk is only simulated. The men do not smear menstrual blood on themselves; that would destroy them. There is no excitement in that, only terror. Instead, they do as the transvestite does; the moment of greatest trauma—humiliation and threatened loss of identity—is transformed, via hidden safety factors, into the point of greatest excitement.

Excitement, then, is a defense against anxiety, a transformation of anxiety into something more bearable, a melodrama. The ultimate danger that I believe lies at the heart of sexual excitement is that one's sense of existence, especially in the form of one's sense of maleness or femaleness, can be threatened (what Freud called "castration anxiety"). To dissolve that threat, I suggest, one calls forth the mechanisms of hostility being described, such as dehumanizing others, and then decks the scripts out with mystery, illusion, and safety factors.

When mystery and its inherent risk diminish, boredom or indiffer- ence intervenes. Normative examples: the capacity of a particular piece of pornography to hold an audience's attention drops off precipitously with a second exposure; Peeping Toms do not stare at their wives; a square inch of thigh in a drawing room is vaster than an acre on the beach; stage managers at strip joints read the sports page while the show unfolds; most couples—heterosexual, homosexual, a fetishist and his latest panty hose—get bored.

There are probably several different states that go by the name of boredom. One is a tension that is meant to replace depression. Another may simply be indifference, the product of one's not having the necessary dynamics to respond, for example the inability of most of us to be sexually excited by a garment. The boredom arising from repeated exposure to the same erotic story (scene) is not related to depression or indifference but is probably a state of frustration moving toward anticipation. It is a hunger for hostility.

Behaviorists explain erotic tastes—necrophilia, fetishism, homosexuality, red hair—as the pairing of intense excitement with a chance simultaneous association, such as, say, a dead body or red hair, especially if this is one's first erotic episode. That simple explanation, however, does not account for boredom. If erotic styles are conditioned, and if orgasm is a pleasure, then repeated episodes should not lead to boredom.

A woman (not a patient) articulates the nature of this boredom:

> When you first start reading a dirty book you can get really excited just by thinking about it. There is something about the dirty words. But when you read the whole book or start on a second book, it just loses something: the same words and the same action; the same thing over and over again. You just say, "I *know* all this." You just kind of put it down.

And if one lives protected from the worst of the endless random true mysteries, risks, and traumas of the real world, there grows a hunger for excitement—hang gliders, cigarette smoking, pacts with the devil, gambling, hallucinatory drugs, bank robbery, art, books written without adequate data. Most people who can have it cannot long bear calm contentment.

A problem in my writing about this subject is already clear: how to mass data convincingly. I have done no studies of populations, have applied no statistics. Anecdotes, quotations, and impressions are interesting but insecure foundations for theory; an appeal to common knowledge is a stopgap at best. But even if it is unlikely to lead to a sense of conviction and certainly does not prove hypotheses, I suggest that there is plenty of evidence lying out there in society, uncollected but in endless profusion.[19]

As you review the myriad forms of sexual behavior in our society, it is important not to hide behind such conceits as "the normal," or "the heterosexual" when it is used as synonymous with "normal." If we look closely, areas considered normal shrink away, leaving only a few that need to be challenged by any research more acute than simple gross inspection. If we carry out this assignment scrupulously, the "data" of normality will boil down to generalizations, clichés, folk tales, anecdotes about paragons one rarely meets, or last-ditch statements of disbelief. (A colleague, on first hearing this theory of excitement, said, "I simply cannot believe this explanation! I have *never* felt hostile when excited," an argument difficult to contradict in open discourse.)

So in place of carefully assembled data, we can refer to such examples as: pornography (perhaps here the reader should turn to pornography that does not excite him or her, for that is the best way to sense how odd it is); the uses of fashion; the erotic value people place on anatomic parts of others while discounting or ignoring the persons attached to those parts; sexism; conscious erotic daydreams; the need to choose as sexual partners only certain restricted categories of people (or the inability to choose certain people who are enticing to others); the voyeurism of males in non-nude cultures; the masochism of women in "civilized" cultures; the ubiquity of unmistakable sexual aberrations; the rapid onset of indifference and boredom; the need for many men to get away quickly from the body of a woman with whom they have been intimate (some men seem to consider femininity an infectious disease[20]); the fear, disgust, or envy most people suffer with regard to the bodies of the opposite sex. If from now on, those who wish to do research on sexual excitement will not be satisfied with generalizations on such subjects but will demand details—what is done, with whom, where, what is wanted, what is thought, what is felt—I predict that permutations of hostility will be found far more frequently than is acknowledged today. We ought then to be closer to answering the next question, whether such mechanisms are universal or just ubiquitous.

When we get these details, perhaps we shall become more lenient, or more aware of our hypocrisy when we allege—as in law codes—that all sorts of behavior that does not damage others must be massively punished.

We try to make the outlandish folk function as scapegoats for the rest of us, but anyone—not just analysts—who collects erotic thoughts knows that many citizens, avowedly heterosexual, conspicuously normal—not just the subway frotteurs, erotic vomiters, sheep lovers, coprophiliacs, or dirty phone-callers—are also filled with hatred and wishes, if not plans, to harm others: *chacun à son mauvais goût.*

There are thousands of books and papers on "sexuality." Yet almost none I know in the psychiatric literature take up this matter of excitement, except indirectly, as in studies showing that men and women are becoming more alike in their ability to be turned on,[21] or in the research done for the Commission on Obscenity and Pornography;[22] an earlier study of mine approaches but does not fully engage the issue.[23] Except for the writings of those analysts who note the scenarios that guide their patients in perversions (e.g. de M'Uzan, McDougall, Reik, Smirnoff[24]), the dynamics of excitement are dealt with only obliquely in psychoanalytic works (for example, with an anecdote that reports an episode of excitement, or with a study of the dynamics of a perversion though not of the excitement experienced). There are studies in which sexual attractiveness is part of an experimental design,[25] but the stimulus—attractiveness—is a given, taken for granted rather than itself examined. And there are those that attempt a behavioristic explanation, a viewpoint that leaves out fantasy as an agent in excitement, using instead a flaccid language that talks of "instrumental stimulus search and stimulus presentation"[26] or "reciprocal instrumentality."[27]

There is, of course, a huge and essential literature on biologic aspects of sexual excitement, which I shall not deal with here, except to say that the biologic is not the whole story, even in lower animals; monkeys, too, get bored with the same partners.[28]

I turned to the anthropologists and read several dozen books and articles that, in the mass, survey the anthropologic literature (in English) of the last generation on sexual excitement. Although the innumerable descriptions, discussions, theories, and hypotheses have brought us knowledge and an understanding of factors that contribute to sexual excitement, these works stop their investigation at the point where the individual's excitement begins: although the influences of anatomy and of the environment (such as mythology, customs, and family attitudes) are well considered, the mind is not examined.[29] Omitted is the mental content of an individual's sexual experience: why or how certain preferences lead precisely to sexual excitement in that particular person, or what anyone thought, felt, or imagined when sexually excited and what got him or her excited. There are hints or brief descriptions, of course, but no extended study. The following, found at random while I was looking for something else, is typical of these useful, unsystematized data:

> Margaret Mead, in various writings but notably in her book *Male and Female*, goes beyond the bare bones of such reporting to suggest that human societies evince two polarities in regard to sexual arousal. One is a tendency toward erotic specificity, so that sexual arousal depends upon particular conditions. The nape of the female neck in Japanese lore of the past century is one instance of cultural specificity, whereas intersexual bathing and nudity are alleged to have had no such connotations. Among the Ute Indians, whom this author has studied, it is claimed that female breasts are devoid of sexual meaning. On the other hand, positive sexual arousal, including homosexual arousal, has been described as being stimulated by a wide and diverse range of nonspecific sources.[30]

I know, however, of two teams that are on target. The first, the sociologists Gagnon and Simon,[31] look at scripts that people create in their minds in order to get excited. To their ideas I would add that conscious scripting, although an essential piece for a theory, serves mainly as the vehicle that carries underlying dynamics, not so much as a force that in itself creates excitement.[32] The second group—Abel, Blanchard, Barlow, and Mavissakalian—using a transducer to measure changes in penile size, tease out, most ingeniously, which elements in a subject's full script are exciting and which not.[33] In addition, Bonime has stressed the functions of erotic daydreams as problem solvers and as "aggressive" depersonalization maneuvers.[34] And Nydes has noted that "the masturbation fantasy is itself a power operation . . . to confess the fantasy is to confess to a crime."[35]

We thus cannot—yet—investigate this subject by questionnaires or even by massive interviewing of populations (though some workers are in the neighborhood). Such research, as exemplified by the Kinsey people, does give us powerful data but does not tell us why John becomes excited by Mary's stockings or Mgbubu by Djala's buttocks, or why in Western society men can be turned on by putting on women's clothes while it is almost unheard of for women to be by men's clothes, or why ankles or feet or eyebrows or skin color or hair distribution that is exciting one year—or century—is only a joke another. Questionnaires and mass interviewing techniques do not get such data, nor, at the other pole of inquiry, does psychoanalytic theory. It is odd that such a powerful, intense, dangerous, gratifying experience as sexual excitement, one that has even been of central importance in the researchers' own lives, does not provoke more investigation.

Most of the new sex researchers, too, have been unable to take on the study of individual erotic experience. With no interest in psychodynamics, they not only do not have a way to plumb subjective states but even deny that such states exist. At times, this failure is disguised by referring the problem to the physiologists, with the implication that the emergence of an episode of sexual excitement is a matter only of hormones, nervous system, and anatomy; or to the behaviorists, with their belief that at the right moment a chance association of excitement with any object or sexual style links the stimuli together; or to animal psychologists, who are not obliged to confront their subjects' awareness of selfhood. In private life, researchers know these explanations do not fit their own histories, but curiously, in publications, the subjective experience is ignored, as if the researcher did not live in his own self.[36]

One might say, then, that the techniques for collecting data on societal, cultural, subcultural, and biologic inputs to sexual excitement are competent and that the data already collected have essential value; but the next step, which moves the investigator into the mind—the subjective experience—still has to be taken. The missing link, the essential clue, lies in the detailed study of erotic fantasy, the conscious daydreams people tell themselves or live in the real world, plus unconscious fantasy, the private, idiosyncratic, unrecognized meanings people attach to their behavior and to the objects on whom their behavior is worked out. Perhaps such studies come last because they are the most difficult to do. The data are hard to collect. We know that fantasies, conscious and unconscious,* function best if protected by secrecy, disguise, and repression, being powered more by guilt, shame, and hatred than by simple, joyous lust. Then too, the data are difficult to validate (since no outside observer ever sees a psychoanalytic interchange, much less a fantasy). But especially, the experience is strong, occurs rapidly, and is sensed as a unitary event rather than a synthesis of components no one of which is the excitement. Most of what we label sexual excitement is made up of several parts—different experiences of excitement felt simultaneously—only one of which is "erotic." Others are triumph, rage, revenge, fear, anxiety, risk, all condensed into one complex buzz called "sexual excitement."

Until recently, the study of sexual excitement was badly flawed; an essence of the scientific method, the need for directly observed data, could not be honored. But when the times changed enough that pioneers could dare, the naturalistic study of sexual excitement began with the revolutionary work of Masters and Johnson. And just as it is important to measure how a body reacts, is it not also of use to know what the person experiences who inhabits that body? That research problem has two parts. We have to find a methodology for measuring a mental state that contains a heavy charge of fantasy. And we must create a neutral environment that will improve our chances of being objective about a subjective phenomenon, without the environment itself participating in the phenomenon that is being observed and thus distorting it. Regarding the latter, what probably made the studies of Masters and Johnson possible was that these workers interposed between subjects and observers a three-dimensional fantasy—the laboratory—that relieved everyone's guilt and anxiety by saying that erotic fantasies were not to be present. This objectivity changed the manifest content of the subjects' fantasies, pretty much removing from the room (maybe) conscious fantasies (daydreams) or attitudes toward sexual partners or investigators, thereby reducing the power of such fantasies. The rules of our culture still make any other setup unbearable.[38]

There is another subject, partaking of but not synonymous with fantasy, that we must also study someday if we are to understand sexual excitement: the interpersonal communication that carries fantasy out of ourselves and into other people, making contact with the others' fantasies and turning the participants on. But how is one to observe

---

*Even if there is no conscious daydream, we can sometimes find the script. Belle says she masturbated last night without fantasies; besides the erotic sensations, she was aware only of the shape and feel of the tissues beneath her fingers. Of course, she adds, her fingers "visualize" the tissues: she knows the parts she touches. Silence. Surprise: "Actually, I guess I was picturing my genitals. No, that's not quite right. I was a man picturing my genitals and getting excited. Because he was excited, I got excited." The term for that experience is "fantasy."[37]

people communicating their excitement to each other? If it was naughty of Masters and Johnson to have observed the physical side of excitement and pleasure in a laboratory, think what shakings of society must still occur before a virtuous researcher could investigate *in vivo* the signals that start and increase the process. Here is a suggestion that might yield only partial data but on the other hand might keep the investigator out of jail: study pornography. The pornographers have skillfully worked the area I am now discussing, though their aim is intuitively to understand dynamics so as to produce excitement, while ours is to make those intuitions only intellectually manifest.

Although we should know the generalizations of sexuality for a culture—such as the criteria for sexual beauty, cosmetics and dress, taboos—these do not tell us precisely what goes on in an individual's head. Here are representative, but by no means exhaustive, questions and perspectives that researchers on sexual excitement could investigate.

1. *Pornography.* In the culture in which you work, is there a pornography or are there pornographic equivalents? By pornography I mean material made available (openly or secretively) for those who derive sexual stimulation from representations of sexual objects and erotic situations rather than from the objects and situations themselves. These materials may consist of writings, drawings, paintings, sculpture, ceramics; private performances, recorded or spoken; performances for an audience, such as recitations, plays, dance, religious rites; performances in which one is a participant.

2. *Physical Attributes.* Here let us ask our researchers to distinguish —as the anthropologic literature does not—between criteria for beauty and criteria for turning on. (An ugly man may be fascinating; some men prefer a woman with an amputated leg.) So we shall want to know about lust-provoking as well as aesthetic ideals of anatomic configuration: genitals; secondary sex characteristics; height; bulk; muscle; fat; hair distribution, amount, color; voice; skin quality and color; special idiosyncratic features of the culture (such as bound feet in old China or scarification in Africa); bisexual qualities; needs to push definitions of masculinity and femininity to opposing extremes versus unisex trends.

3. *Adornments.* Clothes, cosmetics, jewelry, tattooing and other decorations that modify anatomic appearance: what are they; how are they used; what transformations are they to produce? (By transformations, I am thinking of disguises, corrections, amplifications, intensifica-

tions, exaggerations, minimizers, mystifiers, tantalizers, or effects that focus on certain anatomic parts by covering others: brassieres to change breast shape, codpieces, powder to lighten skin color, suntans, filmy clothes to suggest revelations not quite revealed.) Are there negative adornments such as bound breasts, penile subincision, circumcision, clitoral or labial amputation?

4. *Body Styles.* What are the prevailing styles of moving, such as walking, running, dancing, sitting, standing, lying? Under which circumstances are which postures used?

5. *Taboos to Heighten Excitement.* Probably in such cases the taboo is only partial and in that culture associated with something expected to be pleasurable *and* dangerous. Related to this should be (perhaps) another perspective: the use of danger as an ingredient introduced into erotic situations in order to increase excitement. How is danger modulated so that there is not too much, which would produce anxiety and impotence, and not too little, which could lead to indifference or boredom? A study of sexual taboos may also begin to reveal the sexual fantasies of a culture. Whether these taboo-dimmed fantasies are woven into people's sexual daydreams is difficult to determine—but it is worth a try.

6. *Language.* This is not quite the same as pornography, though related. Is language—spoken usually, written perhaps less often—used not just for courtship but precisely to stimulate sexual excitement? When is it used—early on during foreplay, during intercourse itself? What is said?

7. *Daydreams.* Can researchers get precise information about daydreams their subjects use for exciting themselves? This category is related to pornography, which is, I believe, no more than formalized daydreaming in which one chooses in the marketplace the daydreams one prefers (with an added impulse of excitement because the daydream was invented by someone else, which gives the illusion of reality rather than the more meager awareness of its being only one's own fancy).

8. *Masturbation.* Masturbation is the mechanism that puts daydreams to work. Sometimes, when the researcher cannot collect the scenario of the daydream because it is too embarrassing to tell or because it is not conscious, it is possible to get a feel of the underlying daydream from the techniques of masturbation the subject uses or

forbids herself or himself. Regarding the latter, one should determine if a technique's absence is due to its being forbidden by the culture, to lack of interest, or to its being unknown to the society.

9. *Subliminal Communications.* What I have in mind here is subtle, nonverbal erotic passage of information, such as expressing emotions with eyes and face, changes in voice modulation and timbre, and changes in respiration, all of which can indicate shifts in excitement. Which of these turn people on, which turn them off; which frighten, which signal immediate lust, which tenderness?

10. *Looking and Being Looked At.* Elements of this have been touched on above. What body parts excite; what techniques for exposing or covering; what circumstances? (Seeing an anatomic part in one ambience may not excite, but in another the same part of the same person will.) What childhood frustrations and permissions lower or heighten voyeurism and exhibitionism? What differences are there between the sexes in what one can show and what one can look at?

11. *Erotism of Body Parts.* Which body parts can be stimulated to excitement? Which techniques of stimulating are most likely to excite?

12. *Boredom.* This is related to all the foregoing, for an opposite of excitement is boredom. But we should ask specific questions to ascertain how fast, under what circumstances, with which people a person gets bored.

13. *Other Sexually Related Affects.* When and why do disgust, rage, fear, cruelty, pleasure in pain, anxiety, etc., occur in erotic situations?

14. *Different Expectations Regarding Excitement.* What has one a right to expect in that culture in regard to tenderness, love, intensity, potency (degree and staying power), foreplay, styles of intercourse (positions, extragenital intercourse, permission for orgasm), afterplay (stroking or talking versus falling asleep or getting up and leaving), repeat performances? What are the rightful expectations at different ages; with lovers; with spouses? What differences are there between boys and girls, men and women; between those of different financial, religious, political status?

15. *Aberrations.* The cross-cultural literature is understandably meager in this regard. It is obviously a subject about which people in most

places do not easily talk; an alien observer is not likely to be given this information. But without those data, one cannot understand sexuality.

We shall want to know, for all the aforementioned categories, if, how, when, and why men differ from women; rich from poor; the educated from the less educated; anarchists from republicans, kings from the rabble. And if there are other clusters of people within the culture who separate out with differing reactions in any of the categories.

In the absence of such data, especially of conscious and unconscious fantasies, we know less about human sexuality than we should.

Conclusions here, early, before Belle's story. Sexual excitement is produced in varying degrees by (1) general physiologic state, (2) stimulation of erotic zones, (3) fantasy. In this book, I attend only to the third. (But, of course, neither the first nor the second is immune to invasion by fantasy. Think, for instance, how disgust can raise one's resistance to erotic touching. A woman brings off an orgasm by stroking her nipples, becomes intensely excited in foreplay when her lover does the same, but finds it unbearable—nonerotic—with her husband.) Sexual fantasy can be studied by means of a person's daydreams (including those chosen in magazines, books, plays, television, movies, and more outright pornography), masturbatory behavior, object choice, foreplay, technique of intercourse, or postcoital behavior. Scarcely visible but still available for study in the exact details (which almost no one bothers to collect) of these manifest versions of fantasy are, I postulate, memorials raised to commemorate painful experiences and relationships of infancy and childhood plus, as life proceeds, endless alteration of the script for maximal effectiveness. The function of fantasy is to convert these painful experiences to pleasure while still keeping the details of the earlier traumas and frustrations embedded in the fantasy, to allow an endless repetition that reverses trauma to triumph.[39] In order to sharpen excitement—the vibration between the anxiety that original traumas will be repeated and the hope of a pleasurable conclusion this time—one introduces into the story secrets, elements of risk (approximations of the trauma), and safety factors (subliminal signals to the storyteller that the risks are not truly dangerous). Unless this is done, indifference or boredom intervenes.

To repeat, sexual excitement depends on a scenario. The person to be aroused is the "writer," who has been at work on the story line since childhood. The story is an adventure in which the hero/heroine runs risks that must be escaped. Disguised as fiction, it is autobiography in which are hidden crucial intrapsychic conflicts, screen memories of actual events, and the resolution of all these elements into a happy

ending, best celebrated by orgasm. The characters are chosen because
they resemble (though are usually not identical in appearance with)
important people of childhood such as oneself, one's parents, and one's
siblings. Most often, the writer becomes director, moving the action out
into the world of real people or other objects. These are chosen because
they are perceived by the writer-director as filling the criteria already
written into the role. (Prostitutes, for instance, are available to those
without better resources for casting.) If the chosen characters pretty
much fit the part, they work. They should, however, have just a touch
of unpredictability in their behavior; that introduces the illusion of risk.
If unvaryingly predictable, they are boring. On the other hand, if they
do not stick close enough to their assigned role, too much anxiety
results and they are traded in. Every detail counts for increasing excitement and avoiding true danger or boredom. For many people, sexual
excitement is like threading a minefield.

At this point in my work, I am convinced that this use of a story line is
fact, not metaphor, and that it holds for most people (with some elements
conscious and some not, for some people more and for some less). I am
less certain how universally hostility and its permutations, especially
revenge, are found in episodes of sexual excitement.[40] Perhaps the following will turn out to be correct: as one proceeds along a continuum toward
less use of hostile mechanisms, one is proceeding from the bizarre
(psychotic) through the character disorders we diagnose as perversions
and on into the range of the normative, where the mechanisms propel-
ling the excitement are energized by hostility but where affection and
capacity for closeness also thrive. At the far end of the continuum is a
small group of contented people who enjoy (even in fantasy) loving,
unhostile relationships with others and who are not so frightened by
intimacy that they must fetishize the other person. For them the other *is*
a person; they do not have to dehumanize. If hostility is present in their
excitement, it is microscopic (as in Freud's concept of signal anxiety). Is
it, nonetheless, essential? Whatever the answer, we should not equate the
small amount of hostility that powers a daydream with the much greater
degree of hostility needed for hostile acts in the real world.

I fear that some readers will get hung up on the word "hostility,"
feeling that it is too strong to describe the minimal activity present in
the sexual excitement many experience. I agree that a gentler word
would be better. (But not "aggression": that simply implies movement
or action and need not indicate direction. "Hostility" makes it clear
that the "aggression" is purposeful, directed at someone who is to be
harmed.) What is the word for just a whisper of hostility?

Stressing hostility as a central feature in sexual excitement may seem a mistake to those who do not experience frank anger when excited or who feel this hypothesis subverts love. (The hypothesis does not claim that people are fully conscious of hostility as they move to excitement. Some are; probably most are not.) The idea may be easier to take if we recall that a touch of hostility enlivens all kinds of pleasant human activities. Think of the build-up of excitement as a magician teases his audience. In this behavior, too, there is the simulation of risk within the guarantees of safety (after all, this is a show and we know that magicians really are only technicians), mystery, illusion, and fetishization. It is all in fun, of course, but it does not take much imagination to sense the undercurrents of tension (the communication of hostility between performer and audience, going both ways) that make the experience more exciting and lead to a more dramatic endpoint.

Some of the same is found in other performers whose acts build up tension and lead to climax: athletes, gamblers, circus performers, explorers, actors. In all these, it is easy to see an attack on an apparently threatening object—an audience, competitors, the odds, a mountain, a jungle, God—and the way in which that object is forced to give in to their strength. Whatever else it is, is that not also hostility? Perhaps this dynamic holds for all excitements, rites of passage, myths, and miracles. What we call "sublimation" may be a state that has been non-hostilely depleted of hostility.

The trick in excitement is to go to the edge of the cliff and then turn aside at the last instant, converting disaster to triumph. When one succeeds, there is an explosion of energy—laughter, yelling, body movement. An artist makes a revolutionary breakthrough; he could only do it by means of hostility, a tearing down of the old traditions, those out in the world and those inside himself. Art is demolition; kitsch is the corpse left when art loses its anger.

The idea that hostility can be a central feature in a benign, inevitable part of human experience is illustrated also in humor and its physical gratification, laughter. As Freud long ago observed, humor and hostility are closely linked.[41] Take, for instance, slapstick, at which we all can laugh; transform the same amusing act into a real event in the street and one sees the hostility that must be there to generate humor. Humor is hostility subdued and graced by tolerance. Both it and sexual excitement use, I think, the same mechanisms: mystery, risk, reversal of trauma to triumph. And what is left of humor if we extract hostility?* There is always a victim, and our amusement comes in part from the

---

*I think that humor (except, perhaps, for puns) does not exist without hostility. But an episode of sexual excitement can start, as humor does not, simply from a physical stimulus, internal or external.

fact that we always know him: he is us, enough disguised that we can bear it. Once again, as in sexual excitement, the victim has for the moment assumed the role of victor.[42]

Between finding something funny and being enraged by it, there can be a fine line, one delicately negotiated by certain humorists and comics who know that sometimes the story line does go over the cliff to a smashup. One person's joke is another's insult. Audiences can become enraged if not protected by the movements I have called *simulation of risk* in excitement. But when they are protected, audiences applaud and in doing so assure the performer that they forgive—are even grateful for—his attack. Similarly, in sexual relations, one's partner's excitement and orgasm can be experienced as applause, not only for a skillful performance but as acknowledgment that the hostile currents are, as in art, no more than piquancies that enrich love.

Those readers have misunderstood who think I am saying that love, affection, generosity, concern, and other sometimes nonhostile qualities cannot contribute to sexual excitement. I believe they can but suspect they do so infrequently. Perhaps this can be made clearer by our glancing again at the fetishization mechanism. With it, one focuses on and overvalues a part without fully taking in the whole. That in itself need not, however, rule out affection. Rather than keeping two people at a distance from each other, it could be a device that, by increasing the other's erotic attractiveness, promotes closeness, enriches love. There is no absolute law against long-married couples still fascinating each other.

Just as humor can enliven love, so can a touch of fetishizing. Becker underlines this point:

> We are all more or less prone to fetishistic definitions in our sex life when we show a preference for a particular portion of our partner's body. There is nothing per se about a large breast that has any more inherent sexual stimulation to the partner than a small one. Obviously it is all in the eye of the beholder. But our culture teaches us to become committed in *some* way to the body of the opposite sex, and we are eager for cues which give us a passport to permissive excitation. When we learn such a cue, we invest it with rich significance. Each culture heightens the meaning of certain qualities of objects so that its members can easily bring into play the approved responsive behavior: lace underwear and steatopygia for sex objects, tailfins and chrome for cars. The easy mark of "beauty" that serves as a perceptual counter is a promise that socially approved satisfaction will be forthcoming. The identifying body part signals, in encapsulated form, an entire range of meanings—of cause-and-effect sequences to be expected.[43]

The issue, then, is not whether people use fetishization to enhance their excitement. I think Devereux (as reported by Arlow) gives us an essential clue to the ethical issue that hides behind arguments regarding normality when he

> distinguishes between normal sexuality and perversion from two points of view. From the intrapsychic point of view he maintains that the conscious purpose of foreplay is to increase tension and to cathect the partner, whereas the purpose of the perversion is to release tension and to decathect the partner. From the point of view of object relations, normal sexuality is characterized by true object cathexis in which the partner matters as an individual, is not used as a means to an end, is highly cathected, and is valued in the subject's and the partner's sexual gratification. The so-called passionate love relationships between perverts lack these unique characteristics. The pervert's love object is never perceived as a total object. He remains a partial object. There is a quality of incompleteness in the object relations of perverts. This incompleteness is often depicted in literature under the guise of an ethereal quality which invests the perverse love relationship. Devereux compares this ethereal quality of the incomplete object relation with the hazy aura which surrounds the similar relations of schizophrenic patients. [And those madly in love.]
>
> These criteria, the author felt, indicate that a sexual relationship in which the behavior is normal but the object relationship defective is essentially perverted. If this definition is taken to encompass the vast majority of human sexual relations and to place them in the category of perverted relations, Devereux maintained, then so be it. It may be regrettable, he insists, but "only an infinitesimal fraction of mankind is capable of behaving and experiencing even occasionally in a mature manner befitting genital characters."[44]

A balance to my stress on hostility is found in the studies of Kernberg, who has gone a long way toward accounting for those who experience sexual excitement lustfully, joyously, openly, and lovingly without being propped up by heavy doses of revenge and degradation.[45] My description does not disagree with his. Gross hostility is not necessary, only usual.

It is not the presence of hostility per se that determines the value—the goodness or badness—of excitement. Suppose, instead of calling this a study of erotics, I were to say it is an introduction to the dynamics of aesthetics (which I believe), using sexual excitement as an example. Perhaps, then, some readers would recognize that to suggest that hostility is at the center of the experience is not to say it has to be evil or unhuman.

If these dynamics are typical of sexual excitement, then we must bear the idea that sexual pleasure in most people depends on neurotic mechanisms. This may not frighten those who do not equate "normal" with normative; but it is disappointing.

My theory makes sexual excitement just one more example of what others have said for millennia: that humans are not a very loving species —especially when they make love. Too bad.

2

Primary Femininity

PSYCHOANALYSTS HAVE FINALLY begun to formalize again and in
depth the study of the psychology of women: its origins in constitution
and infancy; its elaboration in pleasure, in danger, in pain; its silent
growth in childhood and adolescence; and its forms in adulthood.[1]

For almost thirty years—until the last ten years or so—psychoanalysis turned from its early intense study of sexuality, as if that area had
been mined out. As part of this neglect, we dozed along on the subject
of the psychology of women, accepting Freud's thoughts more or less
as the last word. His position can be stated simply: the psychology that
is uniquely women's is the sum of the efforts made to adjust to not being
male. Because they lack penises, women know they are doomed to
inferiority. The development of femininity in females, then, is the effort
made to salvage something of value from this fateful, originally biologic
fact.

Although several analysts during those decades published their disagreements with Freud,[2] the effect until recently was minimal. Time has
caught up with psychoanalysis, however; social change and nonpsy-
choanalytic research have begun to impinge. From the mid-1960s on,
new data on prenatal and early postnatal origins of sexuality have
brushed the consciousness of our theory. These advances, now probably
known to most of us, fall into two categories.

First, the biologic bases for Freud's arguments regarding masculinity
and femininity need revision. Since he tried to make his speculations
firmer by referring to biologic abstractions, the vulnerability of this part
of analytic theory has become more visible. In brief, we are now told
that the original state of mammalian, including human, tissue is not
male or even neuter but female.

The second area of new research, loosely labeled "learning effects," has been virtually ignored by psychoanalytic researchers or theorists, although it lies between the lines of most descriptions of interpersonal object relations. That aspect of learning theory related to our subject can be given the neutral labels psychologists use: "rearing," "shaping," or "molding." This includes all contacts with parents (and later siblings and others) that impinge literally on a child's sensory systems, producing sensations that at first are probably measured primarily on a scale of pleasure-neutral-unpleasure but that soon, by means of memory and fantasy, become mental impressions that help form object representations. Once we have arrived schematically at that point, we are on ground well traveled by psychoanalysts. But the earliest stages of rearing, when object representations are not yet formed, have only recently been conceptualized or studied by direct observation of infants.

To be considered on this topic are the findings and theories embodied in our understanding of such mechanisms as imprinting, visceral conditioning, simple conditioning, and operant conditioning. These forces may cause changes in the nervous system without necessarily passing through the infant's mental apparatuses. That is, they may never reach any level of awareness and may never be dealt with by mental mechanisms such as fantasy, incorporation, identification, or memory. They may be no more directly sensed than is the source of an "instinct," like adrenal or thyroid or pituitary physiology, even though their effects energize behavior and thus impinge on—contribute to—the mental state we call "awareness." (See Appendix B, "Fixing.")

Regarding that aspect of rearing which leads to gender identity—that is, the mixture of masculinity and femininity present in everyone—the new research describes the process as beginning with sex assignment. When an infant is born, someone, usually an authority such as a physician or midwife, announces the infant's sex on the basis of the appearance of the external genitals. Almost always, assignment is made either to the male or the female sex (though in rare cases, it may be to some intermediate, hermaphroditic sex: for example, "I do not know what your baby is; it is neither a boy nor a girl," or "I do not know what your baby is; it is both a boy and a girl"). This assignment sets in motion a process, the effects of which act on the infant innumerable times a day forevermore. The people of its environment respond specifically to that assigned sex, confirming it, for instance, in the name the child is given, the color and type of its clothing, the ways the child is picked up or played with by its parents, the choice of noises and words directed at it, the styles of holding and feeding it. Within the wide range of possible behaviors that confirm a designation of maleness or femaleness are the endless idiosyncratic variations from one family to the next, but always transmitted is the parents' belief in their child's sex, as a male or a female (or a hermaphrodite). Within this ambience, at first in the intimacy of the mother-infant symbiosis, the automatic, nonmental patterns of behavior noted above are presumably fixed.

But beyond these silent forces is the shaping of permanent aspects of personality that occurs as a result of what parents favor or forbid and the styles they use to get those messages across. This process, the child's response via identification, especially identification that is not the result of conflict and trauma, should occupy our theory-making, I believe, even more than it has.* (Our prototype can be Freud's description of how the collection of functions called the superego is in part formed from such interchanges incorporated.)

If we bring an understanding of this shaping by parental influences into contact with our psychoanalytic information, stronger hypotheses may appear. For instance—a subject introduced by Freud—the development of body ego. Analysts have been increasingly interested in determining to what extent and when do genital, including vaginal, sensations contribute to a girl's gender identity. Awareness arising spontaneously in these organs, from self-exploration and from mother's care, inform the child of her genitals' dimensions and sensations. But these sensory experiences are given full meaning only because they serve to validate for the child the correctness of communications parents have been giving her from birth on about their awareness and opinions of her sex. And the later experiences of comparing her own genitals with those of others, children and adults, of the same or opposite sex, further confirm as well as amplify and complicate her awareness of sex assignment. Only these interpersonal communications give purpose to what is otherwise mere sensation.

What has recently become available to us, then, in the study of masculinity and femininity is the conflict-free spheres of ego formation that Hartmann, especially, signaled would be our concern as we advanced psychoanalytic theory and observation. So far as I know, none of these data and hypotheses are considered in classical psychoanalytic theories of masculinity and femininity, from Freud on. I cannot state too strongly my impression that if we analysts do not take them up soon, we shall have made a historic mistake.

Where does this leave Freud's ideas on the psychology of women— or, as it is usually put, on femininity? In the psychoanalytic theory of the origins of femininity in females as first laid out by him, the first several months of life are not considered in the chronology of the little

*I think the process of identification begins by means of responses conditioned by reward and punishment.

girl's development. We become aware of this, not by its being clearly stated, but rather more indirectly in writing style: *"At some time or other* the little girl makes the discovery of her organic inferiority."[3] Skipping over the earlier period grants the classic analytic understanding of the psychology of women a substantial logic. But we pay too great a price for it; if we must ignore data in order to retain logic, then our explanation is flawed and should be modified.

For Freud, the psychology of women begins with a sense of castration, as if what went on before, in the first year or so of life, did not contribute to the development of masculinity and femininity. Femininity, according to this theory, is just a defense[4] and shows its makeshift origins in its nature: passivity, masochism, penis envy, renunciation, a weak superego, commitment more to biologic imperatives such as reproduction than to social options such as friendship, and restitutive operations that result in such secondary narcissistic manifestations as exhibitionism of nongenital parts of the body.[5]

Starting under such handicaps, a girl is unlikely, according to Freud, to escape without serious damage. At least, she has more barriers to overcome than does the boy. Although he can be knocked off the track or forced onto detours, his superior genital and his start in heterosexuality give him the potential for a straight run—biologically and psychosocially—on his journey to masculinity and adult heterosexuality. Not so for the girl. Her start with that inferior organ and homosexual object choice means she must either put out a major effort in childhood to switch onto a new track or she is doomed to irreparable unfortunate consequences.

We know by now that castration anxiety, penis envy, disappointment in mother, the problems in turning to father as a new sexual object, and the other traumas and frustrations of oedipal conflict are easy to demonstrate.[6] So if we are unaware of an earlier, nontraumatic and nonconflictual stage, the theory fits together (though for those familiar with women less wretched than the ones Freud said typified the species, his system seems somewhat wobbly). But if the first stage in women is different from Freud's description—if a woman can have a fundamental, fixed sense of being rightfully a female—then our psychology of women needs repair. We should look for that earliest stage and try to fill in the empty space in observations and theory.

Freud understood, in fact discovered, the contribution of pain and conflict early in gender identity development, but findings and ideas he did not have, bearing on the earliest months of life, require that psychoanalysis shift its perspective. That shift, modest in itself, nonetheless leads to a different conclusion, a new and more accurate view of the origins and essence of the psychology of women: a woman's psychology adds up to more than her belief that she is a castrated male. Disappointment at not being a male contributes to but is not all there is to, or even the first stage in, the development of femininity. Rather, femininity also has origins distinct from envy. And so, because women have a primary, unquestioned acceptance of their femaleness, they are not inherently, inevitably, unalterably—by nature—psychologically inferior to but simply different from men.

The terms "femininity" and "masculinity" throughout this book will have no biologic connotations (which is not to say they have no biologic origins). They will refer only to an individual's sense of self (identity) and to how that sense permeates role. Thus, for me, femininity is what a person and her (or his) parents, peers, and society agree is femininity; the criteria change from place to place and time to time. Such usage frees us from the impasses produced by biologizing, such as alleging as a biologically induced fact that masculinity equals activity, and femininity passivity.[7]

Although there are physical acts that only females can do, such as give birth, many behaviors commonly called feminine can be found also in some biologically normal males. Trying to pin an explanation of femininity on a biologic bedrock—women are by nature masochistic or passive—can lead to oppressive social consequences as well as be a poor summary of data.

My work in recent years, following that of others,[8] has tried to announce the gap in Freud's thinking about women—the earliest, non-conflictual stage—to point to observations anyone can make of that early time of development, to derive propositions from the data, and to find a theory that explains and predicts. The term I made up, "core gender identity,"[9] derives from a mixture of experimental data and data observable in infant females, girls, and women (and, of course, males). Let me review the concept. Core gender identity is the sense we have of our sex, of maleness in males and of femaleness in females (and in rare cases, of being a hermaphrodite in hermaphrodites, and in primary transsexuals, of being—sort of—a member of the opposite sex). It is a part of, but not identical with, what I have called gender identity, a broader concept standing for the mixture of masculinity and femininity found in every person. ("Male" and "female" refer to sex, or biologic state, "masculinity" and "femininity" to gender identity, a conviction about one's self and one's role.)

Core gender identity develops first and is the nucleus around which masculinity and femininity gradually accrete. Core gender identity carries no implication of role or object relations; it is, I suppose, a part of what is loosely called "narcissism." I postulate it to be the result of the following:

1. A biologic "force": this is an effect originating in fetal life, usually genetic in source (though occasionally nongenetic[10]), springing—so far as we know at present—from neurophysiologic (CNS-systemic-hormonal) organizing of the fetal brain.

2. The sex assignment at birth: the message that the appearance of the infant's external genitals brings to those who can assign sex—the attending physician and the parents—and its subsequent unequivocal effect in convincing them of their child's sex.

3. The unending impingement of parents', especially mothers', attitudes about *that* infant's sex and the infant's constructing these perceptions, via its developing capacity for fantasy, into events, that is, meaningful, motivated experiences.

4. "Biopsychic" phenomena: early postnatal effects caused by certain habitual patterns of handling the infant—conditioning, imprinting, or other forms of learning that permanently modify the infant's brain and resultant behavior without the infant's mental processes protecting it* from such sensory input. The evidence that these "biopsychic" phenomena exist is, in humans, so far weak. This category is related to the previous one and is listed separately for emphasis and to distinguish it from mental processes (also the result of parents' impingements) with which we are more familiar—castration anxiety, for instance—which probably begin appearing later in infancy and which depend on the infant's having acquired the capacity to fantasize, that is, to change reality by its own mental efforts.

5. The developing body ego: the myriad qualities and quantities of sensations, especially from the genitals, that define the physical and help to define the psychic dimensions of one's sex to oneself, thus confirming for the baby its parents' convictions about their infant's sex.

6. Intrapsychic development: the "forces" just described are experienced by the infant and now are available (because of a developing capacity to internalize and fantasize) for becoming parts of a sense of self: attitudes, convictions, conflicts, identifications, fantasies, and stable modes of confronting oneself or the world ("character structure").

In the usual case—by far the most common—each of these factors (presumably, as no one has yet been able to make precise measurements) contributes to the resultant core gender identity. However, it is only when we find an aberrance that we see any of these factors clearly.

*By fantasy, a process that empowers the infant to *explain* perceptions, thereby reducing their potential to traumatize.

In other words, they have been discovered more in the pathologic than in the normative. Here are examples:

1. *Biologic "force."* This exciting new information need be only briefly reviewed since it is becoming increasingly familiar. Without the addition of fetal androgens, in all mammals, including humans, anatomic maleness cannot occur. This is true whether the chromosomes are male (XY) or female (XX). But if these fetal androgens are present at the right time in the right amount and are of the right chemical structure, both anatomic maleness and postnatal masculinity will be possible regardless of chromosomal maleness or femaleness. This rule operates in all species tested. Since direct experimental manipulation is impermissible in humans, "natural experiments" have been used, all of which have confirmed the general mammalian law. Thus, for instance, all people studied with the complete form of androgen insensitivity syndrome have been feminine girls and women despite their having male (XY) chromosomes and producing normal amounts of testosterone (from cryptorchid testes). Because these people have a somatic inability to respond to testosterone, their anatomic appearance is female and their gender identity feminine. Comparably, all people with Turner's syndrome (XO) are feminine, there being no fetal androgens present.[11]

2. *Sex assignment.* When the appearance of the external genitals is unequivocal, the infant is assigned to the appropriate sex. Whether the parents are pleased or not, they do not question the assignment, and although their pleasure or displeasure may contribute to the intricacies of the child's developing masculinity or femininity, the child does not question if its body is that of the assigned sex. The exceptional case makes the point: it sometimes happens that an otherwise biologically normal female with adrenogenital syndrome will have external genitals so masculinized that they look rather (in rare cases exactly) like a normal male's. Such infants are, naturally, assigned to the male sex and develop a male core gender identity. Should the proper diagnosis of sex be made at birth, however, and the child be recognized as a female, then a female core gender identity results. In those cases where the sex assignment is equivocal because the genitals are hermaphroditic, the core gender identity is neither female nor male but hermaphroditic.[12]

3. *Parental attitudes.* Let us use the adrenogenital syndrome as our example here also. An otherwise normal female is born with genitals that appear equivocal, neither male nor female but, rather, bisexual. On

delivery, the doctor tells the mother that she has just had a hermaphrodite, that this is not a boy or a girl; his attention caught, however, by a female-appearing part of the genital anatomy, he adds, "You might as well raise it as if it were a girl." She does so and in the process communicates her attitude to this child, who is given no reason to doubt in early childhood that it is a person who is neither a male nor a female but a member of another sex, of which, the poor creature usually feels, it is the only example in existence. As an adult, the patient believes herself to be neither male nor female but an "it" who imitates women. The evidence for these effects and their results is presented in detail elsewhere.[13]

4. *Biopsychic phenomena.* In the rare case, despite biologically normal sex and proper sex assignment, core gender identity can still be shifted by nonmental effects—that is, effects not perceived and worked over by a psyche—transmitted subliminally (unconsciously? preconsciously?) from mother to infant. I believe this occurs in the excessively intimate and blissful symbiosis found in the most feminine of boys (primary transsexuals), those who believe they are in some way female while still not denying their anatomy or sex assignment. Although they suffer from no demonstrable congenital defect and have normal external genitals, although their sex assignment is correct and is accepted by their parents, within the first year or two of life these boys are showing the effects of their mothers' too gratifying ministrations. There is no evidence that these infants were traumatized in the symbiosis or subjected to frustrations that could cause intrapsychic conflict, as is seen in effeminate homosexuals.[14]

5. *Body ego.* There is a large literature on this subject,[15] to which I have no new data to add except a footnote: Even when anatomy is defective, so that the appearance of the genitals and their sensations are different from those of intact males or females, an unequivocal sense of maleness or femaleness develops if the assignment and rearing are unequivocal.[16]

6. *Intrapsychic development.* I need not review the findings on this subject, either; recent analytic literature is filled with good studies.

The concept of core gender identity, then, is at odds with the usual analytic position, represented by the following: "The process of acquiring a differentiated sexual identity rests largely on the child's capacity to identify with the parent of the same sex."[17] Although there is evidence, often described, that identification contributes to the comfortable acceptance of one's sex, my data suggest that there is an earlier process, the one just described for core gender identity. Recognizing this process is, I think, helpful for theory. The development of core gender identity, with its use of preidentificatory mechanisms, contrasts with identification wherein we *invent* a piece of personality because of a need to do so. That is, in identification, the psychic means ("ego structures") are already present that allow the small child to do its own creating. But in the earlier process I am postulating, attributes are *imposed* on the infant and child. (Although it may later say, "I am masculine because that is what I want to be," that will be a rationalization to preserve its feeling of omnipotence by saying "I am creator of everything in me.")

Let us look at the issue of this early stage in girls, primary femininity, from two angles, the first logical and the second observational. The logic is simple. The evidence, first announced by Freud, is that in our society little girls—very little girls, as young as one-and-a-half years—suffer from penis envy.[18] But why, except to preserve a fragile theory, need we say, as Freud did, that a girl envies penises before she knows of the existence of penises? How could she be upset if the discovery were not unexpected? Does not her surprise, dismay, envy, or denial indicate her previous belief that she was intact? Is there any reason why she would not have taken her anatomy for granted prior to the momentous discovery? Did she suffer pain, restricted mobility, deprivation of the chance for early motor, sensory, or intellectual development in the first year or so of life because of a missing penis, as she would have, say, with a missing leg? Why postulate an inheritance of the memory of penises placed genetically in the fetal female brain?[19] Is it not simpler to argue that the little girl, having been informed from birth on by innumerable exchanges with her genitals and with the outside world, has no reason —no way—to doubt her femaleness until she receives new information? And even then, her surprise, disappointment, and envy in themselves indicate that her belief she is female is in its depths unchanged: she reacts the way she does because she cannot give up her sense of being a female.[20]

The second reason for doubting Freud's assertions about femininity in females is simple observation. Freud himself seems to have recognized the primary femininity and then to have struggled against accepting his own knowledge. His awareness is suggested by such comments as, "*When* the little girl discovers her own deficiency, from seeing a male genital, it is only with hesitation and reluctance that she accepts the unwelcome knowledge," and, "*When* she comes to understand the general nature of this characteristic, it follows that femaleness—and with it, of course, her mother—suffers a great depreciation in her eyes."[21]

Unfortunately, I know of no systematic—only anecdotal—reports showing that little girls are feminine long before the oedipal phase, and I believe these reports do not exist simply because no one has bothered to measure the obvious. And it is obvious. Anyone who has observed little girls has seen that they can be feminine as soon as any behavior appears that can be considered gender-related. Only if we were to say that the observed behavior and its underlying fantasy life are not genuine or are defensive constructions used for disguise, or that the little girls are really masculine but we just cannot see it, could we argue that there is "complete identity of the pre-Oedipal phase in boys and girls." If we insist that little girls believe they are little boys who have been castrated, then we must discount evidence to the contrary. If we insist that femininity is defined by passivity, masochism, and a penis envy that will be assuaged only by the substitute of growing a baby, then we may ignore other evidence. But why create such a strange definition of femininity? Why not count the ways little girls move, carry themselves, daydream, play games, choose clothes, use vocabulary? Little girls of two already show differences from little boys in styles, inflections, carriage, and fantasy life. Are not attitudes and behavior as much a part of femininity as such theoretic constructs as "passivity"?

Of course, if direct, systematized observations become available, we shall know better how early in children's lives consistent differential behavior between boys and girls can be seen. We may also discover, when large enough populations are studied, to what extent the observed differences are culture-bound and to what extent universal. (My guess would be that very few universals will be found, and that most of them will be variants on aggressive behavior, such as play in which pushing and penetrating or being pushed and being penetrated are dominant themes.)

Some such work, still fragmentary, is now being reported. Certainly in animals, these differences appear early in life. Observations of monkeys and higher apes, which have gender behavior that is not exclusively linked to reproductive behavior, show sex differences. Mothers and their infant females are closer for longer, while for the young males, separation from their mothers is enforced by mothers' breaking the symbiosis.[22] Play that will in time develop into sexual behavior also differentiates the sexes, with, for example, the males doing more mounting and the females more presenting. (All these behaviors can be reversed experimentally with brain manipulation by opposite-sex hormones at critical periods.[23])

Although the study of neonatal sex differences in human behavior by detailed observation is still rudimentary, there are data available:

> Studies of the human neonate hold promise of isolating the early roots of "innate" male-female dimorphism. Several sex differences have been reported, some replicated, others not, and most are difficult to interpret. They group into displays of greater muscle strength, sensory differences, and the degree of affiliative behavior to adults.
>
> Newborn males are more able to lift their head from a prone position. Mothers have been observed to stretch the limbs of their three-week-old boys more readily than those of their same-aged girls, but more often to imitate sounds made by the girls. Mothers have been observed to hold their five-month-old daughters more than sons, and, at thirteen months, these same daughters are more reluctant to move away from their mothers. The same thirteen-month-old children also show a different play style with toys and react differently to a barrier placed between themselves and the toys: boys tend to hurl toys about, girls tend to gather them together. They also react differently to a barrier placed between themselves and the boys: boys more often crawl to the barrier's end (in an attempt to get around it) girls more often sit where placed and cry.
>
> In an elegant research design, differential mother-attachment behavior by *opposite-sexed co-twins* was demonstrated. Female co-twins looked at, vocalized to, and maintained proximity to their mothers more than did their brothers.
>
> Other differences during the newborn period have been reported, sometimes of an obscure nature. Neonatal females increase their formula intake when a sweetner is added; boys do not. At three months, females can be conditioned to an auditory reward while boys respond to a visual one. At six months, girls show cardiac deceleration (a measure of attention) while listening to modern jazz, whereas boys decelerate to an interrupted tone.[24]

In Kleeman's reports,[25] we also find descriptions of what seems to be primary femininity, and on reading these reports, we are reminded that the feminine behavior of these girls is part of what all of us have observed. Were it not for Freud's theorizing, would anyone have doubted the existence of primary femininity?* Here are "experiments" that test the hypothesis:

*This is not to say that anything that seems obvious is to be accepted. Freud made us aware of the dangers of believing that the manifest is a complete statement of reality. But we would also be remiss if we took the position that the manifest is never an accurate view.

Marked Femininity in Males. If we want an "experiment" that makes the first stage of femininity manifest and that does so regardless of anatomy, we can look at the male primary (or true) transsexual. The type of person to be described begins to show femininity sometimes as early as a year old. Feminine behavior is found exclusively; there is no masculine development at any time in childhood or later. In childhood, the boys are taken for girls by strangers, even when dressed in boys' clothes; as adults, their femininity is accentuated, as is seen in women with hysterical personality.[26] It is not, however, contaminated with caricature as is found in effeminate homosexuals, the caricature being a marker for a hidden masculine urge that shows itself in its mockery of femininity. My data suggest that this femininity is not the result of pre-oedipal or oedipal conflict but is rather the product of the failure of the infant to sense himself as separate from his mother's female body. The process is nonconflictual, in fact, is an extremely gratifying experience of excessively prolonged mother-infant symbiosis.[27]

Throughout life, then, the male transsexual retains "her" feminine appearance, behavior, and position vis-à-vis other people. "Her" fantasy life and its manifestations in everyday living are feminine in style and heterosexual in object choice. But, as has been described elsewhere,[28] the rest of femininity—the second meaning, the second phase that is the result of the oedipal complex—is not found. These people have no impulse for pregnancy or mothering (except that which is expressed in clichéd manner in order to simulate the patient's image of a normal woman). I experienced this absence especially in the transference, a great silence in the patient's capacity to relate to me, unlike transference with other kinds of people—except, perhaps, very exhibitionistic women, such as models and starlets. For years I believed there was no transference until I realized that this absence *is* the transference. It is the recapitulation of an infancy and childhood in which father was absent and mother treated her beautiful son as if he were a *thing,* an ideal feminized phallus that she had grown from her own body and then kept all too attached in the unending symbiosis. The trouble is that this boy—this creature of his mother's need—has never experienced oedipal conflict. I have never seen a true transsexual (by my restricted definition, not by the one generally used: that the person requests "sex change") without this "empty" transference; and some of these patients have been seeing me for ten to fifteen years.*

*In keeping with the odd attachment to mother that I experience in the transference, none of these patients has ever accepted my offer to treat "her" psychodynamically. They only use me as an effective caretaker who knows how to ease reality for them or who is to listen attentively and benignly.

It seems to me, then, that this stage in femininity can occur in early childhood in both males or females and results in a femininity that is genuine (a natural, unstudied, nonmimicking appearance). This primary femininity is, however, lacking in other qualities also designated as feminine, such as impulses to be a mother (the urge to be pregnant, to give birth to an infant, to nurse, to cuddle a baby, to raise and educate a child) or to take on the role of companion or wife. These latter, when not merely transitory imitations, are the products, in the form our society takes in this era, of later experiences, that is, of oedipal conflict and its resolution. They are not just a matter of appearance, but demand commitments to oneself and others beyond the reach of primary femininity. (One can see, then, that primary and later femininity, arising from different processes, may be rather independent of each other, so that a woman not very feminine in demeanor may be a wonderful mother and vice versa.)

Marked Masculinity in Females. A further test of a theory of the origins of femininity in females can be made by the study of the most masculine girls and women, female transsexuals. In the absence of demonstrable biologic (including anatomic) defect, these patients develop from childhood in a most masculine manner. Sooner or later, usually while still children, they ask that their bodies be "transformed" to male.* If the thesis is that the male transsexual's femininity results from a too-intimate, gratifying, unending symbiosis with the mother, encouragement of feminine behavior by their mother once it appears, and their father's failure to interfere, then opposite parental influences should produce masculinity. Were these opposite influences at work in the infancy and childhood of the female transsexual? The answer seems to be yes. Not enough cases have been reported for confirmation, but so far, our research team has found that the most masculine female children and adults (numbering fourteen)—and only the most masculine—have fit the thesis.

In brief, the findings show that sometime during the first year or so of life, the mother-infant symbiosis is severely disrupted.[29] The mother, usually because of severe depression but at times for other reasons, is unable to nurture the infant girl. No other woman is substituted as a mother (as might happen if this mother died), so the little girl is not given adequate mothering, only subsistence. Yet mother is somewhere in the household, out of reach but a tantalizing presence (which leads

*They do not merely daydream of being men or at times represent themselves in dreams at night as having male qualities, but consciously, insistently, vociferously demand that their bodies be changed.

to a lifelong yearning on the girl's part to save and protect feminine-appearing, mothering women).

Father does not assuage his wife's suffering. Instead, the little girl is made to sense that she should function as her mother's cure. Rather than serving as a supportive husband to his wife, father appoints this daughter as the succorer. Unhappily, such cures do not work; mother does not get well and enfold this daughter. The little girl, however, establishes a good relationship with her father, to whom she turns for comfort and closeness. They become comrades, and in the process, the father encourages behavior like his own: masculine. So, by three or four years of age, the girl is already acting very much like a boy, unwilling and unable to submit to demands that she be feminine. By this time, she dresses only in boys' clothes, plays exclusively with boys in wholly boy games, and imagines herself as having a penis or prays each night that God will affix one. (Disrupted mother-daughter symbiosis, unreachable mother, and encouragement by father to identify with him are found, though in different proportions, in two other categories of women with powerful masculine components: mothers of male transsexuals, and women who believe—hallucinate—that they have grown a penis.[30])

There is reason to believe, therefore, that just as excessively close and gratifying mother-son intimacy can produce femininity even in a biologically intact male, so can massive disruption of symbiosis cause masculinity in a female child; just as a psychologically absent father can contribute to femininity in a boy, so can a close relationship based on identification with father (rather than on father as a heterosexual object) contribute to masculinity in a girl; and just as a mother who encourages graceful and nonmasculine behavior in a boy can contribute to his femininity, so can a father who reinforces nonfeminine behavior encourage masculinity in a girl.

These factors are indicated, even in the guarded circumstances of a conference, in the most recent female transsexual seen by our team; the patient* has lived as a man for several years. We learn about femininity by studying masculinity:

> PT. My primary relationships [in childhood] were with males, my father. But that doesn't answer anything to me. Because I was around a lot of women too, but my deepest affinity was with my father.
>
> DR. B. Yes, but often when that happens what ensues is an attraction toward men rather than an identification.
>
> DR. N. How about the other way around? Was there any evidence that your

*Dr. Howard Baker's patient.

father was attracted to you? In other words, that he thought that you
were pretty or cute or lovely?

PT. No, my father always treated me as a son.

DR. N. What do you mean by that? He knew you weren't his son.

PT. Well, my father and I had a—I don't know. I don't know how much
that played a part in our relationship until I was about thirteen or
fourteen, you know, when the breasts developed, and I started singing;
and it was obvious that there was a beautiful voice there. Then he
perhaps treated me more as a daughter, but before that he treated my
brother and I identical.

DR. K. In what way?

PT. Going on hunting trips and fishing, and when he built churches we
went out and, you know, built and did plumbing and electrical stuff
and mixed cement and cut the lawns and whatever else.

DR. N. He never put you on his lap or kissed you?

PT. Neither of my parents were affectionate. The most my father would
do . . . My mother never touched us, but the most my father would
do, and he would do that fairly frequently was, you know, pat us on
our shoulder.

DR. B. What about your sister; did he treat your sister that way?

PT. No, no, no.

DR. B. Did he want to?

PT. No.

DR. B. Why not?

PT. Because she wrecked everything she touched. She had no ability that
way at all. My sister was very poorly coordinated. And also her head
was always in a book, and he never interrupted that.

DR. B. So there was some kind of feedback between you and your father that
you were receptive to the requests he made upon you, and your sister
was not.

PT. Yes. I helped him do all the carpentry work, built cabinets and all that;
he taught me what he knew. He taught me to use power tools by the
time I was eleven.

DR. N. What do you think he thought, the two of them thought of you as you
were growing up before puberty?

PT. Well, I can only answer that from a couple of months ago when I
talked to my parents about this. And their response was that they felt
the way that I was living now and attempting to live [as a male] was
far more satisfying to me and to them than the attempt at the gay life,
and they said they had known from the time I was ten that there was
a real problem there, but they didn't know what to do about it. And

my mother just said that she often blamed herself, and I said I can't see where that could be; she was pretty much at fault—she wasn't an average mother because she was, I mean for that community, she was one of the few professional women there, but in terms of the way that we were raised, we were raised pretty much as other kids were. You had to be on your own young.

DR. B. When you were very young do you recall whether or not your mother was ever ill?

PT. My mother was sick constantly.

DR. B. Can you tell us about it?

PT. Well, I think it probably started with the back injury she had, but she had periods of really pushing herself hard and then going into total collapse, and so lots of times she would be sick and nobody would tell me what was wrong with her. And I would think she was dying.

DR. B. How old were you then?

PT. When I was really aware of it I must have been six and it really reached a peak when I was ten or twelve.

DR. B. Was it going on earlier?

PT. I would presume so because the accident—I can remember a little bit about early childhood, and I remember once my sister and I took a walk down the highway, and when we came back she told us we caused her to have a heart attack or something. But I used to always think it was my fault that she was sick.

DR. B. Who took care of her when she was sick?

PT. I did. I did most of the time. Because I never would leave her when she was sick.

DR. B. Could you tell us something you remember about that?

PT. I don't really remember a great deal about it except that I used to be terrified when she was sick. I was afraid of losing her. My dad was gone all the time and so I would stay out of school. That's where I developed the ability to do a semester's work in three weeks, and I would stay home and cook for her and keep the house clean, because my sister would not do anything, and I would nurse her and if necessary go get the doctor, or one of the missionary nurses, and I would give her her medication. I would sit, and lots of times she was not really in her head because of the medication. It was very frightening to me.

DR. B. How old were you then, the earliest time?

PT. The earliest time I remember doing that was when I was six.

DR. K. Do you know what her illnesses were?

PT. It turned out later that it was a thyroid condition, and the back; she had been very seriously injured and when she would overdo she would go into a problem of sciatica; but she had a thyroid condition too which was not diagnosed for years, and she had a lot of problems, but she carried on quite well in spite of it. I was very protective like. I learned to drive when I was eleven because every time she would drive, she drove into a telephone post. She could not drive; so I learned to drive. I had my brother take me to the airport, and I learned to drive, and then I drove her everywhere she went.

DR. N. You said your father was absent so much because of his work—the over-all picture that you are describing. How important do you think you were to the functioning of the family?

PT. I ran the family when my mother was ill. My brother was working in construction. We did not have a lot of money. So he was working, and my sister worked; so I really ran the house. I did most of the shopping.

DR. N. What would it have been like if you were not like that; let's say you were more like your sister.

PT. God only knows; it would have been a disaster.

DR. B. Meaning what?

PT. My dad would not have been able to function in that capacity.

Comparison of this material with that published elsewhere on transsexual females shows the same factors at work.[31]

By now we should know that major aspects of character structure develop from two different ways of learning. The one that has been especially the domain of psychoanalytic study is learning that is the result of frustration, conflict, trauma, and resolution of conflict via defense mechanisms. Freud's theory of the development of masculinity and femininity is almost exclusively of this sort (except for his firmly held though vaguely documented belief in biologic contributions).

The other, conflict-free learning, was introduced into our theory to restore balance, but it is still not well secured. Theorizing on concepts like "self" and "identity" are preliminary attempts to absorb these intuitions into analytic theory. We are open to using these ideas, perhaps, when we agree that a major piece of character structure cannot be understood without our investigating the contributions of both ways of learning.[32]

And so it is with the development of femininity in women. I would suggest that this development can be conceptualized as being of two different orders.* In the first, which can occur in either males or females, learning takes place that is conflict-free and mostly egosyntonic, consisting of behaviors the little girl identifies with or is taught

*I am indebted to Dr. Lawrence E. Newman for discussions in which these ideas were clarified.

and encouraged in, especially by her mother. Mechanisms like conditioning, identification, and imitation contribute heavily to such learning, resulting in the automatized behaviors and convictions, attitudes, and fantasies of the core gender identity. The manifestations of this stage—such as what clothes the little girl prefers, what dolls she plays with, how she carries herself—these external appearances are culture-bound, fashions, changing as parents' desired image of their daughter's femininity changes. (This does not in the least imply that an infant's development is conflict-free, only that certain behaviors are learned and maintained by conflict-free processes. And of course, unpleasure increasingly plays its necessary role in creating and maintaining gender identity.)

The second, but by no means lesser, order of femininity, the one on which psychoanalysis has concentrated, results from conflict and envy in the oedipal situation. It brings a new desire and danger to affection, erotism, awareness of anatomic differences between the sexes, and to wishes for children. And it gives depth and richness, via the fantasy systems the girl creates to manage these problems, to those behaviors we label feminine. This form of femininity is made from conflict and its resolution and simply cannot appear without such creative tension. For instance, the switch from yearning for her mother to longing for her father will be negotiated in a girl's mind by conscious and unconscious fantasies on such themes as how to be rid of mother and how to get father's attention and then desire. She creates these fantasies to correct the traumas and frustrations of reality. The little girl's play will be shaped to promote satisfaction of these fantasies. And then she will fill out the play world with something more substantial, more fully experienced in bone and muscle, belly and chest: imitation and automatization of behaviors observed in the real world that clearly do or possibly might appeal to father. If the subject that preoccupies her is what father likes about and wants from females, she will gather in clues from her environment, and to the extent that she comprehends and refashions these in line with the progress of her development, she will convert the observations into behaviors. Those that feel right are likely to be repeated, rounded off for a good fit till automatic; they become chronic—what we conceptualize as "a piece of character structure" or "identity theme" or "identity." And when these fantasy-systems-become-behavior focus on certain topics, we call what we see "femininity."

This is not to deny that girls pick up defensively masculine qualities early in life. But I believe this occurs only after the desires and behaviors have been laid down that mark the presence of primary femininity.

Recall the woman described in the preceding chapter (pages 19–20) who was attracted to men she sensed as dangerous. Men with this attribute were dehumanized by her in that her excitement occurred only when she rid them of their individuality and responded to their common characteristic: they were phallic. That is, they were brittle-strong; erotically driven; unable to sustain intimacy in a woman's embrace; hard and forceful in carriage, speech, and expression of feeling rather than showing such "weaknesses" as tenderness or generosity; fiercely competitive professionally without loving their work; unreliable. Every man of this sort was exciting, for she saw them all as equal. (I believe dehumanization is the main motive behind promiscuity—"indiscriminate mingling," says the dictionary—as different from other styles of liking and wanting a variety of sexual objects.)

As soon as her figure developed at puberty, she discovered, to her surprise and relief, that her femaleness served her wonderfully in the attacks she needed to mount against men. It would not be quite accurate to say that she equated her body with a phallus but rather that she used it phallically, as a weapon to destroy the phallicness of men. But she made it clear from the start of her analysis that the fundament of her being was her femaleness; her purpose in being analyzed was to free her sense of the value of her femaleness from the contaminating, defensive phallic overlay. She used her vagina in the way she experienced that her lovers used their penises: to ruin the sexual object in the act of love. When she finally discovered her vagina again as her female organ for intimacy, love, and erotism and as a reproductive organ, she was no longer excited by these phallic men. Promiscuity ended.

Certainly, as Freud discovered, penis envy and blaming mother for the lack of a penis can turn a girl to masculine behaviors; and these can be used in the service of a homosexuality that tries to win possession of mother. But that struggle does not kill the earlier femininity. Both —primary femininity and defensive masculinity—persist into the next phase, wherein successful resolution of oedipal conflict—resolution that is gratifying and without flooding hostility as the blighted harvest —brings about a more complex femininity, modifications more likely to allow a girl to convert the tasks ahead to congenial, productive womanhood.

From such chronic and successful resolution of conflict come attitudes and behavior attached to tasks assigned to females by biology or culture, such as ways of expressing sexual excitement (differences between men and women in response to pornography, in parts of the genitals from which one draws erotic sensations), desire for or pleasure from the fruitfulness of pregnancy, capacity to mother infants and rear children, etc., etc.

There are implications for treatment in these ideas.[33] Although the ideal of the nonjudgmental analyst may be neither attainable nor desirable, most of us feel that the less we introduce our biases and idiosyncrasies, the more likely transference manifestations will remain free to be analyzed. Regarding the question whether primary femininity exists or not, we find that a theoretic issue is likely to become a living pressure insinuated into the analyses of women. For instance, one analyst may consider his work finished only when a woman accepts* that she believed herself a castrated male in childhood, renounces her wish for a penis, and expresses true femininity by graceful admission that maleness is better. Such an analysis will look different from that of an analyst who believes this woman had an early, uncomplicated phase of primary femininity before the disappointments due to the discovery of penises. That analyst may at times judge as genuine certain expressions of joy in her anatomy and its functions, while the first analyst, attached to a different theory, will hear the same joy as being defensive, manic, evidence of reaction formation, denial, or splitting.

When, as in treatment, envy of men's phallicness dies down in women whose commitment to being feminine and to being female has been overlaid with anger, competitiveness, and desire for revenge, they may still dream of wounds or excisions. But one must distinguish between castration and debridement. In contrast to earlier dreams that were about (or were accompanied by associations to) mutilation, dangerous hemorrhage, or permanent crippling, there is now a new theme: the removal of excess, ugly, or diseased tissue so that the flesh can return to its former healthy state.

And a woman may even have such a dream of repair—by cutting— at the start of analysis; it is a shame if an analyst misses that announcement and thinks only of castration.

If primary femininity exists and the analyst does not believe it, what happens to the patient's trust in her analyst? On the other hand, if primary femininity does not exist and the analyst acts as if it does, what trust will a woman have in an analyst who, even silently, gives her false support?

Although it is old-fashioned to say they exist, it is no secret that there are women with richly textured and complex femininity who meet anyone's criteria for psychic health. Their femininity is the product of a solid core gender identity, permanent and non-conflict-laden identifi-

*Translate: acknowledges masochistically and passively.

cations with feminine women, and successful grappling with and mastery of oedipal conflicts in which they participated with their mothers and fathers. We need not doubt it; they unthinkingly, comfortably accept having female bodies that are sources of physical pleasure. Should they marry and have children, they draw from their femininity a capacity for mothering in which there is so little hostility that, with the help of their masculine husbands, they raise their sons to be masculine and their daughters feminine.

PART 2

Data: Belle

3

Case Summary

LET US CALL her Belle, for that suggests how she felt she was when analysis began: old-fashioned femininity; a touch of exhibitionism; gentle masochism; a slightly addled yet refreshing innocence; soft, round, dreamy erotism; an unbounded focus on males, romance, silken garments, flowers and bees, bosoms, bare behinds, and babies.

At the start of her analysis she was twenty-four, a quiet, intelligent, attractive, well-groomed, feminine woman, white, American, Southern, middle-class, college-educated, single, Baptist (fundamentalist sect, her mother heavy on the dramas of sin, her father bored with church). She was an only child, whose parents—both descendants of famous Southern families, her mother's still intact, her father's only a rumor from the past—had separated when she was six. Her father had died a year later; her mother died a year after the analysis began. Belle entered analysis with a sense of distress she could not clearly articulate, a feeling that she was wasting her life and would continue to do so forever, and especially that her wish to be a wife and mother would be thwarted by fate. Fate took the form of a belief that men, whom she desired and envied, were banded together in a brotherhood of scorn for women like herself. Although she claimed full commitment to her belief that she was doomed by the power inherent in men's masculinity, she contradicted this belief to the extent that she sought analysis. Two asides that came to dominate treatment were mentioned during the evaluation in a tone of voice that implied the subjects were hardly worth noting: she was a bit self-conscious except when alone, and she thought her sexual pleasure was impaired but was not sure how. (Unlike most of my patients now, she did not enter analysis because of a marked gender problem or as the parent of a child with a gender problem.)

Other information, such as her profession, is not mentioned if not pertinent to the limited goal of this presentation: to understand her sexual daydream. The price paid is that the reader's picture of Belle's true character is incomplete. But since my purpose in this book is to concentrate on a primarily intrapsychic event—sexual excitement—I hope to get away with leaving out the facts that would be necessary were I explicating other aspects of her existence. That could not be done without compromising the confidentiality or accuracy of the data. When one falsifies a fact in order to disguise a patient's identity, one damages the material somewhat. Therefore I am lucky to be working in an area of study in which so much is made up of fantasy and of events from the distant past that few external facts need be changed to preserve Belle's privacy.[1]

Her mother was a tantalizing, vain, frivolous woman, a milkless breast uncommitted to the child except as it served to display Mother's feat of having produced a baby, and incapable of sustained contact with the infant Belle. The first dream Belle recalls ever having in her life: "Candy is falling from the sky, and I am all excited about it. It was going to taste marvelous, but when I picked some up and put it in my mouth, it melted away without any taste, worse than cotton candy." Her father, who was old enough to be her mother's father, was a professional athlete who at times made a lot of money. A passive man, he accepted himself as others saw him: all muscle and no culture, hypochondriacal and unreliable. He took up with a teen-age girl when Belle was six. The trauma of his leaving was compounded within a year by his death, and within the next when her mother became successful enough in the entertainment world to be away from home for weeks and often months at a time. During these separations, the child was left in the care of her father's brother's widow, a woman of pious and forceful character whom Belle would refer to only as "The Caretaker." Although Mother returned at times to visit, the understanding was that her profession, which required her to live for long periods anywhere in the world, precluded more frequent visiting. Throughout these several years, Belle was made to believe that plans were afoot for her mother to rejoin her for good. When this finally happened, Mother returned with a new husband, a retired European army officer, who, in contrast to Belle's real father, was her mother's age. The three of them lived together until Belle was eighteen, when she came to Southern California for college.

She remained here after graduation, going to work for the company with which she continued until the last year of her analysis. She is now self-employed. Because her life in the real world has been orderly, without crises, and even without unusual excitements, it does no damage to our limited purpose to concentrate on her inner life. In fact, to do so will not create an artifact but rather will establish accurately for the reader a sense of what was Belle's experience: her fantasies were the focus of her daily existence from the time she went to college to the time of analysis. Outer reality served mostly to provide props and characters for the conscious daydreams she created all day.

She was not considered neurotic by those who knew her, except— when observed from the odd perspective of analysis—herself and me.

This is the skeleton of historical reality on which shall be hung Belle's fantasy world.

"I shall be abandoned" is the theme,* with its connotation of betrayal, that dominated her childhood. I place it here at the start of this discussion of her so that you will think of it as part of all the aspects of her with which you will become familiar. My main clinical thesis is that Belle, from birth on, had to suffer and somehow cope with her parents' inconstancy—their not caring enough for her to concentrate on her needs.

Several other important "identity themes"[2] run through Belle's analysis. In order to give you an overview of her before getting more specific, I shall describe them briefly.

First, the theme most dangerous for her future and for the treatment, was her expectation of disaster.

She was cheery enough when we met and during the hours of evaluation before formally beginning analysis. Her life had proceeded without catastrophes, dreadful symptoms, or manifest failures. She was young, lively, intelligent, sensual, attractive, stylish, educated, and nice. Her first dream in the analysis, however, troubled me. "It was a hilly place. There had been a plane crash and debris was littered about. Somehow [in a way that was not portrayed visually or aurally] there was a list of survivors and the dead; I was listed as dead. Still, I was walking with a group of people. It was not clear who they were, but I think they were supposed to be my family and other people I had known." But, she adds, the most important feature of the dream—then she says, of all her dreaming—is the scenery, not the people: landscapes, streets, houses, neighborhoods. And that was true; for a long time the landscapes dominated, and even as the people gradually became more significant, the importance of the landscapes and settings never diminished. (The change was in the increasing delineation of the humans' features and personalities.)

---

*Themes are related to but different from scripts; a script, we know, is a story line with characters taking their parts in order to move the action along, while a theme is not a story but a persisting idea, concept, or presentation. Themes are in scripts, but a script is not a theme.

The same hour she reported a second dream: "I am walking along a street. There is no sidewalk. There has been a holocaust of some kind, but it's not clear what has happened. I am walking with a young woman, and we come upon what seems a sleeper train. Everyone senses there are crises coming. There are dull explosions in the background because there is a bombing going on."

These first dreams state the theme, on which endless variations (earthquakes, bombs, huge waves, runaway cars, fires, floods) would be played with diminishing intensity as the analysis proceeded until they faded out toward the end. This theme, that probably no good would come from living her life and that disasters were impending, gave me a most uneasy feeling; at times when she was suffocating in her self-destructive passions, I felt I was hanging on by the fingertips.

I had not sensed her really to be working as an analytic patient for some months after we started. She was so superficial. She had no free associations to speak of. Dreams were reported just for the sake of presenting dreams. Nothing moved. Then, during a few hours, the process opened up; she stopped blotting everything out. She reported this dream: "I am in an institution or on a campus or in a small city [UCLA is located in a part of Los Angeles called Westwood Village, which, when she was in analysis years ago, was like a village] and in the basement of a building. In some way I was responsible: there were a lot of children, already dead. It had been arranged. They had been sentenced or something else like that; and so they were dead. There was a woman in charge of this operation. The whole thing was very secret, going on in the basement. The woman was maybe fifty or maybe sixty, and she had two different faces. I gave her the face of a woman who was sweet and kind, but in the dream she did not act that way at all. Also, there was my child, a girl, who was involved in some way, who had to burn up the bodies after the children had been killed. She should not have had to be involved in this way. I wonder if she was in some way supposed to be me. It was an ugly dream and painful and frightening; it makes me afraid I may go crazy." Again the catastrophes, but now the analysis had begun to move; I had sensed that in the previous hours. And she was ready to reveal that there were secrets in her basement.

A second identity theme—perhaps two themes—was the conviction, held by the family at large and put into her as a truth, that she was damaged—appearances to the contrary, and she was told clearly that she was supposed to develop appearances to the contrary—because she was her mother's daughter. This was compounded by a second "inheritance": that she was the daughter of that inferior, despised man. Believing herself composed of these two substances, she had never generated much sense of worth, despite the more positive themes built into her. ✡

In addition, by accepting these two avowedly unalterable qualities, she internalized the war between them: if we are each of our parents, we are also their hatred of each other, or, if lucky, their love. (I am presuming that when we take in—identify with—our parents, we not only select attributes of each but also accept our versions of some of their scripts.) The relationship between our parents is preserved in us, not just their separate pieces.[3] These identifications, then, are among the givens—the building blocks—from which our scripts are created.

I believe there are such stages as oral, anal, and phallic, and that a piece of behavior-become-character-structure can be shown to originate at a particular time. But I do not agree that the conflicts are primarily instinctual in nature, that specific neuroses or psychoses result from instinctual vicissitudes occurring during a particular stage (that hysteria, for example, is a product of the phallic stage). The interpersonal should be emphasized more. Still, oral, anal, and phallic themes are found in everyone. A few examples from Belle will suffice for now: oral —dreams of kitchens, restaurants, locusts, cannibalism, vacuum cleaners; anal—dreams of laundries and mud, fear of humiliation from secretions; phallic—envy as a child when looking at little boys' penises; or mixed types—dreams of food smearing.

On getting to know people, we sense another theme that permeates them and that they transmit: the age they feel they are—say, a child, or a teen-ager, or a young adult, or old—regardless of their chronologic age.* One even, though rarely, knows people whose chronologic age matches their "identity age." (Some people present the same stage of development all the time, while others have more than one. This sense of "identity age" is, for me, independent of a person's neurotic or even psychotic symptomatology.) For Belle, I sensed two ages, both of which gave me a better feeling about the prognosis than did her often primitive behavior. Mostly she seemed somewhere just beyond puberty, but when pushed to it, she could be herself at her present age: neurotic, but full-grown.

A person's style of dreaming is as distinctive as a fingerprint. This may change over the decades. Analytic treatment and other powerful life events speed up the process of change; not only do elements and moods, story lines, and types of characters (such as humans versus animals) shift, but more tidal movements occur, hard to describe but

*One plays these ages-of-man themes chronically and with appropriate clichés: brave, confused, passive, nasty, long-suffering, silly, altruistic, stubborn, exhausted, bawdy, dour, naïve, blasé, wise; and with appropriate props: clothes, haircuts, styles of smoking and alcohol use, cars, inflections. In time, the themes are fixed in anatomy.

deeply felt. For instance, a jittery, flickering unfolding of dream stories can quiet down to a more gentle flow, nightmares can disappear, brightness grow darker, death retreat or advance, greed soften or turn fierce, and biting rage die down to peacefulness—or vice versa. You could pick Belle out in a crowd of dreamers by her endless dreaming on these themes: female anatomy and physiology; feminine roles such as sexual partner, wife, mother, companion; clothes and fabrics; colors; music; houses and furnishings; and—an odd break from these "sensible" elements—her feeling (not hearing or seeing) words, phrases, or ideas: nonsense words, nonsense names of people and animals, names of songs that do not exist; musical concepts (not music heard); geometric patterns, sometimes seen or just felt but not seen; or unadorned oddness, of which even she could not make any sense, sitting in the middle of the dream's story line: for example, "babies were to be passed out according to intervals of hamburgers." For me (of earthbound, nonartistic sensibility), these, coming in the midst of a dream report, were like stepping into empty space. (Did they represent for Belle some sort of infantile aloneness or sense of not being supported?)

Here is a shower of dreams in her typical first-year-of-analysis style (probably more useful to the analyst than to the general reader for getting to know her): "There was a bus. Someone said, 'Get out,' and we got out and saw there was a policeman. He was shooting at a bomb that was in the street. We thought that was crazy, because that would just ignite the bomb; so we didn't want to get out. It turned out it was only a joke to see if we would react.

"There was another part to the dream. There was a room with a lot of objects. Some were very nice, and some were just junk. I then masturbated, but I stopped when I heard a man coming." This makes her think of a dream from the night before: "It was a shadowy room. I was eating with an old teacher and his wife, and I was supposed to tell the story of Pignora and Gullah [neologisms]. The story I was supposed to tell was about a woman dressed in Victorian clothes, who had on a wild hat. She was to be Pignora. She was bad and mischievous. Then there were pigs in the dream. There was something about throwing water on a man by mistake."

Then there was another part: "We were driving a car and almost hit a woman who was dragging a laundry hamper. We got out, and I saw there were three intelligent animals standing on the hill by the road. One was a tall pig, one was a cow, and one was a dog or a wolf. I liked them. Some hippies in Arab costumes and blond hair came by on camels. Then I was riding a pig; it was a fat, black, little pig. It was really too little to ride on. I was in shorts and I had on no underwear.

I had a lot of vaginal discharge, and it was getting all over the pig."*

Modes of identification could be another theme, but this is too unclear for more than a brief mention. There are identifications formed pleasurably and not for solving conflicts, and there are those used for conflict resolution. The latter, I think, are invaded by anger, hatred, or sarcasm and are meant, at some level, to harm the loved but pain-creating object. For instance, as noted elsewhere,[4] sarcasm is an essential ingredient in homosexuals' effeminacy, a mixture of a desire to be like women, fear that the desire may go too far, and envy and anger at not being a woman; the result is caricature. Belle's sense of herself as a liar is another example.

She believed she was a liar, and of two sorts (I am talking now about being a liar, not about self-deception, rationalization, denial, or repression). In the first category, she was an ordinary liar, and she felt guilty about that. In the second, she was granted the privilege of lying because her mother had that right (as we shall see), but more subtly because, in lying, she was not only being like but also was making fun of her mother. At any rate, unlike the ordinary liar, she often felt no conscious guilt. It was quite a problem in treatment; for a long time I did not even sense it. Then I sensed it but thought it was some sort of crazy distortion introduced into her thinking by a psychotic-like irruption. Only after she delineated her mother's habitual lying did I begin to sniff it out as partly an identification. That insight forced it to take a different form. She gave it a masochistic twist so that she was now lying so grotesquely that she could not get away with it; she told the truth by telling lies badly. In the final form, many months later, she caught herself the moment she told a lie; after that, the device disappeared (almost) from the analysis.

It was a difficult and unpleasant symptom to deal with, and yet I always felt she was honest. The lying was not important, simply an analyzable symptom, but the honesty—desire for honesty—there at the beginning and persisting throughout, was essential to the treatment. (More and more I think success in analysis depends on the patient's need to be honest.)

She constantly thought I was lying, that I was always lying because I was by nature a liar. But in time she recognized that the reason she stayed in treatment for years with this liar was her deeper belief that I did not lie. Only the latter gave her the freedom to say I was a liar.

Another theme. Belle's "paranoid leak," as she called it: her uncom-

*Associations: Alice in Wonderland, an Indian story with a wallah, Pygmalion, Ibsen's Nora, a boyfriend's slovenly sister and alcoholic brother, Circe, sloppy sex, me, her mother, her father, the Director, Baptists, baptism, Catholicism, candles, tallow, Jews, Dachau.

mon capacity to live in the real world, apparently in full contact with reality, yet be heavily committed to a daydream. "Last night I met a man named Robert, and he is sexually interested in me. So I knew today that you would be sexually interested in me." A more complicated falsification was her insistence that some of her acquaintances were in contact with me. Her employer, she said she was sure, regularly called me, which was why we both said a similar thing to her during the same week. An aunt was phoning me to check on Belle's treatment, no question about it. Whereas the feeling I would get from another patient reporting such tales would be that the latter *was* paranoid, with Belle I thought only that she was nutty; that is, she had me believing she really believed it, and at the same time I was thinking, "No; she can't!"

Near the end of treatment, she made it clear. She knew none of the tales was true and yet she was simultaneously living another of her scripts to the hilt. The power came, not from the paranoid manifest theme, but from the latent theme below: They are constantly keeping an eye on me *for my welfare*. It may be painful to believe you are constantly watched and talked about, but such harassment certainly proves that you are not unnoticed—abandoned.

Everyone out there was a character in her script, and she would run through, and display, appropriate emotions for the script. No; not quite appropriate: like (but less than) professional actresses,* she was often on stage, and those who looked closely could see she was usually laying it on a bit thick. In fact, this was the result of her continuously playing a character in her own plays. Those who are genuinely paranoid are even more committed to believing their acts are real (though a careful piece of therapy can wring from the most paranoid patient an admission that he sometimes knows he is a playwright).

Other identity themes could just as well be emphasized by those with different theoretic interests or purposes from mine. For instance, had this been a study of creativity I would have described the experiences, from infancy on, that contributed to Belle's aesthetic and artistic sensibilities. I would then have emphasized a theme that I shall not mention further: her musical ability. Although it might occupy her for hours in a day, I leave it aside, along with other interests and delights that are as much a part of her life as the ones I have chosen. Obviously, if we are going to focus on sexual excitement, we shall see a grossly distorted picture of the whole person.

Belle had been an incessant daydreamer as far back as she could

---

*I suppose that many actors and actresses, when abandoned in childhood, hypertrophied their daydreaming skills, forcing make-believe to take on the feeling of reality. As adults, they often know that they do not sense themselves as real except when on stage.

remember. In early childhood, daydreams filled in for her parents' abandonments. (Before age six, when she thinks her daydreaming began, her favorite fairy tale was about a beautiful Snow Queen who lived far in the north and had a gnome working for her—not an ideal oedipal configuration.) Loneliness produced daydreaming, and because she could make it so gratifying, daydreaming guaranteed greater loneliness. She says, "I never played as a child does after I was six years old." Though comfortable with girls, she had no close friends throughout her school years. Instead of playing with children, she says, she had experiences with them. Her real life was inside; the people outside were all too much just characters for her scripts. (I certainly came to experience that in the treatment.)

While she was still a child, then, her sense of being a forsaken person became fixed. We can conceptualize that sense as a belief, an expectation, a piece of character structure, a chronic defense, a tactic, whatever: its retrievable form was fantasies. These were unconscious, the proximate source ("force," "energy") behind innumerable forms of her behavior. Having constructed, from actual desertions, this sense of identity as the abandoned one, she found daydreaming a sharply pleasurable way of soothing fear and anguish. Loneliness encourages such script-writing.

4

The Erotic Daydream

HERE IS BELLE'S prototypic daydream; we shall try to understand its origins and functions.

A cruel man, The Director, a Nazi type, is directing the activity. It consists of Belle being raped by a stallion, which has been aroused to a frenzy by a mare held off at a distance beyond where Belle is placed. In a circle around the periphery stand vaguely perceived men, expressionless, masturbating while ignoring each other, the Director, and Belle. She is there for the delectation of these men, including the Director, who, although he has an erection, makes no contact with her: her function is to be forced to unbearable sexual excitement and pleasure, thereby making a fool of herself before these men. She has been enslaved in this obscene exhibition of humiliation because it creates erections in these otherwise feelingless men; they stand there in phallic, brutal indifference. All that, however, is foreplay, setting the scene. What sends her excitement up and almost immediately to orgasm as she masturbates is not this scene alone, for obviously, if it were really happening, she would experience horror, not pleasure. Rather, what excites her is the addition of some detail that exacerbates her humiliation, e.g., the horse is replaced by a disreputable, ugly old man; or her excitement makes her so wild that she is making a dreadful scene; or her palpitating genitals are spotlighted to show that she has lost control of her physiology. And, behind the scenes, a part of herself permits the excitement because it (she) knows that she, who is masturbating in the real world, is not literally the same as "she" who is the suffering woman in the story. In the story, she is humiliated; in reality, she is safe.

My task in this book is to take that daydream and, as Belle and I did in her analysis, separate out its components.

A year or so into her analysis, Belle first mentioned the daydream.

She had been struggling during this hour not to express—not even to feel—anger toward me that was set off by her belief that in the previous hour I had subtly implied she was not feminine. When I said it was odd I had never seen her angry, she replied that perhaps it was odd but that it made sense to her nonetheless. She said there was nothing that had ever happened with me that she had to be angry about, but her next thought was that after the last hour, she kept gagging from being so upset. "But that really isn't anything," she added. And then, without feeling, "You hate everything about me." She thinks of a battleship, of a childhood fantasy of being peacefully underground in a silent and happy community (a fantasy reported before, to be discussed later); and then: "Did I ever tell you the first sex fantasy I ever had? There are men and women performing on a stage. They are defecating and urinating." The hour ended shortly thereafter. (Only months later did I learn that this was not the first erotic daydream.)

In the next hour, in response to her diffuse remarks about masturbation daydreams and technique (vagueness was a strong defense in the analysis this far), I expressed the belief that there was value in detailed description, in that way urging her to say openly what she was thinking. The result, in the following hour, was the first report of the daydream. With more embarrassment and struggle than I had seen before, she said there was a daydream: "It's about a horse having intercourse with me." Silence. I then nudged her, asking her not only to announce what the fantasy was about but to reveal its details. (The resistance of secrecy often takes the form of people telling what they are thinking *about* but not *what* they are thinking.)

She continued, saying that in the story she is watching herself having intercourse with a horse. Then, "No, that's not quite accurate. It really isn't myself that's watching. It's some man, and he is watching me doing this with the horse. And the reason that I am doing it is because if I do this with the horse, it will excite the man who is watching. So I do it for his sake, and in that way I can prove to him how great he is and that I am willing to make a fool of myself, humiliate myself, in order to gratify the man."

The following hour, she reported two dreams, both of which were composed of elements I subsequently heard often enough. The first: "I was wearing a blue crepe thing that I have. It's very feminine. I was sitting in a chair. There was a fountain pen which had splattered all over the hem. I got a solvent and used it everywhere, but I just couldn't get rid of the ink." The second: "We were in a cottage, which we were showing to other people who also wanted to rent the cottage. A lot of dirty laundry, and they were ripping up the bathroom and all the plumbing. And then it smelled bad. The maids were in there trying to clean the place up. They were very sulky. The man who was in this cottage was very annoyed because he had clients there, but I didn't feel at all rejected that the man was angry. And that was surprising."

In free-associating to these dreams, Belle had thoughts about being well-bred. These touched on factors present in childhood regarding her family's social status and the odd place assigned her as the daughter of her mother, who was accepted as a silly, irresponsible woman, deviant from the other—classier—members of the extended family; on cleanliness and dirtiness (condensed in the fountain pen, with its connotation of indelible dirtying by ink despite the cleansing allusion in "fountain"); and on the terribly important subject that now moved into the center of the analysis: masturbation, a practice that undercut all attempts at neatness, proper clothes, and good breeding.

This discussion frees her up enough to continue.

She says she has used the horse fantasy for many years (how many and the details and origins of the daydream will take years to reveal). No more description for this hour.

She touches on the daydream at times in the next weeks. She adds that, to keep her positioned for the horse, the man has tied her up; she cannot move. She thinks she may have begun relying heavily on the daydream—using it as her only means of getting up intense excitement —around age twenty, while having an affair, lasting a couple of years, with a man who always suffered premature ejaculation. On his entering her, she would get voluptuous vaginal feelings but could not move lest he lose control. Caught between her need for penetration and the danger of his impending collapse, she fell back on the daydream invented years before, polishing it up by introducing a few details (for example, she was tied down but still on the way to orgasm) that were to prevent and undo the frustration she was suffering at that instant. So, consciously stopping her body from moving, and daydreaming that she was forced to this by being tied down by sadists (or one sadist; it was not yet clear), she converted her angry suffering into growing excitement. Since her efforts were of no use in the actual intercourse, for he came in a moment anyway, she learned that she must invent details exactly right in order to cause quick excitement. There was no mistaking who was in control: only when he was finished did she have an orgasm.

Over several weeks, she began to fill in the picture of the man she had said was there in the daydream. He ran the situation. He was rigid, tough, unfeeling, brutal, perverse; nothing about him was admirable.

He had no interest in her as a person; she was there only for his gratification, as a fetishized object.*

Some months later, she mentioned—merely a sentence and with no elaboration for a year or more—another sexual fantasy. Only years later did she say that this daydream was the immediate precursor, in puberty, of the horse fantasy. In this first announcement, she said that around age thirteen, when masturbating, she would picture beautiful, Amazon-type women who beat each other while she watched. At this age, she also daydreamed of boys chasing her.

Gradually, more elements of erotic daydreams were added, often only a sentence at a time. I did not get the feeling that the horse story was a central one, nor, for years, was I interested in knowing its complete form.

Although new details were brought into the horse fantasy to take care of frustrations and pains of day-to-day reality, the main themes and characters were constant. The action takes place in a space, an arena, perhaps a stage. Standing around, watching silently as the horse —stallion—blindly ravishes her, are an unknown number of men of unknown age, without emotion but with erections; sometimes they are masturbating themselves or each other. The man running the performance, called the Director, promises in his cruelty that at the right moment he will have intercourse with her or will arrange for another man—handsome, virile, heterosexual—to do so, the right moment being when the horse has gotten her so excited that she cannot bear it without now having a man. But the Director never grants her wish. Instead, the horse is removed and a disreputable-looking, old, lower-class, stocky and muscular, physically dirty, fumbling, incompetent man is substituted. When this occurs in the story, she is on the verge of orgasm in the real world. The old man is the final straw. Up to that point, despite her mounting excitement, she has lain silently without moving, resisting the overwhelming pressure to humiliate herself by losing control. Finally, for all her reckless bravery in opposing the men and her struggle to keep a ladylike composure, she suffers the ultimate humiliation with the dirty-old-man. Instead of having a mature, womanly sexual relationship, she is fixed there on display, in uncontrollable excitement. Her orgasm occurs simultaneously in the daydream and in reality.

The manifest trauma portrayed in Belle's story is that she is being forced to lose control, to lose her lovely, feminine appearance, and thus be fiercely humiliated. What solutions remove the depicted trauma and

*This earliest description, as we shall see, was incomplete and subtly inaccurate.

thus allow her to have pleasure? First, what is happening to the girl in the story is not taking place in reality. Second, there is another audience present but not in the script: the decent people of the world, God and his heavenly host, all the laws of morality and goodness in the universe —a throng of understanding and sympathetic observers who recognize her suffering and know she is finer than her tormentors. Despite appearances, the odds are stacked for her.

More details emerge. The tourney takes place in a cold, austere concrete area with no interior furnishing or outside foliage. Whether inside or out is not made clear. She has no clothes on. Sometimes she is forced to masturbate.

The horse is a stallion; the men fasten her to him with rope or a leather device. He becomes wildly excited but not by her: the men have set a mare in heat off at a distance, at which, over Belle's nude body, as if she did not exist, the stallion stares.

Although the elements changed, this was always and each time her primary erotic daydream, with variants. It began when she was six or seven and was rewritten as she grew older. The main themes, which were concerned with the fundamentals of her identity, were the following. Heterosexuality: sex whose ultimate goal is marriage and babies. A touch of homosexuality: women's voluptuous breasts and buttocks, especially when seen through flimsy cloth. Anality: the interior as a place for both unbearable tensions and peaceful tranquillity, and inner contents and external orifices, whatever their pleasures, that threaten to sell one to the enemy (males). Abandonment: a constant threat always overcome in one detail or another of the script. Masochism: to be publicly humiliated by losing control. Sadism: to be revenged when it is recognized how unjustly she has suffered. Audiences: one—portrayed—that, in watching her, is the agent of her humiliation, and the other—implied—that stands witness to her martyrdom. Femininity: graceful, tasteful loveliness of face, body, carriage, clothes, and orifices. Femaleness: a natural, wanted state she would be glad was hers if only maleness, for no fair reason, were not better (except that some females —purely female—are equal to men). Oedipal rivalry and primal scene: as when the stallion ignores her for the mare tethered beyond. Guilt and redemption: heroic suffering redeems one's being oversexed.

As she grew, shifts in inner and outer circumstances called for script changes, details for which were always at hand, as in novels or movies. In the earliest version recalled (age seven to nine), powerful women whipped weaker women, the strong equipped as warrior types, the weak portrayed as defenseless slaves. Belle was not one of the characters; she only watched the scene, as if it were a movie, the real Belle just an audience. Later (around ten to twelve) she changed the script to men urinating on women because babies, she thought consciously, were created by men urinating on or in women. The action took place on a stage. Standing aside was a silent, powerful woman, a Queen, who had ordered the whipping but did nothing but watch. This story was erotically exciting, with the urinating activity as foreplay. The high point came the day Belle introduced herself (minimally) as a character present in the story, a girl who watched the Queen: watching the Queen was the excitement. Then, at thirteen, she became one of the victims of the Amazons. Within weeks, however, she needed men, for the excitement, which had been diffusely genital, became focused in her vagina. I presume that was one reason why the Director as Amazon Queen had to become male; Belle needed someone competent to penetrate her. In the transition from Amazon Queen to the male Director, the director is a madam running a harem. She watches as Belle is penetrated by a penis. If the girl makes any sounds due to excitement, the woman spanks her bottom. The madam is stern but also lascivious. Shortly after, the Director took the place of the Amazon Queen.

Belle was nine when she learned that intercourse occurs by a male putting his penis into a female; she had known her vagina since she was six. Then, she assumed, the man urinates. At this point, Mother was gone, but exciting stories were told of Mother being the center of attraction for innumerable glamorous men. Belle was filled with ideas of lovemaking, sex (whatever that was) as beautiful, pregnancy lovely, delivery an ecstasy, and motherhood a glory. Although it was also clear to her that she would never approach Mother's desirable womanliness nor be a marvel of the sex, she saw herself as able to get some leavings from the feast.

But the news about the anatomy of intercourse shattered the all-too-susceptible child. She tried not to believe it but also knew it was true.* Then she thought that somehow it just could not happen, that though males could, they would not really do this, or that though adult women did, *she* would not. When the friend who told her insisted that babies were produced this way, she gave in to this truth with a fear that persisted through childhood. From that day on, she felt shame; not only did someone push that thing into you, you were supposed to enjoy it —be thrilled by it, as her mother had endlessly warbled. That was impossible for Belle. Yet by this point, she was fully committed to femaleness and to its life-plans of heterosexuality, marriage, pregnancy, childbirth, and motherhood. These had been so clearly laid out to her

*She briefly forgot this knowledge at puberty, when she had the men urinating on, not in, the women.

and in such enticing (even if ambivalent) ways, as we shall see, that she had no other options. She contemplated the boys she knew and wondered how to come to terms with this dreadful news. Daydreaming became her method of planning and her means of relief, as it does for other children.

The problem was how to convert shame and fear to pleasure, and since the focus of the issue was her genitals, the end product would have to be sexual pleasure. She now also had to adjust her image of women, and especially the family mythologies, to this awful truth that women before her had accepted. And so, she says, "In order to survive, I taught myself that I liked it." Developing the daydream, working on it until it fit, reworking it to keep the fit as the years passed, became a crucial piece of the work of acceptance that, as earlier analytic workers pointed out (Freud, Deutsch, Bonaparte), is done by feminine women via masochism. (It is hard to imagine a little girl, confronted with this task, who would not envy boys and their aggressive, penetrating, hedonistic, arrogant, unfettered, God-granted, antisocial, unsympathetic, humiliating penis.[1])

So the problem from childhood on was how to take men in and yet maintain integrity. Belle "solved" this only at great cost, during the moratorium called latency, when most children in our culture can put aside, somewhat, the insoluble sexual problems of early childhood. But with puberty and adolescence, the battle was again joined; Belle was once more in the throes of these issues when, in the company of her peers, she had to solve in the real world those painful identity questions carried on the vehicle of anatomy.

The trouble was that the more she daydreamed, the more excited she became; so the more she daydreamed. She was unable to reach orgasm when she masturbated (she felt that something big, strange, unique lay ahead but did not dare proceed to discover it until she was twenty). So she was left in a chronic state of excitement (which she controlled when she learned to introduce nausea into the mix) from age six or seven into adult life. This made her see herself as oversexed. It was clear evidence of an inborn, permanent, and therefore hopeless part of her self.

The element of almost uncovered female flesh was another complication with which she had to deal; for instance, around age thirteen, her head was filled with Amazons,* barely clothed but not nude. At first, on finding them in comic books, she had them just "running around," her excitement coming from watching them, especially their breast-

*Derived from Wagnerian Rhine Maidens, comic books, *National Geographic* magazine illustrations of Egyptian women with breast harnesses, etc.

plates and underlying breasts. Gradually the stories developed: the Amazons were chasing other women, whom they would capture and put in chains. Sometimes she only watched; sometimes she was one of the victims and was forced to humiliating acts, the worst being that she had to display herself nude (her figure was just forming). This daydream was a precursor of the adult version.

The elements in the preadolescent daydreams that deal with beautiful women and their almost nude bodies were taken from life with Mother, who was interested in Belle only if the girl was a dazzled audience for Mother's endless tales. In these, Mother portrayed herself as a ravishing morsel men frantically devoured; she never claimed that the men excited her erotically, only that her femininity drove them crazy. Since Belle was allowed no time with Mother except during these sessions, and since the price of admission to the show was rapt attention, the girl was fiercely motivated to be enthralled. These scenes were staged in Mother's bedroom, where this luscious marshmallow lay nude, flesh awash in the bedclothes. Any thought that these stories were histrionic (a suspicion she had to suppress from early childhood on) was dispelled by the pleasure she derived from Mother's lavish descriptions of the romantic and sexual treatment provided by the men.

By age fifteen, when Belle's own breasts had developed, she was fascinated with looking at herself in the mirror. She would drape herself in gauzy cloth, plump up her breasts with her hands, and become excited by looking.[2] She even took photographs of herself during that year, pictures she rediscovered later in analysis. In time, we found that the excitement, which seemed to spring instantly and spontaneously when she saw herself in the mirror, came from condensing into one conscious experience the memories of her mother's seductions plus the wish to be the man who devoured that feast. Her eyes were a man's and they looked, in the mirror, at another woman's breasts, an intricate bisexuality in which each character assumes a heterosexual role. The genital she then masturbated was hers in its sensations, but her hand was a man's. Each had a part in a different play, all of which were plays within the larger performance of which she, Belle, was the author, director, and audience.*

During the year when she switched from Amazons to males, she was also preoccupied that men were in the bushes outside the house, peeping. At first, she decided they were looking at her mother, who napped every afternoon nude; but as her own body developed, the idea evolved

*Another imagined audience was the men of the photo laboratory. She was astonished that the film had not been confiscated, and was amused years later when, during analysis, she looked at the prints and saw they revealed nothing of her flesh.

that they were looking at her. This was frightening, not overtly exciting. (These voyeurs, I believe, also stood for herself looking at her mother's body.)

Another element in Belle's adolescent erotic development was her concern with guilt and redemption, underlined by the hellfire churches she attended. To make her incessant, evil, erotic thoughts compatible with the religious teachings, she introduced two devices. The first was that her stories, during this phase, had no ending. This was to represent uncertainty, for she knew, years before she allowed herself an orgasm, that there was an ending that would place her squarely in hell. But in time, convinced she was destined for hell, she lost her commitment to religious practices. They could no longer protect her, for her daydreams were the overriding evidence to be used against her on Judgment Day.

She heard, however, from a Catholic friend that, with good works, one got days off from purgatory. So she did her addition; even if on the way to hell, she could reduce the sentence a few days at a time. Therefore, in her sexual fantasies, she suffers for others. This means there is, besides the frozen men, another audience, unseen and unmentioned, watching her suffering. It is God, his holy assistants, and, to a lesser extent, an undefined band of good people—all who witness the evil done her and judge it as unfair. (Analysis caused quite a mess for years: by precipitating the erotic fantasies, our work was adding up more points against her. There she lay on the couch, excited because on humiliating display, stretched out before the sadist "analyzing" her.)

The Director gradually became clearer, especially by the third and fourth years of the analysis. A detail was mentioned for the first time, elaborated the next day or perhaps days later, another detail coming up weeks, months, years later. Sometimes Belle reported spontaneously; at other times, she could only hint and I ask for clarification. During the two or more years in which this material emerged clearly, I began to think dimly some of the ideas now being made fully conscious in writing this book. I did not think them and then transmit them to the patient; it was the other way around in that, in time, she revealed the structure of the daydream and, with her associations, its roots. Meanwhile, I was showing her how she had transferred her daydream into our relationship, so that she believed she was there to resist being humiliated in my presence by excitement that was the result of my directorial sadism. (Erotic excitement felt for the analyst is not so easy to analyze. It carries into the treatment a sense of reality, for it is actually experienced, not just a memory from another time, or an intellectualization, or even an insight. Being a sensation, it is a truth of the body.[3] It also, of course, fit into Belle's key fantasy, for my analyzing rather than sleeping with her was the equivalent for her of the Director's refusal to touch her, his exciting her from a distance without involving himself.)

An essence of the daydream is her personalized theory of masculinity and femininity. Being female and feminine is good. These are traits she has, admires, and wants. Though she envies males, she does not want to be one. She divides females into two types: the girls and women who are secure and are therefore as good as if not better than (though different from) males; and those, such as herself, who are inferior.

As for her theory of males, she breaks the possibilities into four classes she says she has experienced. The audience of silent men exemplifies the first—males in general—drawn from the boys of childhood and especially adolescence: all the men she wants are sadistic, uncommunicative with her, banded together, phallic. She does not believe she created their cruel amusement at her vulnerability or that her capacity for humiliation is also her invention. The Director stands for the second group, the particular men she gets to know, her stepfather being the prime example. In the Director is focused even more sharply than in the group of observing men the cruelty, the pleasure in exciting and frustrating her, that she has always experienced with men. The third class of men are portrayed in the dirty-old-men, who are, she knows, all that fate will offer her (except for the almost completely disembodied phallus the stallion represents, the beastlike passion hidden in masturbatory daydreams). These dirty-old-men stand for her real father. The fourth class are defective men—effeminate, homosexual, transvestite— the male equivalent of what she must never become. At different times, I fit into each group.

My thesis is that the paradigmatic daydream recapitulates the primary relationships of infancy and childhood,[4] trying to undo the frustrations, traumas, and conflicts that resulted therefrom. Every detail is chosen, each has its necessary place, each contributes to a script that seems to reproduce the traumas and conflicts but that then resolves these painful issues. The function of the daydream is to change a victim into a victor.

As we proceed, we shall see how the members of the oedipal drama become characters in the daydream: mother, father, stepfather, the woman (Caretaker) who substituted intermittently for mother for several years, and Belle—as depicted star, hidden but dimly recognized writer-director, and silent (unconscious) person for whom, at bottom, all the others are only stand-ins.

The Director is the crucial actor. More feelings are attached to him than to any other figure, more important parental figures, more trauma, and more hopeless hope condensed in his portrayal. The person who most immediately contributed to his creation, when it was time to switch from the Amazon Queen, was her stepfather. As she became more excited (excitable) in her teens (which is saying a lot, for she had been in a state of excitement throughout latency), she was also confronted with a physically attractive man in the house, not available since he was married to her mother, but on the other hand, not as taboo as a true father. As the analysis proceeds, she recaptures memories of frank genital excitement in his presence that help explain the never-forgotten memories of being almost always angry at him and not knowing why. Ramrod straight, inhibited, quiet, meticulous, and proper, he seemed invulnerable to her. With her already well-developed sense of inferiority, she presumed she could not make him unbend; and she did not dare daydream conscious erotic ideas about him. At any rate, that is how she described him for years. The reality, she finally recognized, was that she did not try to reach him, for, in order to protect herself from loving him, she had to deny he was ever kind.

Television shows and movies of Nazis fed her details she could fit with his being European (though not German) and a cavalry officer early in World War II. Modeling the Director on a Nazi guaranteed that the unseen audience would distinguish good from evil and silently but implacably witness the terrible things done to her (as long as she kept him faceless). Her story construction was also helped by tales of the Inquisition and bonbon novels of English queens locked up in dungeons.

No one, not even her stepfather, had the essential qualities the Director had. Only he was absolutely stiff, without tenderness or gentleness. Only he could not be corrupted by her techniques. She was in a bind with me, therefore. Whenever she imagined I was kind or trustworthy, she would have to protect herself by defining my behavior as weak. If not, she would succumb to trust and in doing so, give to the other person the power to abandon her (before she could do it to them). "To protect myself against feeling tender toward someone, I tenderize them."

Only when we found that the Director represented (among others) her stepfather could we effectively analyze her relationship with the real man. Therein, with the return of the memories that showed her rewriting reality to comply with the masochistic fantasies, she recalled working on the details of the daydream and on the version of the world she had come to believe in as true. Now, in analysis, she saw how she had chosen from the real world only those events that fit her scenario, ignoring, denying, or reinterpreting observations that did not conform. She had had to create her stepfather as being naturally (not neurotically, which one can forgive) cold, sadistic, and tantalizing. With this second look that analysis promotes, she found him to have been in reality stiff but not unbending. He had made efforts to reach his frightened and inhibited stepdaughter, who, with her own rigidity and anger, had pushed him away, leaving him puzzled and unable to establish the bond with her that she now recognized he had wanted but did not know how to make. Where formerly she remembered only how he failed her tests, she now recalled how well she had created her provocations.

There is another quality in the Director, latent but necessary to protect the excitement. For all his cold sadism, he is nonetheless safe in that, in the fantasy, he will sexually excite her and not spoil the excitement by being sweet, tender, or foolish. This means that he is not a failed man like her real father, and it also allows her to maintain the fiction that her stepfather had no kindness in him.

An element I missed for years, not represented visually in the script but used in her relationships with all people important to her and present but unknown in the transference until I caught it in the daydream: the advantage in always being the victim was that her two Directors (he and I), though they mistreated her, concentrated wholly on her, unlike her undependable mother. Even if she was an irritating, unpleasant little girl, at least that way she got people's undivided attention. Before understanding this, I was simply her victim, puzzled as to why she was doing this to me. Insight is a relief.

The Director may be frozen, but he focuses only on her: she is the main character. Everyone watches her. The play's action proves she is not abandoned; the past is undone. Secreted in the apparent suffering is the triumph. The way is open to full pleasure. What better disguise than to display publicly the opposite—suffering—of what one is secretly or unconsciously experiencing: revenge, undoing, triumph. She has even more control than all these brutal, powerful men. They try to dominate her, but nothing they can do, not even putting the excited stallion on her, enslaves her. Instead, she belongs to herself, ultimately at the mercy only of her own oversexed nature.

Another detail in which her strength is hidden: the silently observing men have erections and, sometimes, emotionless ejaculations. Only when the daydream lost its power to excite did she recall that this represented their tiring, being overmatched in the script by her capacity to come indefinitely without exhaustion. (Variant: the men watch, get erections, ejaculate, leave, and are replaced by a second phalanx, and that by a third.) Her belief she is disgusting because oversexed is repaired by the reassurance that the men are inadequate.

In all this, the Director—her version of the strong, silent type popular in movies—stands like a rock, without sympathy for her predicament, unaffected by what he observes. Even when he has an erection, and even if he ejaculates (and that is never while penetrating her, for he never even touches her*), he does not experience these. He just appears before her in these physical states, which indicates that he can but, with her, will not. The audience of men (representing the boys and men she had known throughout her life) are minimally movable, but the Director is not. Still, there is this comfort: as she believed was true with God, she might not be able to stir him but he is always present, dependable, potent, watching her.

The analysis proceeded. As we worked through an obstacle, we could then experience the obstacle that lay behind the earlier one. In that way new details of the scenario became visible, each illustrating for us, as we worked, how the daydreaming process fit into—made possible—sexual excitement.

Detail. The story has no introductory phase, in which the characters might have entered the scene, positioned themselves, and by their actions or words indicated why the event will occur. Instead, it begins abruptly, adding to the inhumanness she needs to create her victimhood. I learned this detail when she told me that one time, years before, she played it differently and did not get excited: a beautiful, voluptuous, but proper and efficient young woman, dressed in a suit, appears. It is precisely established that she enters at the start, creating the idea that she does not know who the men are or what is to happen. (In the usual form, the woman knows throughout what will happen.) This variant, which did not work well, has her being then forced to undress before the Director, after which the action proceeds in the typical manner. This exemplifies the process by which she experimented with rewriting or retaining elements of the script. When a new detail not only corrected a day's little trauma but also fit in with more common problems, it became a permanent feature. The test was what it did for the excitement.

Detail. The daydream never clearly portrays how she is attached to the horse. It was not, Belle said, necessary to make that exact. During the analytic hour when she told me that, she next remembered being tied into her highchair while being fed. Her mother was gone. Her father was not even an empty space whose absence was noted. She was with a baby-sitter, missing her mother, strapped—wet, sticky, uncomfortable, no pants—onto the leatherette seat, feeling abandoned.

To what extent, I wonder, is the horse also her mother, the detail

---

*A screen for Mother's nursing failures? A reason for an infant learning to reach mother by its eyes when it cannot otherwise get back to her body?

about being strapped to it a reference to the fear of being and the wish not to be deserted?[5]

Detail. At times the Director is being masturbated or fellated by one of the men while she is with the horse. This detail serves to underline that she cannot hope to reach him, that he is so cold, so distant, that no woman will ever excite him. This idea then allows her to feel more frustrated and more humiliated, and therefore more excited. But it also indicates that no one else will have him either.

Detail. The watching men sometimes masturbate. She says she does not understand why that should be exciting, especially when she has no interest in reality in watching a man masturbate. Thinking further on this puzzle, she realizes that the exciting element is that, if the men are masturbating, she is being tantalized. That is, although they are excited and could be serviceable to her, they are just putting it there in front of her and then refusing her. She does not get the penis in her, and, with their ejaculation, she loses any chance of it. Yet what is exciting them in the fantasy is her excitement. No one touches her, only the horse; not one of the men is within reach. This element of no contact is crucial and did not disappear until its analysis helped her to make contact more intimately in the real world. With that, of course, the daydream lost its ability to excite her (or, to see it from a different viewpoint, she no longer needed it for excitement). "My sex fantasy is changing. It's as if it's giving me up. I just can't get any excitement thinking about the Director any more, and I've also changed." And from this time on, the intense, provocative, and yet self-victimizing sexual excitement toward me began dying down also. Where she had formerly pictured me as sitting behind the couch, stiff, erect, and ready to pounce, she now felt me "not as a hard-on but as a soft-on."

As an early manifestation of this change, she met a man who, despite his interest in her mostly for sex, could also treat her warmly at times. One day, she reported that when he was tender the last time they were together, she began disconnecting from him, and the more tender he became, the more she drifted off. (She had done that to me innumerable times when, following an hour during which she felt especially close to me, in the next she became so distant that her dullness almost decorticated me.) There she is with a man who is tender, which is what she has wanted all her life—and she drifts off, as if floating in space watching the two of them. This is the sadness of neurosis and the devastation of masochism: people prefer their defenses to the lost, original desires.

Why did she avoid the intimacy she craved, endlessly repeating instead the old trauma? Freud explained this kind of behavior as being a repetition compulsion, ultimately a biologic drive, antecedent to mind. The data used to confirm the repetition compulsion, however, are flawed. Although it is said that people mysteriously repeat these original traumas, I disagree. Rather, if one takes a closer look, it turns out that the repetition only *simulates* the original trauma. And in that simulation, we can find subtle, easily missed changes in the story line, details that give away the secret that the original trauma is not identically experience.*

Or rather than using a hidden change in a detail, the script-writer makes do with hiding his intent, as when the masochist buries the portrayal of safety in a story of pain. For instance, the Director torments Belle by promising her she can suck on his penis. When she jumps for the bait, he reveals that he was pretending. Her associations to this story led to the underlying trauma. After having left Belle for the longest time ever, Mother returned to a great public welcome. Belle had anticipated the day for months, dreaming of being the center of her celebrated mother's attention. She would be swept up in a perfect embrace that guaranteed an end forever to abandonment. Instead the child could not get Mother's eye, much less arms. Finally, with a peck on Belle's cheek, Mother turned to more exciting people.

Trauma like that is only simulated with the Director. This time, Belle, the true director of the scene, tells the Director how he will perform.

The analysis finally became almost synonymous with the daydream. I, a male, had to make her suffer the same indignities, which she assuaged with the same erotized masochism. Obviously I was one more experience with males to be confronted and survived. As much as she wanted me to be an exception, I could not be without her understanding the origins and functions of her masochism. Thus, my every act and silence was evidence of arrogance, disgust, coldness, determination in the service of hatred, and indifference to her tender tissues—the notorious characteristics of an unfeeling, mindless phallus. She invented, accepted, her conviction that I had a natural right over her, that I was just the most recent version of the lifelong ascription and inevitability of her inferiority. My being an analyst only added to my power. Analysts sit up, patients lie down; analysts interpret (penetrate), patients accept or are flayed with insights. So the problem was the same as with the Director: how she could maintain her integrity while exposed to humiliation. Like the Director, I did not touch her, much less have intercourse with her. She felt such propriety was not intended to allow her freedom but rather was a further exercise in her mortification. For

---

*And that differentiates this experience from traumatic neuroses, in which there is *no* accompanying pleasure, secret or open.

years, when I reached her with understanding, she, in order to maintain independence, replaced her first impulse of relief and gratitude with disbelief and anger.

These episodes of emptiness and noncontact with me that followed a piece of analytic work that brought her relief or understanding should not be labeled as evidence of our old analytic excuse "negative thera-peutic reaction," or of that poetic sentiment called "death instinct," the inherited desire—intention—in humans, in all living organisms, to re-turn to total quiet (entropy).

A note on the composition of the plot's characters. She never (till treatment made it possible) used people she really knew, either from the past or the present. I think this was to ensure that she would not discover the meanings of the daydream. The few times she introduced a feature of a known person, her excitement flattened out to zero. On occasion, she would invent a story with the same masochistic themes in a new script, but it deteriorated after a single use and was never used again.

Night dreams, we know, can be divided into manifest and latent content. But we also know that even the manifest content, the dream as experienced by the sleeping dreamer, never comes close to being reproduced in the telling. Some of the manifest story line is clear and intense, but much else is scarcely noted or even subliminal. The same is true for daydreams. Although they are to bear more of the burden of simulating reality, they too are filled with the business of disguise. Interesting yet not dealt with in analytic theory are the daydreamer's prestidigitations, the tricks he or she uses—is driven to use—within the realm of consciousness, to push away from awareness all sorts of knowl-edge, of insights.

For instance, Belle had to teach me, when she felt it was safe to do so, that she was consciously aware that the whole Director story, all those years she used it, was a mass of exaggerations. It was necessary for her excitement that she know this, have it in mind during the excitement, and yet have it tucked away in a corner so that it could be ignored at the same time it was acknowledged. Had she not been aware always that the daydream was ludicrous, she would not have become excited. Even as a teen-ager, she knew she must beware of constructing daydreams that would be dull, ordinary, and cheap. If ever she had sensed those qualities, excitement would have disappeared instantly, and so, instead, she put together what she knew was a flamboyantly exaggerated story.

Equally known to her, and unattended to in the same way, was the fact that all the details about the Director's cruelty were, to a degree, hokum to disguise the crucial point that, as opposed to the abandoners of childhood, he never wavered in his concentration on her. The absolutely essential factor was that he was eternally and without a second's break concentrated on her, never threatening, never traumatizing, never even bored: the total antithesis of abandonment. "In time," she said, "punishment ends; abandonment never does." So she gladly threw into the script any price to be paid for that undoing of her ultimate trauma: "I put everything I had into it." The Director needed no past history, no clear personality: "I always had to be sure not to allow him to expand his personality. I don't know anything about him. I don't know whether he went to college or he didn't or does he work or not. He's invented to be very narrow." The greatest secret, one I learned only after years, was that she had always experienced him, every time, as *admirable*. On admitting this, it was easy for her to clarify the horse. It too is admirable, a beautiful, unsadistic, but wild creature (an aspect of her ideal she could never reach as well as a hidden admission that she found her stepfather admirable). It does not hate her, despise her, or want to humiliate her. It is not the horse's intent to screw her; it wants only the mare.

The horse also served, in part, to screen out known facts—earlier memories. After dreaming of a cute baby girl of eighteen months, she asked an aunt (her mother being dead) if something had happened when Belle was eighteen months old. Her aunt said that she was quite fearless before that time but became very phobic thereafter. Now, in the hour, she remembers clearly for the first time that—as it feels now— when she was around two years old a dog chased her. Although it was only a puppy, she was terrified: "My parents were watching me, it seemed from a long distance, inside the house from a window. No one ever responds to my fear." As time passed, she recalls, she had transformed the puppy into something dangerous. It remained in her memory, surfacing intermittently, gradually taking on new form so that the memory became a screen memory, then an element in spontaneous fantasy, and then an element available for scripting daydreams. Around seven or eight it became tied to stories, told by a nursemaid, of Christian martyrs chased in the arena by wild animals. And it had arrived, now in the proper form for erotic masochistic daydreams, waiting to become a horse.

(She considers this puppy event perhaps her first memory, along with another at the same time of "my mother and father making lion noises in bed," a nice association for a daydream of oedipal trauma. During this period, she had "long strings of nightmares of pursuit by a goat but mostly lions and being swallowed.")

This summary covers several years, during which most of our work was concerned with issues other than those artificially isolated here. Then, a year or so before the end of treatment, the unchanging structure of the daydream began to crack. She was now regularly warmer, closer, and more open with me, and her efforts to recover from these feelings by means of masochistic fantasies became less convincing to her, shorter-lived. They often ended with an awareness that she was boring herself or with a chuckle of insight. Details were sharpened, origins found, new variants introduced that softened the hostility or even hinted at kindness, and, toward the end of treatment, a new script emerged: normal intercourse with a potent, loving man. Here are examples of details discovered in this concluding phase.

The Director, a man of indefinite age, would, depending on what was occurring in the analysis, take on attributes of her mother, her father, the cruel but desired boys of her adolescence, and especially myself. Only late in treatment did she look at him closely and discover that his age had always been the same as hers. This clarification of the visual image occurred when she discovered that her suffering was of her own making, not the result of her fate to be dealt with cruelly by men, and that she used her masochism to drive the rest of us crazy. Only then did she also know that the Director was an aspect of herself. Thus it is not surprising that until late in treatment she never reached orgasm in intercourse as a result of what the man did. Instead, she had it by herself. She managed this by masturbating on his penis to the bidding of her fantasy, ignoring him as he pushed grimly on; or, after he was finished, she would take over and gratify herself by herself.[6] Only when the masochistic fantasy had been understood did she have orgasms during active intercourse and as a result of her lover's action.

When the fantasy had lost its erotic power, she saw what she had earlier only dimly perceived: the action is staged in a factorylike place, one huge area, not separate rooms. But perhaps—she was not sure—there are other areas in which other women are being used similarly. The main event—herself—takes place on a dirty old mattress. The men are looking at her genitals. They will become excited if they catch her getting excited because of their looking. But she disappoints them; she does not become excited from their looking that way but simply from her old condition: she is oversexed. *"They* don't excite me; I'm excited because of my own inner need." That crucial detail lets her maintain dignity in these outrageous circumstances. Despite everyone—including herself—knowing she is too easily aroused, she has withstood what everyone knows gets her: being watched. So now her performance is even more remarkable. In reality she suffered indignity from being excited day in and day out "because men are watching." But in the daydream, although her humiliation is portrayed, she is nonetheless *dignified,* thereby becoming an admirable, lovable, sympathetic victim, not the adolescent mess she considered herself in real life.

One day she reported that the day before, the audience men had not just watched but talked to each other, saying she likes to have her breasts fondled. So one of them obliges. They do this because they know she likes it, *not to humiliate her.* Not being humiliated now can cause excitement. A few months before analysis ended, she told me the Director had had another function. He had not only been present in the daydream but had also been used, into her adult life, as an imaginary companion. "He was a comfort. He was like a mother. He would tell me that it was all all right. And he would call me stupid if I had really been stupid. He was very hard but he was very fair. The only time that he wasn't like that was in the daydream."[7]

A change in a variant script when, as the analysis progressed, her hostility was decreasing: a dirty-old-man is watching her masturbate. Instead of being humiliated, she has an assignment: to teach him (mother, father, stepfather, me*) about her excitement. If she teaches him clearly, he will know how to handle her erotic needs skillfully. She is on her way to becoming a child, a better role than that of victim. In the next phase, although the men may be depicted doing things she considers perverse, they do so to help, not humiliate, her.

Then: here is a dirty-old-man, with no erection, drunk, a derelict. He sucks on her nipples and gradually gets an erection. Then he goes down on her. At this point, another man comes along, pushes the old man aside, and takes over. He is attractive, virile, lovable, and does not act from sadistic motives. The only masochistic element in the story, she says, is that he has a large penis, and as he is about to put it in, she, as the character in the story, fears for a moment it will be too large. It is not. Then (for the first time in her life, she says), "I had a fantasy of having completely normal intercourse and everything just went perfectly all right; and I came in the fantasy"; at the same time her orgasm occurred in her masturbation. She adds that he is nude, which she had never fantasied before. This indicates his willingness, that he is not hiding, that he is loving, that he is not trying to humiliate her. It is therefore not a squalid but an intimate relationship.

In the next stage, lasting several months, a girl (sometimes labeled as herself, sometimes an unknown child) is being taught about sex by her father (never portrayed as any man she has actually known). He

*My interest in analyzing her excitement was always in the analysis, years before I imagined writing on this subject.

treats her tenderly, courteously, and with respect for her age and ignorance. They do all the erotic things she likes. They both have orgasms:
he is good for her and she for him.

In the last transformation, used only with masturbation or when
things were a bit desultory with a lover, she used a story of free,
swinging, lustful behavior ending in intercourse with a masculine, potent, kind man, someone she had actually seen—a stranger, an ac-
quaintance, a friend, me.

But on a day when her pride was hurt or she had had a run of bad
luck, she fell back a notch to the mentor–innocent-girl story. The
Director, however, never returned.

By the end of analysis, she knew (most of the time; like the rest of
us, she had her episodes of backsliding) that whatever may have been
done to her in the past, in the present she is the victim of herself: she
can be free if she knows that she is the Director's director.

In describing how Belle's daydream grew and then evaporated, I
have also tried to reflect some of the therapeutic process that influenced
the changes in the daydream. You will undoubtedly agree that analysis
should reduce our patients' need to harm people in the present in order
to retaliate for harm suffered in the past: if analysis works, it should
reduce neurotic hostility. Since my hypothesis is that most sexual excitement depends on this kind of hostility, its reduction would be
reflected in changes in erotic fantasies, the most obvious being that the
need for hostility would die down and the daydream reflect this with
a changed script. At any rate, that is what happened with Belle.

5

The Underground Fantasy

ALTHOUGH THE DIRECTOR fantasy was the dominant one, there was another that ran, as it were, parallel to it. Here is its typical form (the details and story line could be moved around to suit the moment). It is an underground fantasy. All action takes place in a city below ground, with numerous levels, artificially lighted, without natural landscaping. The feeling is one of great coziness. There is no danger, no uneasiness, no excitement, sexual or otherwise. All is quiet though not silent, for the city is populated and busy with people going about their activities. Nothing special happens. Instead, Belle wanders through the streets and on different levels, looking at the people and buildings.

She is under no strain; there are no obligations; nothing is to be accomplished, nothing will happen. She is always alone. She knows none of the many people who populate the town, has never talked with them. The outstanding qualities are calmness and aloneness without feeling lonely.

Associated with this daydream were firehouses. Since childhood, whenever she had passed one in the evening, the same tranquil feeling had come up in her, accompanied by the urge to move her bowels. This persisted to the period of her analysis. It was not related to fire engines but, as she discovered during analysis, to the feeling that firehouses are places of cozy peacefulness where the men inside are quietly, gently, without speaking, comfortably going about their business: all is safe. (There was no such feeling about police headquarters, of course.) She looked on firemen as men who are not sadistic, not dangerous, dedicated to the safety of structures, especially to putting out, not starting, fires (the eternal task with which she struggled because of her never-ending sexual excitement). Firemen gave her a calm feeling, because, although they were fully men—unquestionably male—she categorized them as less educated than she, from a different class, with different expectations from society, without ambitions; in other words, nonpenetrating, nonsadistic but still masculine men who caused her no anxiety and no sexual excitement. They were not castrated but rather neuter: categorically male but noninflammatory. (Once I showed up in a dream as a Dalmatian, the quiet, trusty, nondangerous fireman's dog. Most of my dog appearances were of a different sort: dogs hound.)

The ultimate sense of coziness came when she would think that the firemen were in there all through the night, benign, prepared, unexcited.

The underground fantasy began, as did the erotic one, around age six or seven, as she tried to bank the fires—the intense, unbearable emotions—caused first by her father leaving and then, shortly thereafter, her mother. After desolation, she began coming to terms with disaster, and one of the techniques was the underground fantasy. It produced a lovely, soft, happy feeling, continuous and unchanging, for there was no build-up, no story line. In the underground community, it is warm, dark, comfortable, and safe. Everyone goes about his and her business without watching her; often they are couples, content.

Additional details, in time: a firehouse is a dark place inhabited, though that is not their home, by lots of people who keep strange hours, even getting up in the middle of the night, and who are away from their homes and families. To pass one is to lose precipitously any sense of tension; that instant vacation produces a sudden opening of her bowels —"a lovely feeling"—so that she has to have a bowel movement immediately, an experience in which she does not feel she has control. It is a happening in her belly. Yet the tranquil feeling in the daydream comes from all being under control (obviously, a different control from that featured in the Director script, where it is a necessary element in creating excitement).

As in the erotic daydream, she makes no contact with others. She touches no one. No one touches her, not even to brush against her. She talks to no one, and no one talks to her. In contrast to the other story, no one looks at her. They just go about their business without excitement, leaving her free to wander contentedly through the nondramatic scene, its ordinariness in sharp contrast to the frantic sex scene.

Most of all, the underground daydream solves the problem of abandonment: it changes loneliness to aloneness.

On our campus at UCLA there were converted fallout shelters. When Belle passed one, the same bowel loosening occurred, especially in the evening, for then the campus was empty. Without consciously thinking the underground daydream (until this came into the analysis), she had the same marvelous feelings. Then, for a short time, while this was being analyzed, the experience spread so that other buildings, quiet and cozy in the evening, would give the same effect.

The underground fantasy, though identified in treatment as vaguely ("perhaps") erotic, was never associated with genital sensations until near the end of treatment. Then she began responding to men—and in the transference, to me—with loving and quiet feelings. These became part of her sexual excitement, causing not only physically deeper but more profoundly emotional feelings. Besides the erotic sensations, she now felt that all her insides—her whole body—were more trusting, available to herself and to the men. Along with this, her fantasies had changed: loving men had nonsadistic intercourse with her. And in masturbation, she sought out the more interior regions of her vagina. She found a part of the vaginal wall, somehow never before located, that gave a new and more profound orgasm.

Each fantasy tended toward its own anatomic locus. The Director story, with its high excitement, worked where sensations were sharpest —clitoris and introitus—while the underground fantasy, quieter and calmer, stirred her more deeply. Thus two different psychic experiences literally overlapped so that a feeling of completeness, tranquillity, safety, strength, and gentleness got introduced into sexual satisfaction late in treatment when she found in herself the capacity for full and deep vaginal pleasure and orgasm. This occurred when the need to feel she was in control, safe from attack by desire for males, had been reduced. Only then did these two separate genital experiences merge and overlap to contribute to what was for her a complete gratification.

> The feeling inside is completely different from the feeling with my clitoris; it is very important for me and feels very powerful. Since I first felt it, I have never lost it. It is there every time I get excited, and it's part of my orgasm every time except if I just touch my clitoris. But I don't like to just do that. When I masturbate I have to [meaning most of the time, not invariably] get into my vagina also. The two places—the feelings in each of them—are completely different in their feelings. But in my vagina, it is not just some kind of general erotic pressure. It is a precise place with its own precise quality just like with the clitoris but as different as the difference between scratching your head and rubbing your feet. It's way up, too high to reach with my fingers unless I push in very hard. But penises reach it. When I daydream and am having feelings up there, the fantasies are loving, more peaceful, where a grown-up and handsome man is making love to me with normal intercourse. With the clitoris, it was always the Director and the dirty men.

Those who announce that vaginal orgasm does not exist or that it is the same as clitoral orgasm are women who are projecting their own lives into the political arena or men who have never known a woman who has these different orgasmic experiences.

Along with finding the anatomically and psychically deeper sensation, her daydreams changed. Now began the daydreams of a loving man, the mentor who teaches the inexperienced girl or young woman to admire, trust, and be turned on by her body's parts. He is potent yet tender; and his penis finds the ultimate reaches of her vagina. The same finally happened in reality also.

I choose not to interpret this underground daydream in terms of intra-uterine experiences but to make do with more reportable data. Let us look at her anality.

6

Anality

ANALYSTS HAVE LONG known that sadomasochism is linked to experiences—traumas, pleasures, anger, stubbornness, humiliation, independence—centered on the sensations and communications in the power struggle that can dominate toilet training. Despite hints from Belle (as in dreams) and despite my expecting, because of her sadomasochism, to get significant associations of an anal nature, we were almost two years into treatment before such information began to come into focus. The introduction to this phase of her analysis came about as if in passing: she said that she saved up going to the bathroom to see how long she could wait. Only at the end of the hour did I find that she meant urination.*

This hour is typical in that regard. She says, "I have this bathroom fantasy." I wonder: A fantasy in the bathroom? A fantasy about going to the bathroom (excretion)? A fantasy about the bathroom but contemplated at other times than when in the bathroom? Ten minutes or so of shuffling around; then, for the first time, the underground fantasy: "It started around age seven. Everyone goes underground to escape disasters on the surface. There is a train-track. There are a lot of people. I don't know anyone; so I don't have to talk to anyone. I feel fairly safe. It is always night. There are blankets there, and if there are structures [the "if" means that, this being a repeated fantasy, there are times when she depicts structures and times not], I don't want to have to feel that I own them, that they are part of me. So I move to another level. But as the years passed and the place got to be more and more wonderful

---

*Over and over, when necessary, Belle acted as if she had been open and informative; yet she had been too vague for me to understand. Doing this served as a major resistance. It was also a salve for her conscience, letting her represent herself as a cooperative analytic patient. Best of all, she could say to herself or to me, weeks, months, or years later, "But I already told you that."

and even to having streetlights, it felt much safer to me. So I then began to always have structures. The main thing about it was the marvelous, safe feeling, and yet it was sort of a sexual feeling. How odd that is. How can safety and sex be part of the same feeling?" Only then does she explain that by "bathroom fantasy" she means that when she was little, she would have the underground fantasy when she was on the pot or just before, when she felt her bowels starting to move. It is, in fact, a bowel-movement fantasy, not just a bathroom fantasy.

Two months later, at a time of heavy menstrual flow, she reports a dream: "There was a big bread oven, but it was me." (This is not an intellectualization; she often felt during a dream that an inanimate object or a person contained a something that was herself. This was clearly represented in the dream and was not simply an association afterward.) A few days before, she had been searching unsuccessfully for a word, which she now suddenly recalls: "cloaca." She returns to the dream. "You're [RJS] at one end, and things are shoved in with a shovel at the other end. There was an obstruction in it. You were at the wrong end." In some way not clear, the words "anal" and "analysis" were represented in the dream, not spoken but floating about in her thoughts (another common style in her dreaming). "It wasn't messy inside, however. It was very clean except that there was that one large obstruction."

The previous day, I had remarked on her pulling her skirt down over her knees; both of us had subliminally noted that her skirt had been rising and falling to this point. (This exhibitionism had its anal roots, as we shall see.) She now becomes terribly vague. I point this out, and she says, "It's because you don't like me. It's because I'm dirty. I'm cruddy. You try hard to stand it, but you really can't. That's because you really can't stand women, and you can't stand the cruddiness of women either. You think this is all a bunch of crap. Oh, shit!" She has relaxed a bit. "I certainly do obstruct things in here and shouldn't. I should just let everything go through." She notes she is dressed so cleanly today, like a dental assistant. She has on a white blouse and white shoes. She was aware, when dressing that morning, that she had to counteract what she is convinced is my feeling, that she is by nature dirty. Also, dressed this way, she is businesslike, not provocative (as she had felt she was the day before, when her skirt hiked up). When I remark that the dream makes her an oven clean enough to cook in, she says, "I'm obsessive about sex. I think about it all the time. But that's obvious. We don't have to talk about that."

Innumerable times, she reported dreams with bathrooms, laundry rooms, other washing places, white clothes, clothes cleaners, dishes being washed, washing machines, dirty houses, dirty walls, dirty floors, messy sanitary napkins, stained clothes, leaking cars, mud, and white donkeys (which are not dirty asses).

We shall look at the many stories, experiences, transference reactions, in which she is portrayed as a victim. This is such an important item that it can be considered a central fantasy (which is usually called character structure). It has powerful roots in her bowel, as does a crucial part of her erotic life, such as liking intercourse from behind, anal stimulation, fantasies of anal intercourse, and exhibiting her rear end.

Even after about three years of analysis, the word "shit" is the worst that exists for Belle. (Remember, this was long ago; it would be hard today to maintain a comparable horror at the word.) She feels, she once said, that the world is filled with shit just below the surface, that at any time, on looking at a person, she can be grabbed by thinking: They are capable of shitting; or: What do they look like when they shit? or: He [I] shits. As a child in class, she often was so uneasy that she could only conceal her tension by thinking: The teacher shits.

A "random" association one day: the Netherlands. Next; this refers to her genitals, the Lowlands—low on her body and low on scales of morality and cleanliness; Dutch Cleanser; the reputation of the Dutch for cleanliness.

A common theme woven into her masochism was her dirtiness. For years, until we were near the end of treatment, she spoke of my "justifiable" disgust with her sweating or her bare legs touching my precious couch; of her messing up the room just by being there; of her rumpled clothes, of her smelling; of her genitals being unacceptable to me no matter how often she bathed or how secretly lovely. In all this, I am portrayed as a hero because, despite my being naturally disgusted, I stay with her, trying my best to disguise, though I cannot overcome, my disgust.

Contrasted with these messy qualities, to which all females are subject (though few, if any, are so liquidy-filthy as she), are the same traits as manifested in males. It is, she says, unfair but true: the dirtiness of males is wholesome, rugged, masculine, and not infected with anality. If they smell, sweat, or even shit, it is phallic and thus superior. This is especially true when she contrasts male genitals and hers (though hers would be fine, even lovely, if men only knew how to appreciate them).

Now let us look for origins of these beliefs. During the years of childhood, whenever her mother abandoned her, she was the prey of her Caretaker, who raised bowel movements to the highest importance in the relationship, in the actual communication that passed between the two of them day in and day out. The issue of this woman's concentration on anal functions became more and more visible in treatment until a key hour in which a major shift occurred, leading to the final phases—over a year long—of the resolution of the analysis.

Frequently, Belle's anal associations were intermingled with oral ones. For instance, one day, she had been talking of the Caretaker's insistence that you either had a bowel movement at X o'clock or an enema; of the forcefulness with which enemas were given lest the "return" not be good enough; and of the child's struggles with the pain from so much water in her bowel, the desire to expel it, and the need to keep it in even longer so as to avoid this woman's impatience. These associations were followed by a memory from earlier childhood of sitting in her highchair and spattering food about. After this memory she recalls another, of her mother putting her in the tub because she had made a mess with her spinach.

Here is a dream from midway in treatment that shows how anal issues could be turned to our use: "Dick was throwing a cat in the air repeatedly. It was paper-thin and finally it was just pulverized into a purée, and it was dead. He put it in the back of my car between two pieces of fur, and it really stunk." She says, "Dick isn't anyone. That just means 'prick.' It means that that's what a masculine, unthinking man would do." I ask her whether yesterday she was in any way involved with her genitals. She says yes. Associations pour out in a tumble: she was sitting on the toilet having a bowel movement, smelling it and her genitals—it is during her period—then she announces for the thousandth time that men and in particular their genitals (Dick) are cleaner than and superior to hers (the defenseless, smelly cat: pussy); there had been another dream that night—of God and gods; I, she says of me, am Godlike but as frozen as a stone phallic carving; raunchy Henry Miller and his fetishistic interest in women's genitals and smells.

It suddenly hits her that I am not driven off by this discussion, which is in part a test to see if I will show disgust. Not having destroyed me with her imagined shit-storm, finding that I do not even strike back under attack, and sensing that the enema-induced flood has passed through her and out, she eases up: "I really feel much closer to you." She now realizes she was beginning to feel that safety earlier in the hour even while it had seemed she was attacking; for she had realized this was the first time she had ever actually said in words to me that she had sat on a toilet and had a bowel movement.

The analysis of her anality exemplifies the well-known process of working through an issue as it recurs in different forms innumerable times: a bit of a dream, a way of resisting me, a fear of talking about manifestly anal matters, a detail of erotic behavior, a style of vocabulary, a theme in a daydream, a feeling of being clean or dirty, physical sensations in the hour. Then a coagulation, when these many analytic events fell in place and became permanently hers; and the treatment moved on to a new level.*

Now, although it has barely been mentioned, let us put aside the Caretaker's role in her anality and instead, just as Belle did with me, go over other issues that had to be understood before a crucial clarification.

For Belle to come to terms with her anality, and especially to reach the point where she resolved these attacks, took much analytic work. The first issue was exhibitionism. Let us consider now only the aspect of it that was enmeshed in anal problems. The process of discovery began, not in content given as history (such as childhood memories), but rather as behavior in analytic hours.

For many months at the beginning of analysis, Belle was (her version of) a model patient. She was never late; she walked into the office looking neither to right nor left, placed herself neatly down on the couch, and began talking, usually giving a summary of a dream, drawn from a written report. None of this had been my instruction. When, months later, I asked what it meant, she said she was trying not to upset me. Since I wore a tie and more or less shined shoes, she decided I needed complete neatness from her. To show gratitude for my treating her, she would try not to stir up my male responses: rigidity, closed-mindedness, unfeelingness, obsessive neatness, hardheartedness, veiled irritation if not explosive anger, and automatic distaste for femininity and femaleness. Her orderliness was a gift I had earned because, more than other men she knew, I at least struggled against these natural male tendencies and was trying manfully to be decent. She felt she was being good to me, soothing me.

She was dismayed when I one day said—showing, she was sure, ingratitude for her gratitude—that there was hostility hidden in these fantasies. From then on, this way of treating me fragmented and was used only momentarily, usually with an edge of sarcasm. In its place

*Experienced colleagues know that attempts to describe these movements in analysis are impressionistic and do not adequately portray the way analyst and patient communicate. More important for a research pursuit, the data are altered when filtered through my mind and then pummeled into new shapes for the sake of writing. Even saying that the subject is "anality" blurs (as well as organizes) the data, for "anality" was also "orality" and "phallicness" and "oedipal" and "pre-oedipal," with still other major themes interwoven. Labeling an event "anality" only indicates that most of this experience was focused on buttocks, bowel, anal, or perianal sensations, contents, memories, or fantasies. But we must never forget that these associations and sensations also, simultaneously, were on other subjects and drew their strength from other body parts as well.

came naughtiness: periods of lateness, door-slamming, frequent (but decidedly not continual) statements (though softened with semantic devices) that I was a bastard, a drizzling crying to indicate I was harassing and degrading her; this ended only in the last year or so of analysis.

By naughtiness, I mean she felt she was being naughty; to have been more overt or severe in the "rule-breaking" would have been unbearable for her. The quotation marks signify her notion that I had a complex, unannounced, arbitrary, silly, hidden set of rules she had to discover. By maintaining that, she could imagine not only that I was a nit-picking sadist who had to establish senseless rules but also that then she could break them. The "broken rule" that in time opened our understanding of anality linked to exhibitionism was my supposed demand that she lie down and never do otherwise till the hour ended. So, bravely though nervously displaying the immense risk she was taking, she would either sit up in the middle of an hour or start by sitting up, sometimes eventually to lie down, at other times to sit for the whole hour. When *in extremis,* she even sat on a chair at the far end of the couch. This was to indicate total disconnection and despair about me, that she had no other device left to deal with this cruel, cold male.

At first in this "naughty" period, her dominant mood was a plucky defiance, poured out in a flood of words meant to choke off any other reaction in herself to me and therefore to make me so irritable I would explode. In doing so, she imagined, I would finally reveal true feelings that, although terrible, would nonetheless show we were in contact. When this did not happen, the sitting-up occasions changed; they now had an erotic tinge. I did not know why, and free-floating attention did not provide clues. So instead I paid closer attention.

At this point I observed her mastery of her skirt. She knew how, at the edge of awareness, to manipulate the bottom of her skirt so that, often without her touching it with her hands, it moved up and down her thigh at just the level above her knee to indicate accurately that moment's erotically tinged exhibitionistic feelings. I began to observe how she managed the business: with slight movements of the legs, a turn to the side, a moment's flailing in pain, and, especially, preplanning: knowing (unconsciously? preconsciously? consciously? all three?) in the morning, when she chose her clothes, which style and material would serve later in the day for her analytic performance. Without saying a word, she taught me about fashion. So in time I knew at first glance, when she entered the room, what to expect in the way of erotic expression: her clothes predicted the tone of the hour, unless insight intervened.

So now I was paying attention to her legs; or more accurately, I was now paying attention to her legs from the knees up. From the knees down had never been the arena for exhibitionism. As with most women in contemporary life (though not ninety years ago), that part of her was given away free, which meant it was not erotized.

With intuition raised to full gaze, I sensed the next subliminal layer becoming conscious, again a months-long process completed in a rush of awareness, experienced by me as the ability to make convincing interpretations and by her as new insights and memories, the interchanges between us tumbling head over heels, making available the next stage of confusion.

Together, we slowly learned that she showed her thighs as a last-ditch attempt to hold my interest when her fantasies told her I was about to abandon her: when she thought I was fed up with her behavior; or when I was going on vacation and she was afraid I would use that excuse to announce the end of treatment; or when, pleased with a good piece of analytic work, she presumed I would say she needed no more treatment; or when she had revealed a secret she thought I would find disgusting; or when I would simply lose patience. Being a man, I would eventually drop my disguise, she was sure, and act as men do—cruelly. In the hour after one of these abandonment numbers, I would get an expanse of leg, the amount depending on the depth of her anxiety. When really frantic, she would sit up and lean back against the adjoining bookcase with rump and feet on the couch, placing herself broadside to my view, so that while her dress covered the anterior of her thighs, the posterior was plenty visible.

At the first display, I said nothing, nor did she. The next time, she ended the show after several minutes by pulling her skirt down. This indicated some awareness, and so, a few moments later, when she paused in her associations, I asked, "What did that mean to you?" She was genuinely puzzled, having no idea why I had interrupted with a bizarre question. I spoke again, "You just pulled on your skirt; were you aware of it?" She was not. The next time it happened, I again noted it to her, and this time also she did not remember having done it, for it was still an "automatic" act, though she did remember that I had pointed it out to her some days before. A couple more occasions like this, and with the next one (weeks had now passed), she herself noted that she had pulled down her skirt. There were still no answers, not even usable associations, but at least the behavior was in the analysis.*

*This sketch of the start of a process of working through of course scarcely touches on how much more intricate these clinical moments are than the accompanying description indicates. What is more difficult to describe is why one chooses the exact moment for an intervention, why one

However, the show did not diminish. Rather—happily (not just because she had nice legs)—it increased; whatever else she was up to, she was making this behavior available for analysis rather than hiding it in an erotic disguise (for it was, in part, a disguise, an effort, put in terms of adult sexuality, to keep me from abandoning her).

Although she occasionally became self-conscious about showing her bottom (as she labeled this action), it impressed me how often she indulged, with enthusiasm and with sustained erotic mood, even though I was not reciprocating. This persistence means to me that she was not enjoying an adult, erotic exhibitionism but instead was involved in her own playlet, not needing me to participate—at least, not erotically.

There was another level to this behavior that was less frivolous and yet inadmissible: she did want me to be her analyst, to observe dispassionately, and to help her find herself. It was not until late in analysis, however, when her masochism lessened, that she admitted such trust and hope to consciousness. Before that, her display served such fantasies as: I, the male, who—clean as males are—would be disgusted by her female body and impulses; or I, the sadist, who, on becoming disgusted, would lash her (silence was a lashing, as were interpretations and questions); I, the object of her sadism (seducing me would destroy me; persisting in the behavior despite my attempts to analyze it would harass me, defeat me, because, she decided, in proper analysis the patient is not allowed to sit up, much less sit on the couch, much less put her feet flat on the couch, much less show her ass).

The key word is "ass"; others—legs, thighs, buttocks, bottom, rump, rear, back—are only euphemisms during the approach phases of analysis. But though "ass" is not a euphemism, that is not to say that "ass" had only one meaning; it could mean buttocks, anus surface, anus interior, upper thighs, or a conglomerate of all that anatomy.

Following an hour when she has been especially busy trying to irritate me—with repeated remarks like "You won't want to hear that," or "You can't stand that," or "I won't tell you about this"—she starts the next by saying I have a disgusted look on my face. She follows this with a long and extremely dull episode, which is abruptly interrupted with her report that she is picturing herself as a little girl, squatting and piddling. She thinks then of a woman she saw after yesterday's hour, whom she imagines to be my patient, one I prefer. At the same moment,

---

chooses to intervene with just those words, why one attempts to be tactful or thinks it best not to be, what puts those particular inflections in one's voice rather than others that would make the same words mean something different, why the next intervention is at just the time that it is, why it is in the style chosen, and on and on: the stuff of treatment, about which little theory has been developed, few descriptions attempted, and no serious research performed.

she says she feels she has been boring me. So I wonder to her whether the memory of squatting and piddling does not serve to introduce the impulse to get my attention (after being naughty to me by trying to bore me, and after being frightened by the thought that I have another patient) by showing her bottom. Although she has not described it, I imagine to her that the memory of squatting includes picturing herself with a naked bottom, the impulse to show her bottom shaken loose in the fear that I shall abandon her by succumbing to boredom. "Yes." She then tells how she chose her skirt today: it is very ladylike, but the material is such that it moves with her slightest movement. She knows this dress and can rely on it to do its work even if she is not fully attentive to exhibiting her legs. In fact, for the show to work, she must not be aware of her stage directions.

Now she is less frightened of what may lie ahead in her associations or my interpretations, relieved that her machinations are in the open: she admits she manipulates me "all the time" (that is, whenever necessary). She says—for the first time, and with pain—that she knows no other way really to make contact with me. By "really" she means making contact in a way that convinces *her* that she is in contact; anything else is mere possibility. I ask her where she got the idea that her bottom could serve this crucial, delicate purpose, more than, say, her elbows or her feet. She recalls an experience mentioned before with no conscious effect on me. When six or seven, she had seen a beautiful child show her bottom. On viewing this display, Belle had instantly become genitally, sexually excited without comprehending what or why. From then on, she had used this device of bottom-showing; imagining it excited others excited her. "My first remembered real audience excitement was in first grade, a reading circle where I arranged my dress and panties to show my bottom at the front of the class, imitating that other girl. The excitement was genital and all-over body heat."

Then come shy-amused-interested-embarrassed thoughts that balloon-busted *Playboy* girls turn her on. The hour ends with her feeling in contact with me, not because of the ass-to-eyes connection—she has long since ended the display—but because she is no longer angry toward and fearful of me. Now she feels that my curiosity to find the links between childhood and the present guarantee, for the moment at least, her safety.

The memory of the other little girl's bottom recurred at times in the next year; bit by bit we got a more complete picture. The child had been wearing frilly, "sleazy" feminine underwear, which by chance revealed a lot of buttock. On seeing that bottom, Belle became interested in her own underwear; thus, in the first grade, her underpants became erotic for her.* She was sure this was not so for the other girls, whose under-pants, she noticed, were not pretty but plain and of less "feminine" material, or were dirty, indicating these girls did not care. She immediately became a fashion expert in underpants, conscious of little-girl-underpants styles, wanting only those that were expensive, "sensible," pretty, feminine, and fashioned to show her bottom "by chance."

Even at age six, she recalls, she had sensual feelings on and in her buttocks, which she has felt to the present. Inside, also, in that part now known as her vagina, was a feeling: "It felt warm and it felt good; and I guess it was sexual. But it was not my clitoris." She could clearly distinguish these buttocks sensations from those in her anus; none of these, though erotic, required a conclusion (an orgasm or some equivalent to end the tension). These were simply warm, pleasant, and without much build-up; she would have liked them to persist indefinitely.

Next, she vaguely mentions nightmares at an earlier age, when she was "put out and my bottom exposed." She recalls at age four being left outdoors to play with no clothes on; this was frightening and involved no sensual pleasure. It was even physically unpleasant; her only memories are of sitting on sticky surfaces or being herself sticky from foods like ice cream. At this moment she realizes that a constant element in the nightmares was a sidewalk, a detail that had, when she was little, no apparent part in the nightmare story. Now she remembers that the yard in which she was placed was rimmed by that sidewalk.

In these childhood years before her underweared bottom was erot-ized, she had already been focused onto underwear, because her mother had liked the child to be dressed as stylishly as possible (to emphasize social status). Her next association is to the several years from age seven on, when, pretty much abandoned by her mother, she lived with the Caretaker. This woman, older and stronger than Belle's mother, dis-liked sensuality, let alone erotic pleasure. She was powerful, opin-ionated, and a source of anguish for the child. Yet when Belle was feeling lost and despairing, this woman would sometimes hold the child in an embrace that was genuinely loving and far more comforting than any mothering behavior Mother had ever provided. But the Caretaker's adequacy was contaminated. She was usually not concentrated on Belle, and when she was, it was in regard to bowel movements: when inquiring if the child had had one, or when inspecting the results, or when discussing the importance of bowel movements, or when plotting

---

*This is not fetishism. Her conscious experience, as different from that of the fetishist, who is excited by the garment per se regardless of the setting in which it appears, was not that the underwear excited her but rather her feeling that when people looked at her lovely-underwear-covered bottom, the view would excite them as it had herself when she had been the audience looking at the other girl's delectably covered bottom.

out life-styles that encouraged healthy bowels, or—the great horror—
when, so frequently, administering long-lasting, high enemas.

This woman came into the household within a few months of Belle's
seeing the other little girl's bottom; in a matter of months, Belle's father
had been driven from the family after an affair with a teen-age girl, her
mother had left to follow her career, and the child was placed in the
Caretaker's hands. That is a lot of sensations, traumas, and fantasies
to put into a little girl's rear end.

In contrast to the fierce attention focused on anus and bowel, buttocks—those signifiers of erotism—were offensive to the Caretaker,
who felt they should not exist and commented frequently, disparag-
ingly, on women who wore clothes that emphasized their bottoms.

As Belle talks, she feels pleasant and unpleasant sensations moving
simultaneously across her bottom. She thinks then of anal masturbation, which, by this time in the analysis, has little conflict left in it. She
recognizes at this moment that, when touching her anus, she produces
not only erotic pleasure but also more diffuse sensual (though not
precisely erotic) feelings, the same as the good ones of childhood.
Especially when masturbating, but now too, she thinks, "It's my own.
No one can give it to me; no one can take it away. That's one part of
me that *I* own. All by myself." Perhaps in that thought is an element
of the coziness of the underground fantasy.

Belle is progressing chronologically during this hour of anal associations, bringing the development of her anal erotism into contact both
with her genital erotic sensations and with the fantasies of love and its
complications that one expresses in the genitals. The two streams of
associations—anal and genital erotism—meet in her next associations
on masochism. I have said nothing.

She thinks of erotic daydreams she used before puberty, before the
Director appeared. She recalls these "normal" fantasies, because in
them men and women were having intercourse. Nonetheless, the necessary element was that powerful, cruel men were forcefully taking the
women. Especially exciting was the idea of a woman approached for
intercourse from behind. Her thoughts then move to measuring how,
at this point late in analysis, her present lover is far from cruel though
more phallic than tender. The hour ends with her saying she still does
not have daydreams about me.

About a month after, in an hour when she is talking of recent pleasant intercourse (while images of real horses' penises come spontaneously to mind; no longer is the contrived, exaggerated Director daydream needed), she shifts to remembering how, when little, she
anticipated a wonderful gift her mother was to bring her. Instead, she

got only an uninteresting, useless toy. With this change in associations, her skirt falls upward, showing me a bit of leg. At this point I remark that her bottom is not only a breastlike, generous locus of seduction but also, from the anus in, both a secret sanctuary and place of wrath: her bottom serves for loving and hating.

She responds by recalling how she goaded her stepfather, whom she loved but who, she says, could scarcely stand her. Next thought (never before admitted): she is impelled to a loose bowel movement just before many analytic hours. At this point in the hour—its end—she reveals for the first time that the Director sometimes forced her to the humiliation of anal intercourse with dirty-old-men.

How can I indicate the day-after-day work on anal themes that continued for years, and convey a sense that there was an ongoing process that was gradually freeing her up to expose to me—and, when conscious, to herself—her anal preoccupations and the part they played in her behavior, including her excitement? I can only present glimpses: the sense of the analysis as an anal experience, sometimes with spontaneous and well-formed movements and sometimes with results forced out by my "enemas"—interventions; a dream of a plumber and a plumber's helper, with associations to black-soled shoes, to her getting the couch dirty, to her ugly, deteriorating, and wrinkled body (a real turd); concerns about smelling; dreams of open doors that lead down passages. Here, an example from many, is a fragment of a dream analysis, the dream remembered only when she relaxed after reporting on smells, skin dirtiness, a dream of a house with "lots of doors, but I was not shutting the doors":

> I was in an outdoor restaurant by myself. I was in a nightgown, and I was really messy; it just looked all wrong. I didn't want anybody to see; so I snuck up to the counter in order to pay my bill. But I found I was in the wrong place. I went by some rooms with the signs "men" and "women." Then I went through a turnstile and was outside. There, outside, were some young girls in bridesmaids' dresses, but they had dressed too early. They were going to get all wrinkled.*

Because of the element of messiness, I said, "The young girls?" Belle: "Yes, that's right. They were not just girls: they were young girls around thirteen." I said that my question had implied that, referring

---

*Certain details of the dream refer to other issues than that now being discussed; and anal elements of the dream draw also from other issues. I shall ignore here—though I did not in the analytic hour—these other themes, such as the interplay of issues of masculinity and femininity and reproduction (bridesmaids, wedding); or excretion, as portrayed in the rooms with the signs "men" and "women," which were not seen in the dream as "men's rooms" or "ladies' rooms" (toilets); or the universe of maternal-oral ideas behind "restaurant."

to the time "when you were on the verge of becoming disgusting and messy by your standards, growing pubic hair, getting your smells, finding your sexual feelings so intense, your body changing so much. That must have been the onset of what you felt was your dirty sex and your dirty body. Also, in the dream, the girls are dressed early and are soon to get messy, suggesting that the age of smooth-skinned childhood is ending and young womanhood imminent [wrinkled labia]." In recent years, Belle had begun anticipating the approach of the fateful age of thirty, but from this time on, the battle in her died down—unconscious scripts with their themes—between smooth-skinned, upper-class girlishness and the wrinkled realities of womanhood; after this, she still wished she could look like a young girl but knew she never would again.

During most of this analysis, Belle did all she could—which was plenty—to drive me crazy with her sadomasochistic tricks, to get me to hit back as she distorted my words, meanings, and motives. It is one thing for the analyst to know this behavior is related to childhood anality and battles over control but another to be able to let one's patient know this and have it make a difference. I might think my efforts worked to chip away resistance so that insight could shine through, but for Belle each confrontation and interpretation was one more thrust into her bowels. Then one day, because of the previous years of work, it ended; after that, the analysis was never the same.

This was an hour in which the anticipatory moves, not surprisingly, had anal content: about advertisements for hemorrhoids, smells, little girls' heavy curls that looked like bowel movements, childhood excretory games, and then—once more, as so often before—her mother's and the Caretaker's unending, overpowering interest in her bowel movements. Now, as one comes to expect as the dividend for adequate working through, she remembered these times with a different clarity, telling me much the same as I had heard before, and yet telling it just differently enough—directly, openly, wanting me to know—that I was allowed to accept it in a new way.* Every day Mother's substitute probed. There was only one proper time; and it had better be that time and every day, for failure was corrected with an enema or punishment.

Now as she talks, I too fill with her experience, finally and fully knowing what this little girl, abandoned by her mother and father, had to feel and then feel again and again, without hope that she would be rescued, against which there was no recourse on earth or in heaven; she

---

*I can accept it differently, of course, because working through occurs in both the analyst and the patient, or it does not work. But I do not know quite how it happened. I gave no new, powerful interpretation or special gesture of support. Rather, for reasons not clear then (and beyond retrieval now, years later), she felt safer and therefore able to let me experience her insides. I do know, however, that the work we did the previous hour—to be described shortly—helped.

could not even tell herself that this was immoral, uncalled for, illegal, heartless, outrageous. It could only be borne. Except for daydreaming.

And now the material flows out of her; for the first time, we both feel the formerly unconnected bits and pieces of history and fantasies fall into place. The associations proceed as follows.

She thinks of the early erotic daydreams, of men urinating on bound women. It could be a number of men or one man alone. Then she recalls the preadolescent stories of big, beautiful, huge-breasted Amazons. At that time it was these women who were trapping and binding defenseless women.

Her thoughts return to the enemas, the threat and agonizing excitement that became the dominant, conscious theme of the days without escape from these anal-rectal manipulations and sensations: her Caretaker's sharply focused attention on her anal performance. The manifest form was, "How are you doing? Did you have a bowel movement? You'll be sick if you don't," beneath which lay the chance of inspection followed by enemas. At the core was the threat that if she was not compliant, she would be abandoned. And it takes little insight to sense how threatening it is to one's innermost integrity to have to submit one's interior to another's will. No wonder the underground fantasy portrays sweet, safe, internal silence.

It is clear to her, as the hour moves on, that I finally know—have it in my body that I know. And she lets me in because she knows I know, and that I know only because she let me in.

I note to her that loss of control is the central feature of the Director daydream: the prime exciter in each version is the sense of erotic sensations increasing, rushing faster, beyond control. When she portrays their breaking loose, in fact they do: she has an orgasm in the daydream and in reality. She has lost control; the whole audience— every masculine (that is, sadistic) male in the universe, including the grand macho, God—has seen her. But the portrayed defeat is not the disaster the enemas were. First, the orgasm only seems to be forced on her; in reality it is her doing. Second, defeat—end of struggle—leads to the great peaceful silence of early infancy.* Third, don't worry: disaster did not hit this time. That was only theater, a script. She knows she is alone, safe, secret, undetected. There really is no hostile audience and no Director—just herself.

Even during her rare sojourns at home, Mother was out of the house most evenings: "She was evasive, affectionate, and avoided unpleasantness at all costs." The Caretaker went to her room to read after dinner

*This is the satisfaction suicidal people propose to themselves.

—silent, dependable, protective though not palpable or visible—leaving Belle to do schoolwork, to read, or to daydream. So that was the quiet, safe time when, if she had not had an enema, she might be lucky enough to have a spontaneous bowel movement. (On passing a firehouse when alone in the evening, she repeats these peaceful moments in the impulse to move her bowels; the same feeling of quiet and safety, of someone there who will prevent dangers but who is not a noisy presence.)

She now backdates from age four to around two, at the beginning of memory, her mother undressing her, putting her outside in the sun, and leaving her penned in, buttocks open to public view. (Obviously, for another child, having a bare bottom need not cause exhibitionistic feelings.)

So Belle was prepared a few years later, on seeing the little girl's underwear-covered bottom, for the onset of excitement. Already, at that young age (not too young), she has converted her trauma to a sort of triumph: sexual excitement. She has moved a long way from un-protected trauma—from the inability to control her body, from humili-ation, from being unable to defend her insides—to a game in which she portrays the trauma (pretends to relive the trauma) but controls the action herself. With this use of fantasy, she arrives at a new ending: trauma moves to anxiety, to excitement, to gratification.

You have seen how this analytic progress through her gut began simply as a minimal movement, as "just a habit"* of adjusting her skirt while talking about what she felt were far more important issues. (If it takes this much work to piece together the origins and meaning of an act as ordinary as adjusting one's skirt, imagine the difficulties still ahead for anthropologists who jet out to an alien land, pluck up a few songs about a lizard god and some observations on rain dances or roof raising, package them, and fly back to the campus.)

The hour is almost up: time to put together the ideas elaborated above. I review the story of her Caretaker's invasions and victories, speaking so that Belle knows I now have that understanding fixed also within my guts. (Otherwise she would not hear what I am to say.) On the side of insight is the fact that if I interpret correctly, she will really learn what she already knows, has always known, could not face, and therefore left split off in a separate fantasy system from the one we usually call "sense of self." I remind her that, however cruel, the Caretaker (as did the Director) cared, was focused on her in contrast to Mother's casual abandonment. I describe, as I imagine Belle ex-perienced it, the threat; the invasion of questions, suppositories, ther-

*To quote her and our colleagues in academic psychology.

mometers, visual inspection; the suggestions about proper diet; the assaults with foods that must be ingested if bowels, skin, and soul were to survive; and the discussions of the relationship of bowels to general physical and moral health; the enema tube that went in; the water that filled her; the increasing, painful, almost unbearable and yet exciting bursting pressure, going beyond what seemed to be her limits when she still had to hold it longer and take in more; the uncontrolled blast with its fierce sensations of relief, so sharp and profound that they had to be erotized. It is the nature of mucous membrane to be charged with potential for that form of pleasure we label erotic. The quality of the sensations is ultimately of physiologic origin and so is hard to deny.

The second part of the interpretation reviewed the interpersonal relationships interwoven with the sensations: the terrible bind, on the one side that abandonment by each parent left her the choice either to be compliant or to be without support or hope, and the opposite extreme, that to commit herself to people meant total, profound connection via her bowels and—the ultimate attachment—the enemas' explosive invasions, certainly a primitive and shockingly one-sided version of love. I wanted her not to minimize the latter, to recognize that it was the love that she extracted from the trauma (pleasure, attention, loss of the terror of abandonment, praise for good performances, all this converted into erotic and neurotic experiences) that bound her to her anality, a never-ending presence conceptualized in the term "character structure." The task that confronts the child is how to take sensations, traumas, threats, and fantasies, to put them together and make them work to preserve sanity and integrity of body and being, and even to eke out some pleasure. It is amazing that children almost always manage this.

The third part of the interpretation served to link all this with the present as it was experienced in her relationship with me, that is, the transference. Repeating what had been said at times before, but this time under the different circumstances of all that had just happened during this hour, I told her how the analysis reproduced these childhood anal experiences: the need to protect but also reveal one's secret parts, outer and inner; their sensations, the fantasies that reinvented them, the traumas, the pleasures, the battles for control as my invasive interpretations moved up her intestines.* I reviewed the many ways she tried to retain control: the sadomasochistic interplay with me; her insistence that she disgusted me with her dirtiness; the defiance that was

*At another time, a comparable description would talk of femaleness, genital penetration, and reproduction, and at still another, the appropriate interpretation would be about her nose and lungs or her mouth, her gullet, and the digesting part of her belly.

covered with her "lovely" niceness and gentleness. Most of all—perhaps because I wanted relief after all these years—I emphasized the roots of resistance in her defense against anal attack: you say no, silently and secretively so that I shall not know. "No. I will not hear what you say; no, I will not agree with you; no, I will not speak my thoughts as I think and thus let the shit flow spontaneously; no, I will not be on time; no, I will not close the door the way I think you want; no, I will not lie down in the manner you want. And even if I say yes, you had better know it is no. No."

I ended with this comfort: "I want you to know that I understand you had to do this with me. Yes."

Here is the hour preceding the one just described. It tells you, now, in part, how the one above came to be.

She comes in a few minutes late. My custom is to open the door to my office and call waiting patients in, but if they are not there, I leave the door open and sit at my desk, usually reading. For years, in this latter circumstance, Belle has walked in breezily, briskly, buoyantly, nonchalantly throwing the door shut behind her as she enters chattering. The impression to be made is that she is a fresh, lovely, lively, cheery young woman without a care but nonetheless willing for my sake to embark afresh on another day's analytic voyage. Every effort to analyze this show has been avoided (stubbornly, think I; if she heard that, she would genuinely wonder why I had such a strange, dangerous idea about such an insignificant moment). This, then, is a subtle show of defiance.

She lies down and reports subjects suitable for associations, in a voice appropriate for a grocery list: I am thinking of such and such; now I am thinking of such and such; now I am thinking of such and such. Then she says she has had a dream last night, but does not tell it. I picture dirt being thrown to cover something. She reports the dream: "There were some boys in a yard. They were being helpful, like boys usually are. [I presume this is sarcasm.] I was trying to be private. I was in my house with some girls; it was night-time. There were lights on, and we could be seen. So we pulled the shades down, but the shades were transparent."

They were boys because they were wearing tennis shoes. She went to a funeral yesterday in a Catholic church; one of the altar boys was wearing new tennis shoes: that is what has happened to the Church. She has heard that it used to be beautiful and majestic, but now it is like a Methodist service, people shaking hands, the poetry gone, the language English instead of mysterious Latin. At this point, she says something about being coerced; it is so insignificant to me that I do not write it down. (I take notes, just a word or two every few minutes so as not to deflect my concentration from her to the notes.) The subject is insignificant, but the sense of being coerced is strong for her, and the hour suddenly turns around. I can feel it palpably shift, and for the next moments I sense (and then I consciously think) that she came in prepared for a shift (no evidence consciously in me why I feel that). When dictating from the notes after the hour, I recalled that at that moment, it was as if she had offered an opening into which I could move; so I did. The metaphor became the feeling that I literally was allowed to move into her body, and yet her resistance was still present. But now it was resistance-plus-opening.

I then make an interpretation, the same one made a number of times before but now put a bit differently, to fit the opening. I tell her that she has felt coerced in here all the time, and by that, I say, I mean that no matter what else has happened, in every minute of each of the hours, she has felt herself being forced, having to cooperate, and that there has been nothing I could do so far that has freed her from that. I say that every moment, every movement, every word I said, every word I did not say, the furniture, the books, the paintings, the plants—they all forced her to do what I wanted. I remind her how that element dominates her sexual fantasies, and as I talk, I realize (and say to her) that I have never fitted into place the other fantasy, the underground fantasy. Now I dream it with her and experience out loud the underground places populated by people all of whom are benign though—because—not talking to her, not even paying attention to her; the firehouse fantasies and the feeling as she walks past of her bowels literally opening up because of those firemen quietly and safely contained inside the building. I ask her, knowing the answer, if there ever was an erotic quality to the underground fantasy, and she says no, not quite. I talk then of her genitals and her anus-rectum, suggesting she may feel that her goals for treatment include using her genitals more for sex and her anus-rectum more for uncomplicated evacuation, with each area less contaminated by the fantasies we are discovering. She responds with surprise—quiet and undramatic, with no thrashing about as she has done in the past. She simply is herself, a state that up till then I have rarely seen. And she remains that way for the rest of the hour.

First she says she has just noticed that her muscles down there—and she gestures toward the pelvic floor—are always tight. I say that she does that to prevent humiliation, to prevent things from going in or coming out, not just her thoughts and feelings, not just free associations, but literally her shit and urine.* (The grocery-list voice at the start of the hour had been used on a statement that just then she had

*She did not use the word "piss," only "urine."

feelings in her urethra.) "You cannot believe that anyone, and I especially, can find that your shit is all right; that, as you secretly know, it isn't so bad; that it can be interesting to smell or feel. You believe that if you actually had an accident in here it would *not* be all right with me."

She replies, "I cannot believe it: I did not know you knew that." She says this in complete contact with me, without exaggeration or other games; I have never before heard her accept a remark of mine without reservation. I say, "You have never been able to let your bowels loose in here, only when you're alone, in private." She mentions the Caretaker's obsession with bowel habits (the lead-in to the next hour's full openness about the enemas) and recalls—for the first time in my presence—the details of how the bathroom was furnished; the description pours out for a few moments and then stops.

This happens when I clear my throat. To her, that means I am bored. But she knows somewhere in her that in these circumstances I could not be bored; to be safe, she has fallen back to a masochistic position ("I bore you"), which rescues her from the unaccustomed and still dangerous outpouring of genuineness. With masochism, she returns to the familiar and comforting accusation that she is being coerced.

Who knows how many times in the past I pointed out her retreat for safety to masochism, but this time, as never before, her response is, "I know" (said so genuinely that I put an exclamation point in my notes).

Thinking again about her underground fantasies, I for the first time find myself willing to tell her that these are connected with her bowels and their contents. I think to myself that now she may sense that these peaceful, benign, noncoercive, nonmasochistic, very quiet fantasies of large rooms and corridors underground, populated by silent people whom she does not know but who are not dangerous, who pass her without threatening, are her bowels and their contents, especially as experienced in childhood.*

---

*I speak the language of inner objects only when that feels comfortable, and much less than some colleagues do. This is a big issue in analytic technique and theory now. Sometimes, especially in regard to the way I practice analysis, it is hard to know if, in disagreeing with colleagues, I am right or only neurotically blocked. So, for instance, when I hear of interpretations Kleinian colleagues sometimes give—especially early in treatment—I think they are either applying intellectualized theory, or are not in touch with their patients, or are nuts. At other times, I think they are more insightful than I. But whatever the case, I would feel silly saying things with which they are comfortable. (This does not go for working with psychotic patients; then, many of those remarks come out spontaneously.) How, one may ask, can an analyst spend so much time on traumas occurring so late in childhood—age seven and later—and not more frequently reconstruct and interpret the anal events of the first two or three years of life; or fail to describe the monsters and monstrous events the infant fantasizes occurring in the rectum? Is it even psychoanalysis if the patient is not told that these primitive issues are at work, unconsciously, in her? If I am wrong, I only hope that talking approximately on the subject nonetheless indirectly reaches to the depths wherein the action is occurring.

She responds by describing a pattern in the acoustical ceiling tile. (This is, of course, resistance, but with a difference: for years, she now says, she has done this with the ceiling but never before mentioned it.) In the pattern, she sees a fox, which I take to mean me and also her fear of me—a small, clever, sharp-toothed animal, a warning to her not to trust me, to keep control before she reveals too much. (I refrain from telling her my belief that it is a projection of unacceptable qualities she feels are hers.)

I say, "You just cannot believe—you never have been able to believe —that I wouldn't trick you; even now, when you are closer than usual to trusting me, you cannot."* She responds with another dream: "There was an infant that I loved very much and was holding, even though it wasn't pretty; it had floppy ears and was homely." She then says that right now she has sensations in her bottom. But they are not just in one place; they are, as it were, one big sensation made up of sensations from her buttocks, anus, urethra, and vagina; in fact, the netherlands are flooded. This is pleasantly sensual though not sexual excitement, but she is a bit embarrassed that excretory tissues merge with reproductive to make pleasure.

The fox changes to a dog, and then she talks of "mother dogs": "When their pups are born, how can they eat up all the shit and the afterbirth [long pause]. Nobody ever said before—and meant it—what you just said about my shit." Then, regretfully, "I made a bad choice: I ignore knowing that you are not bad. All I ever do is accuse you." Only now, minutes after first thinking it, I remark that the interior of her bowels became the source for the underground fantasy and that the people and events depicted herein are the bowel contents and movements. I add, "And even if you experience all the people inside you as good and trustworthy, you don't trust any of us on the outside." In response, she mentions for the first time that when her mother finally rejoined her after the many separations, instead of feeling safe and intact, for days she feared she would be physically attacked in an unknown way. "But I put all this away, and I have forgotten all of that. I can feel that there are lots of things I can almost remember, especially about people *not* hurting other people." The hour is up; her last remark is that she cannot watch television interview shows because someone is always attacked.

In this hour, then, while working on bowel fantasies, she felt more trusting toward me. That was appropriate work in anticipation of that next hour when she was able to experience fully with me the traumatic

*At another level, almost always unnoted by patients, she trusts me, or she would not have put up for years with this strange relationship.

enema manipulations and thus permanently change the nature of her work in the analysis, her relationship to me, and her relationship to those she knew in the outer world.

Now, having looked at these aspects of Belle's anality, let us put them aside, and instead, just as Belle did with me, go over other issues that had to be understood before the crucial clarification.

Perhaps equal to our coming to see what had before been mysterious was Belle's relief that I understood what she had been through. Once the anal traumas and excitements were conscious and shared with me, they became no longer active in every cell of her body and psyche, as it were. They lost their power. They were still present—remembered— but they were no longer there as a presence. (The process is similar to that of mourning, in which we finally give up our hope that the lost object is somehow still there to help us, that the loss did not really occur.) The therapeutic effect came as much from her knowing the two of us shared the insight as from the power of the insight itself. (Too many colleagues, who have come to despair of analysis, maintain that the only effect in analytic technique is this sharing; they underline that the insight is not therapeutic, is the result and not a cause of feeling better, is intellectualization. Those of us, on the other hand, who enjoy analytic practice do so, I think, because we have seen what happens when unconscious, and therefore unmanageable, ideas and feelings become part of a patient's volition.)

Another insight was her seeing the underground stories as representing, in part, the interior of her body, mixing together excretory and reproductive fantasies. This fantasy served as a balance—a counterpoint—to the excitedly, masochistically, genitally complicated erotism that was more focused on the outer rim of her body, especially skin, clitoris, and nipples. These two very different complexes of sensations, fantasies, expectations, and perspectives were isolated from each other, each going its own way, until the exploration of the underground fantasy put them together so that she—the subjective "she" that she lives with—could have both available to her, thus enriching not only her erotic life but her other relationships with people.

A fourth understanding, and therefore a turning point, in regard to anality occurred when we analyzed the ways in which she fused her anality and her exhibitionism.

7

Sadomasochism

SADOMASOCHISM IS, I think, a central feature of most sexual excitement. My hunch is that the desire to hurt others in retaliation for having been hurt is essential for most people's sexual excitement all the time but not for all people's excitement all the time. How was it with Belle?

Sadomasochism colored each of her experiences in the real world and in the private world of her daydreams. She transformed every moment so that such themes were dominant; in doing so, she was forever lifting the mundane up to melodrama. I had plenty of chance to study this in our relationship, since her sadomasochism in its most direct form was aimed at me. And it was of course in the transference that these issues were brought under control.*

Her resistance was overtly shaped more by sadomasochism than by anything else. A moment she experienced as filled with distress—usually humiliation—became an attack aimed at me. Even her loving and tender times contained the sadism. For instance, if she was gratified that I understood, she arranged the words in the sentence so that the message was, "Considering that you are a male and therefore have always been and shall always be hard, obtuse, unempathic, and unable to bear my physical presence (because it is female), you really are empathic, kind, and remarkably patient; I love you because you try so hard to contain your disgust." And those were the good times.

She had plenty of techniques available for trying to irritate me, but they all fell within a certain range: never loud in sound or gesture, she still gave a histrionic touch to each moment. Example: she was rarely

---

*I am, obviously, not saying "resolved" or "finished." The measure of success with her—and probably with all patients—is how much the heat goes out of an issue, but the lifelong themes probably seldom disappear completely.[1] She will use this style when pressed, but—as I know through my experience with her—it will be a ghost of its old form.

openly angry but instead attempted to show that she had been unfairly hurt by the brute. For years, there was hardly an hour when tears did not ooze out, to run down her face unwiped, doing their glistening job even when the subject matter changed to the nonpathetic. Example: she often dropped references to people or events about whom or which I knew nothing, doing so as if I were informed and could follow what she was saying. This had a double-edged advantage: either I was left confused (and I *was* chronically confused), or when, infrequently, I asked for clarification, she could feel accused, not just that I wanted information. Example: to demonstrate how cruel I was, she would quote something I had said a day, a week, or several years before. On recognizing what I had actually said, I could see how the change of sometimes only a word or two had shifted the context to suit her purpose. She could then, using her misquotation, show that I was imitating what an analyst should be. She had caught me in the proof that I was a tricky bastard. Example: when, at each hour's end, I remarked that the time was up, she rose sadly, understanding that I had interrupted because I was unable to bear any longer to be in the same room with her.

These exemplified an often-used technique, doing something blatantly at odds with what she knew was reality (as she would later admit). In this way she could be a pest, as she had been with her mother, and so reassure herself that she was being noticed: pests bother you (sadism) till you swat them (masochism); and they know they are pests (masochism).

She kept a script going (it made analysis more fascinating for her) that I, being by nature brutal—that is, male—was constantly about to throw her out of treatment. Therefore, whatever she said or did had also to contain a communication to placate me. By saying something she liked, I was secretly telling her that treatment would end now (and doing it despicably—I was a liar, a cheat, a coward, who did not speak directly). On the other hand, if she decided I was displeased, that also signaled the end of treatment. My going on vacation was a secret plan for the end, and in not responding to the accusation I again displayed that incorrigible need to lie. When we set up an appointment in order to begin again after a vacation, that only meant that I wanted to see her a final time to brush her off. A change of schedule was one more sneaky move toward termination.

Before reporting a dream, she often announced that, although a sterling analyst, I did not want to hear her dream but that, by God, she would report it anyway, no matter what dreadful consequences I inflicted on her. This device was also to indicate that I was only pretending to be an analyst. Beneath that lay her awareness that she knew she was playing the fool by using these maneuvers so grossly; and beneath that, after enough analytic work had been done that she trusted me, was revealed the idea that here was a relationship where she was allowed to play these awful amusements out and be done with them.

Exhibitionism was a great vehicle for her masochism. I was to consider her displays silly, bubble-headed, even disgusting, but she exquisitely measured her moves so as to dismay but not exhaust me. The men in her daydream are bored but nonetheless stay. No matter what she does, the Director is steadfast. His one absolutely essential quality is that he does not leave; he may be frozen, but he is always *there*.

She would test me with ludicrously inept resistance: "You don't want me to talk about this but I'm going to anyway"; "if I tell you something good is happening in my life you will not listen because you only want to hear about the bad things"; "I want to lie down now, but you think I should sit up"; "you never said I *had* to lie down all the time, but that's what you really believe"; "you don't want me to lie on your couch because I may sweat"; "they say you're an M.D. and an analyst but you really can't stand my talking about bowel movements"; "you pretend that you're not a liar, but you really are"; "all right: the treatment will continue but only because you don't have the guts to be honest and throw me out"; "you can't stand me when I'm depressed (happy, angry)"; ". . . wearing these pants (this dress, blouse, sweater); ". . . late to the hour"; ". . . early to the hour"; ". . . talking to your secretary"; ". . . ignoring your secretary"; "when you say yes, you don't really mean it—you mean no" (and vice versa); "you don't want to hear what I'm thinking"; "why won't you answer this question since it's not like the other questions I ask—this time I have to have an answer"; "wouldn't it be more honest if you just told me openly that you hated me"; "I love you because you're so patient and try not to let me see how much I disgust you"; "I won't tell you what I'm thinking because it's none of your business"; "I'm so grateful to you for being willing to change the time of our hour next Friday" (considering that you're by nature such a rigid, obsessive-compulsive son-of-a-bitch); "this time I won't tell you what I'm thinking because it's too important"; "you like it when I'm late because then you don't have to spend so much time with me"; "you hate it when I'm late because you can't stand someone who doesn't keep to a schedule"; "you stick to your mechanical, analytic technique with me but if it were another patient—if it were a man or a prettier woman—you don't treat them that way"; "when you are not showing anger (disgust, etc.) you are doubly a bastard because, first, you're hiding your feelings, and second, no real analyst would get angry under these circumstances and display his lack of understanding, and also because in refusing to show your anger you are cowardly and a liar"; "you don't want me to understand but just to stop the behavior you don't like"; "you can't stand seeing my real feelings, and so I have to disguise them in front of you"; "I hate you right now because you understand me, and so I feel grateful, which humiliates me because you are a man watching me defenseless with these feelings"; "because I get sexually excited so easily and especially because it happens here, I am humiliated all the time with you" (which leads to more excitement which leads to more humiliation); "I am even more humiliated because only poorly bred women cannot control their sexual excitement." These quotations and paraphrases should convey the sense of what went on almost every hour for years. What a relief for us both when, the tricks left behind, their underlying functions were in the open.

She worked from a "can't lose" position, disguised as a "can't win." The other person is always the brute, she always the victim; but at the level where the action really is, she is secretly the victor. She has demonstrated the alleged attacker's cruel inhumanity. The double bind —"no matter what you do to or for me, it is wrong"—is the masochist's device for keeping supplies of masochism and sadism flowing. If an interpretation made her feel understood, Belle thought, "He doesn't mean it; it's just a trick to hide that he hates me." When she did this to people who did not recognize what she was doing, they would get irritated, which proved she was right all along: no one loved her. (The analyst's technique is especially painful for masochistic patients, for our quietness in the face of this pestering never gives them a sure sign they are right.) In addition, she ended up sexually excited, while we poor attackers, if we did not catch what she was doing, ended up—at the least—with a headache. She saw in treatment, then, the same battle-ground that had been her fate everywhere.

It was inevitable Belle would stage the Director fantasy with me, and her doing so made the analysis possible: we know that analysis of the transference is not an excursion into theory or a look at the past as in a book but has its own passionate life. I had to be the Director; and I frustrated her just as he did, though I also added the quantity of time and a real presence to the measure of interpretation, which helps patients change the meaning they read into the relationship.*

Winnicott has described "the holding environment," the physical and psychologic setting the analyst provides, comparable to the infant's

*Perhaps, generalizing about resistance, one can say it not only functions to ward off the analyst and thus to protect the patient from attack, but also is a secret way of reversing the situation so that the apparent victim—the patient—becomes the victor and, by thwarting the analyst, makes him suffer.

security within its mother's calm and attentive embrace. Only if the analyst establishes that and the patient finds it can an analysis occur. (We should also recognize that patients hold us, though in a less visible manner.) Then, for the transference to dominate treatment, this "holding" must be ignored. If either analyst or patient tries too hard to manifest this kindness, games of love are played and real gratifications pulse through the analysis, jeopardizing the delicate ambience that allows the past to be present.

At times, when insight broke in after a correct interpretation, Belle admitted—knew—we did not have a truly sadomasochistic relationship. It was the task of analysis to make that manifest. Had it been my job to teach her what she had never known, analysis would not have worked; or at least, nonanalytic techniques hidden in the analysis would have been the predominant ones, as in supportive and behavior therapies. For I was not the teacher of a child but rather the co-worker with an adult. With analysis, she was able to learn what she had always known.

For years, it was my function to serve as the victim of her masochism without feeling myself a victim. Had I really felt victimized, I would have turned sadistic (grumpy, at least), and the analysis might have ended, no matter how correct the interpretations. (By the way, I do not see how an analyst can for long feel himself a victim if he is serious; he will be too busy thinking about why the patient is doing this, which precludes his believing he is the real object of the sadism. Yet we must sense our patients abrading us, or we deny them the chance to experience and analyze their sadism.)

I rather doubt that, had I been a brave and true sadist, she would have stayed in treatment, just as she would never have had an affair with a real sadist. She had never had a relationship with a cruel person, probably because she is not cruel, despite all the masochistic shenanigans. It was her purpose to irritate people and exhaust their patience but not to destroy them. In behavior and in daydreams, she had to introduce *failing* defiance; only that sustained her excitement.

Belle had her first boyfriend when she was six. They wrestled; he beat her up. "It was with him that I had my first body-contact excitement, when we played cowboy, with me as the wrestled-down loser and him on top. I was in love with him. Even now in sex, I want to be pinned down." From then till near the end of the analysis, she had no relationships with boy or man, in reality or fantasy, in which she did not feel abused. Only late in treatment did she realize that, although he was always in trouble for attacking her, this first boy never did the same to anyone else. Then she recalled that in her teens, her girlfriends had pointed out to her that she was picked on by the boys as the others were not. Not surprisingly, adolescence brought out the most dramatic expressions of her masochistic life-style. It was then that the sexual daydream took its final form: the Director and the audience of unfeeling men. There was scarcely a harder task in our work than for her to see this pattern as not simply the result of males' natural cruelty but of her endless tricks, either to evoke men's cruelty when they were not going about it spontaneously or to interpret behavior as being sadistic when it was not.

The same themes present in the classic form appeared in other daydreams; one needs change: even a wild stallion can be a bore at times. Here, for instance, is another. One man is showing another man how, for religious reasons, women must not move during intercourse. Belle is the woman on whom these two men are working, and each time she moves, they beat her. In the background she sees herself, watching. (Remember her lover with severe potency problems; she could not move or he would come too soon. The fantasy allowed her to convert this painful reality to excitement.)

Masochism was present, overtly or occultly, in every waking moment, coloring all experience; she was a victim in search of a disaster.

Although I am shy about reconstructions of childhood, finding them more effective in treatment than for research (they are unsafe for research if one is convinced they are correct), here is one we can consider: Belle, the focus of the games of her girl-woman mother, was not treated as a separate person, a daughter, but rather as a doll that enabled mother's childhood to persist. Having no choice but to be in the role of a doll, Belle learned to secrete "lovely," a primary femininity in which pretty clothes, pretty face, pretty body, pretty bottom, pretty carriage, and pretty thoughts created a burdensome sense of being constantly on stage, observed, concerned that the imagined audience might not admire her. Her kind of exhibitionism (the nonperverse, nongenital kind) is not usually described as masochistic, but it probably is.

She never had a taste for physical masochism. Perhaps that was because physical pain, such as beating or pinching, was not used in her early childhood to control or punish her and so never became a trauma needing to be mastered as she grew.* Her masochism was related, instead, to humiliation.[2] This theory, however, does not account for the enemas, which not only attacked her integrity but also were acutely

---

*Perhaps the perversion of masochism is a hungry search for skin and mucous-membrane stimulation in people who got too little in infancy and who have decided, as have "moral masochists," that any attention, even if painful, is better than none.

painful. Yet I saw no sign of that pain being converted to symptoms of excitement except perhaps in her mild focus on anal stimulation. I do not know why she converted the *psychic* trauma of being attacked and humiliated into a masochistic life-style, including her style of erotism, but did not convert the *physically* traumatic sensations into a need for anal penetration. Perhaps if the enemas had been daily, or the Caretaker's concentration clearly filled with anger or hatred—brutal, as it was not in reality—and without the woman also at times being comforting to Belle, the invasions would have been hot enough to demand an erotic defense. (Why, in our society, where grossly sadomasochistic fantasies are a favorite of women, do so few practice the perversion of sadomasochism? What ethnographic data are there on sadomasochism in women in other cultures; does one find the actual perversion or mostly—as in our culture—fantasies? Are there—as I suspect—places where women do not rely on masochistic scripts to excite themselves, places, perhaps, where the power distribution between men and women tips more toward the latter?)

Let us look further at the first few years of Belle's adolescence, by which time masochism was already essential for her dealing with the world. She was well along into masturbation (never to orgasm), with her erotic needs increased by puberty and with her figure beginning to develop, when she began worrying about Peeping Toms. Her concern was augmented by her mother, who dramatically embellished the theme. Belle was preoccupied with fears that voyeurs were hiding in the bushes to watch her. (She says that in fact this did happen once.) In order not to be seen, she would go to a hidden, quiet, safe place that gave her a feeling like that in the underground fantasy.

As the boys and girls of her group developed their social and sexual interests, Belle moved with them, though she spoiled her adolescence by masochism. She let herself be displaced by the girls she felt were prettier, more vivacious, more graceful, and had better social credentials. So she did not try to capture the attention of the most desired boys, but chose instead the boy who became a prime model for the audience of men in the fantasy. She saw him (as, to a lesser degree, she did all the boys of her group, and in time all men except the effeminate or otherwise overtly weak) as cold, arrogant, contactless, unloving, superior. These qualities defined masculinity for her. This young man, of course, was a match for her, meeting her compulsive flinching with constant teasing. Whatever he may have been in reality, she saw him as a sadistic, neurotic man who knew her innermost secrets and met them point for point with his uncanny capacity to humiliate her. So she was chronically excited by him, hating him, blaming him, crying, whining, coming back for more. Of all the nonfather males mentioned in her analysis, he was the one most constantly present.

He expended little erotic effort on her though they were constantly together. She interpreted this as evidence that she was flawed; first, because he, unpopular and odd, was willing to keep going with her, and second, because, though he went with her, he never acted either lovingly or as if sexually excited. More exactly, he touched her in openly erotic ways and got her excited (often by wrestling with her), but he never advanced the action or tried for satisfaction for himself (the Director's attributes). She could not have sustained a relationship had it been otherwise. And of course, because she persisted in this manifestly neurotic relationship, she felt—no doubt correctly—that everyone observing her thought her defective for keeping at it. At every moment, in every way, she knew how to keep that picture before her girlfriends' eyes.

He represents one of the two types of men she chose until these issues were resolved in treatment. The other was as follows: handsome and strong-appearing, appealing to other women, giving promise in form and manner of manliness and professional success, but in fact hiding a sense of defeat—inferior social origins, unused potential, professional failure, manifest unfaithfulness to her, and disturbances in potency. With such a man, she mastered the scripts in which she imagined herself an enslaved female who was required not to move during intercourse.

Only once in her life had she been fully in love: with her boyfriend at age six. He was strong and tough, of her age, given to chasing and beating her up but also playing more quietly with her. He was her first sexual partner, who enjoyed taking out his penis and urinating to her respectful attention.

The clearest contribution to her masochism*—the anal intrusions— make up another set of sensations and images, played out as if independent of the scripts that lie parallel, contiguous, or that cross over the narrative at the moment regnant. Let us go back to that to catch another glimpse of how treatment helped change Belle's way of working in the analysis, her trust of me, and her trust of everyone else. We return to the hour after she let out fully the suffering the enemas had inflicted.

The first consequence appeared as this next hour began: she had not turned off her contact with me, as she would have in the past after an

---

*Though not as profound as her mother's inability to stay connected—from the birth of the infant on—with Belle. Bak makes the suggestion that sadomasochistic fantasies, especially those of being immobilized, represent the wish not to be separated from mother.[3]

hour that made her feel we were close. Instead she spoke directly and without exaggeration. She said she had felt enthusiastic and tense after yesterday's hour, the feeling persisting to the present. What we had discussed made sense; things had fallen in place. She now understood why in intercourse she stopped the build-up, holding off her orgasm until the man was flaccid and then doing it herself almost instantly. She now knew this was an experience she created rather than one that "just happened," a matter of control as in the lost battles against rectal coercion.

Then followed an outpouring of associations—memories of bowel traumas, bowel habits, bathrooms she had known, her mother's bowels, rear ends—the significance not being in the material but in her finally opening up to let this pour through. The worst was over.

We understood better the years-long struggle, why she fought the free expression of feelings—erotism, anger, weeping, whatever; why she laid on her histrionic displays of feeling that simulated spontaneity while at the same time she retained control over her body, her emotions, and her thoughts; how she solved the insoluble, to defeat the assault on her anus and rectum, by creating scripts (behavior) that would forever let her retain control after the traumatic discovery* that there were circumstances (the enemas) she could not control; the lesson learned that fantasies and their conscious organizations—daydreams—will, for the moment at least, undo any traumas, with the additional bonus of sexual pleasure; and that, with the underground fantasy, she also gained control, for the opposite of noise is quiet, the opposite of excitement is tranquillity, the opposite of loss of control is control so subtle it can only be called peacefulness. She learned more about the nature of her sexual excitement; some of the origins of her masochistic scripts and behaviors; about the battle for control hidden in the scripts; why certain characters were chosen and why they performed as they did; how her exhibitionism was constructed and used; how she controlled others while appearing always as a victim; why masturbation was so easy and intercourse so difficult; why she contaminated her femininity with masochism; why her accomplishments in the real world were negligible but those in creating fantasies formidable; why she saw me as she did and how this led to our sadomasochistic relationship; why it was necessary to risk wrecking the treatment even at the cost of losing what she felt was her last hope; why reality was worth so little whatever its potential; why her capacity to love was so worm-eaten. Now Belle knew the two main functions of her masochism: hidden sadism ("my suffering will

*Rediscovery; it must have been known in infancy.

pain you"), and trauma control ("I feel awful all the time so that I won't ever have to really feel awful").

At the end of treatment, she summarized all this: "For me, sadism was caring." Caring was to not be abandoned. She seemed to have little choice.

Masochism has long been a crucial problem for analytic theory.[4] Freud struggled for years to understand its origins and functions until it finally became for him the central problem of human behavior. How was theory to account for self-destructive impulses that were manifest everywhere in individuals and society in gross and terrible form? The business, he said, must be instinctual.

If masochism hides in its depths a biologic drive, and especially ideas as magnificently impalpable as repetition compulsion and death instinct, we need better evidence than has yet been offered.[5] Ricoeur reviews the problem:

> The decisive experience that led Freud to the death instinct was a certain difficulty that keeps recurring in analytic treatment in connection with the struggle against resistances: viz. the tendency of the patient to repeat the repressed material as a contemporary experience instead of remembering it as a past memory. . . . What the patient repeats are precisely the situations of distress and failure he underwent as a child, particularly during the oedipal period. This tendency, further evidenced in the strange fate of those persons who seem to call down upon themselves the same misfortunes time and again, appears to justify the hypothesis of a compulsion to repeat that is "more primitive, more elementary, more instinctual than the pleasure principle which it overrides."[6]

The problem with the concepts of repetition compulsion and death instinct is the failure of the facts to fit. If we look closely at these clinical repetitions, we find that the repetition is not exact but only a simulation of repetition (as in pornography with its pseudo-risks). Minute differences distinguish the original experience from its redoing; subtle shifts have been purposefully introduced in order to make the experience *be* different while at the same time *appearing* the same. Hidden in those apparently minute changes is, I think, the mechanism of undoing past traumas and frustrations and repeating them, this time successfully, atraumatically—pseudotraumatically only.*

If careful observation reveals that the repetition is not exact, and if, further, one picks up the scripts that support the minute change, one

---

*There are, however, states in which there is exact repetition; these are the traumatic neuroses. And one can add another category, not yet clearly understood: conditioned responses. Are traumatic neuroses a form of conditioned responses?

can see there was no *compulsion* to repeat pain and self-destruction, only the wily wish, the compulsion *not* to repeat suffering, which, in masochists, is disguised by the use of humiliation or selected physical pains.

Most analysts doubt there is a death instinct and are content with the simpler, semiclinical explanation of masochism as a mechanism in which the ego, caught in a crossfire between the forbidden impulses of the id and the forbidding attacks of the superego, offers itself as a sacrifice, accepting (creating) feelings of guilt and undergoing purgative punishment.[7] Even this less radical theory may be wrong. Regarding origins of sexual excitement (and perhaps most neurotic constructions), I find the involved unconscious dynamics of sadomasochism more clever, more intelligent, and more sly than is suggested by the sacrificial ego model: we inflict punishment on ourselves in order to avoid having to change. It is easier to feel guilty and to pay a prescribed price, even suicide, than to change. In most of its forms, guilt is a bargain we strike with ourselves. Its presence indicates we have decided that doing what we should is too much trouble. Suicide (not all suicides, for not all are self-murders) is a trick.* So also, for most people, is sexual excitement. If we look closely, we rarely find in most situations in which guilt is a strong factor, such as in masochism or its close relative, depression, that the guilt expressed matches the crime committed. I believe instead that people erect guilt that looks superficially as if it is connected to the crime; but close observation will reveal that the punishment—guilt and its consequences—only *seems* to suit the crime. We actually trick our audience (conscience, superego, God, or our other invented idiots) into thinking the punishment is appropriate.† Guilt is not the price paid for being bad but the price paid for the privilege of continuing to be bad. The megalomania of guilt: I fool everyone.[8] Even the suicide, in his last moment, is exaggerating, playing to his audience, falsifying his truths, writing his script, running his number.

For those who believe in an "agency" called superego—guardian and judge of morality, punisher, watchdog of atonement—here is another for which superego may be no more than a disguise. This one, hidden beneath the other, gives permission to fail, to be not responsible, to lie, to falsify, to defend against what one knows is true. It is the boss (the "grandiose self"?) who harnesses "the inchoate libidinal mass" (the

*Not only a trick; it is, of course, more complicated than that.
†And yet we may discover that we believe guilt is appropriate, but for a different, hidden offense: for our success in fooling ourselves and others into thinking our expressions of guilt and our confessions are atonement for the manifest crime.

"id"). To uncover this clever devil may be, just as theologians tell us, as important as any other task in treatment.

And masochism is one of this schemer's devices. I do not think people become masochistic because they truly believe they deserve to be punished. Rather, I think they trick themselves and us into believing that that is what they do, while secretly, they are busy with their foxy little sadisms. We had an example of that in the exhibitionist. Does he get caught because of an unconscious need for punishment? I think not. Rather, he gets caught because getting caught is a *part* of the excitement, not an atonement *after* the excitement. And he invents his perversion as a defense against "castration anxiety,"[9] that is, humiliation, fear due to attack on his sense of maleness.

Smirnoff makes this clear in what he calls "the masochistic contract," where he reminds us that "it is the victim who lays down the rules . . . a consenting and demanding victim." Masochistic contracts are drawn up by people who know what they are doing and who read all the fine print. It is, as Smirnoff says, "the 'casting' of the play." The pain a masochist suffers is simply dust in our eyes; it is there to fool him and us into believing that he is genuinely deserving of punishment. If his conscience and we, as external witnesses, will buy this, then, with minimal effort, he has preserved his old ways of behaving. In masochism, "pain is not enough, or even has little to do with pleasure."[10]

Smirnoff knows Belle's Director and the true purpose of her fantasy:

> Masochism is a defiance. It is expressed through the masochist's apparently passive behaviour, by his compliance with the inflicted pain and humiliation, by his claims of being enslaved and used. In fact, the masochist knows that his position is simply the result of his own power: the power of endowing the executioner [read "Director"] with the obligation of playing the role of a master, when indeed he is only a slave, a creation of the masochist's desire. . . .
>
> Sacher-Masoch does not use the vocabulary of a victim, but that of the director of this play. Thus the masochist does not appear as the victimized accomplice of a sadistic executioner, but as his educator—just as the sadist is the pedagogue of his reluctant victim. It is of the utmost importance to redefine masochism—in any of its clinical forms—not through the "pleasure in pain" element, but as an actualization of a contract which must regulate the relationship in the masochistic performance.
>
> The symbiotic relation, as found in masochism, makes use of suffering, pain, and humiliation, not in order to obtain pleasure, but as a symbolic representative of both the unattainable fusion with the impossible separation from the primary sexual object.[11]

There is no way we can demonstrate that masochism is a manifestation of a drive ("instinct") to suffer pain.* We learn more if we look for the meaning a piece of masochism has for its owner. Berliner's phrases "Suffering is the weapon of the weak and unloved"† and "Masochism is a way of hating without great risk"[12] are the main sermons in this chapter. Masochism is a technique of control, first discovered in childhood following trauma, the onslaught of the unexpected. The child believes it can prevent further trauma by re-enacting the original trauma. Then, as master of the script, he is no longer a victim; he can decide for himself when to suffer pain rather than having it strike without warning. Or, when we have more of the hidden text, we can see masochism as an attack ("suffering is my revenge"). Displayed to suitable parents, clever masochism can elicit a suitably guilty response —and easily become a habit. Or, less conflictive, what about the masochism acquired when one identifies with a parent's masochism? That sort is culture-wide when, for instance, it is part of the definition of "normal" femininity (Freud, Deutsch, Bonaparte), and hard to remove, as may be most identifications not created from conflict.

In reality and in fantasies, the masochist builds his impregnable structure. By taking the power to cause trauma out of the hands of others and into his own, he tries to guarantee that nothing serious will happen. Belle said that by not portraying good things in the daydream —no good men and no loving sexuality—by having the manifest story line concentrate on power struggles and humiliation, "I could represent that I was to be alone for life, and by making the fantasy so bad, I was just practicing making things worse than they ever really would be. Then when they were bad in real life, they would never be as bad as what happened in the fantasy. So I would never be disappointed. I was in good shape for that: I knew since I was tiny that I could get by on very little. You can survive anything if you practice mentally over and over." For instance, when forced to eat food she did not like, she would work that food into a daydream and sufficiently transform the actual situation that she could eat and perhaps even enjoy it. The price—the one she so often willingly paid—was that she kept manufacturing situations that were staged until she had it so constructed that all reality was staged.

*Let us put aside herein the physical pleasure that can be found in pain. We must know much more before being sure that the ubiquitous erotism of pain—so many people like to be pinched, squeezed, bitten, swatted; or they dreamily inflict precise little pains on favorite parts of their bodies—is a biologic drive underpinning the nonphysical masochism with which we are now concerned.

†Retain the phrasing but change the inflection depending on your communistic or fascistic tendencies. (Both viewpoints merge when the protagonists turn to weapons.)

It did not always work: with the enemas, brute physical sensations scattered the protecting daydreams.

There is another grand explanation, no longer popular, that equates activity with sadism and passivity with masochism. In fact, both sadism and masochism are active processes. First, both are active in that they require planning and thinking. Second, one behaves in as complicated and physical a way to let oneself be struck as to strike: it takes as much doing to lay oneself on the tracks as to drive the oncoming train. And the manly exercises of boxing or satyriasis have no significance unless one thinks of the risks involved. One gores or is gored. In both bullfighting and ballet, style is a nice cover for masochism.

If we focus on childhood and the interplay between parent and child, as in weaning or toilet training, we recall how babies learn to bear frustration, to value waiting, and to convert pain to the pleasures of mastery. Fortunately, analysts now speak more in terms of the interplay and less in terms of instinctual vicissitudes.

Reik has discussed much of this in *Masochism in Modern Man*. His ideas were formulated almost forty years ago (and at a time when analysis was not as kind to disagreement as it is now); they are, on the whole, as applicable to masochism as any published since. Although he did not generalize his ideas to perversions at large or to sexual excitement, he stated that masochism is better studied as the play of fantasies than as the manifestation of a primary biologic force; that the masochist —sexual or social (as Reik called it)—secretly invents himself as victor (sadist), disguising tormenting, incessant little sadisms behind the unending suffering; that the masochist seeks revenge in his masochistic behavior; that the masochist does not primarily enjoy pain but accepts it as a preliminary to now earned pleasure; that the masochist is forever playing to an audience that condemns his alleged persecutors; that masochism may hide mockery; that the masochist sets up only the appearance of being passive and victimized; and that good analytic work reveals the exact details of the fantasies, going further to explain the behavior than instinct explanations.

He felt (as I do now, years later) that fantasy was the crucial element in the development of erotic and social ("moral") masochism.

It still stands that the preliminary phantasy has a special importance for masochism. The phantasy is also the primary factor in a historic sense. Masochistic practices are but an acting out of preceding phantasies, daydreams that are transferred into reality. Every thorough analysis shows that the masochistic perversion is a reproduction of previously imagined situations long familiar to the individual. In the beginning there is no action, as far as masochism is concerned, but the phantasy.

The actual scene corresponds thus to the staging of a drama and is related to the phantasies as is the performance to the dramatist's conception. They are exposed to the same accidents, incidents, and necessary adaptations to the means at hand, and are just as dependent on the mood and the co-operation of the actors. Only rarely does the performance surpass the ideas of the author. More often, even as with the masochistic scene, it falls short of the conception. There are cases when the person in the actual scene is unsatisfied or only faintly excited while the recollection leads to an orgasm. The rules, given in such a scene, are comparable to directions to the stage manager.

. . . It is perhaps wrong to emphasize the theatrical aspect in masochism. The analysis of the traits in the ritual of perverted scenes proves that there is a full meaning in every one of them. I am using the expression "ritual" purposely, since the peculiarly rigid rule and order which govern the masochistic scene are to be compared with the conscientiousness in the performance of religious and magical rituals. A change or a disturbance of this masochistic ritual diminishes its lust-value. It can even destroy it. A kind of tradition will develop, which has to be kept as in ceremonies of the church. First this has to be done, then that; words have to be pronounced in a certain manner, and so on. All these traits may seem to be haphazard and unpremeditated, but the psychologist who studies the history of the ritual, recognizes that there are meaning and connection. In no other perversion does ritual play a role similar in importance.[13]

I can only repeat, as still true decades later, Reik's remark:

I only wish to stress here that the importance of the phantasy as the very essence of masochism has not yet been appreciated in analytical theories, that its indispensability has not yet been recognized. . . .[14]

Reik knows people like Belle:

The masochist runs his own show . . . [Masochism is] a staged repetition. . . . The masochistic action has the purpose of enacting a phantasy of revenge by repeating a situation that justifies the feeling of revenge and defiance. . . . The suffering . . . becomes the sign and expression of one's own values. Whoever has to bear so much misfortune and hardship has a right to be proud of it. He is marked by destiny, but he is also chosen by destiny. Simultaneously he is one of fate's elect, one whose peculiarity and peculiar lot raise him above the mass. One who has to suffer so much, who is exposed to so many wrongs, is permitted to look down upon others, is not bound by the laws and rules that bind others. . . . [The masochist] represents the supremacy of will power apparently giving in to the will of all others. In renouncing his own will he shows insubordination. He marks time until the forces of aggression and destruction have worn themselves out against the might of his inertia. He can take a beating now, if he hopes that later on his aggressor will be destroyed. The unconscious revenge fantasy is a permanent companion of his surrender. Submerged, he rises again and again. . . . The masochist does not accept punishment and humiliation, he anticipates them. He not only demonstrates their impotence to withhold the forbidden pleasure, but he affirms and demonstrates that it was they which helped him to it.[15]

Reik, I think correctly, disagrees with Freud and other analysts who believe that the main mechanism in producing masochism (lying, as it were, on top of the biologic anlagen Freud postulates in his discussions of primary masochism and death instinct) is the need for punishment. He does not, however, tell us what provokes the excitement, what impels one forward; rather, he tells us how masochism is used to protect the excitement, to allow it to pass through dangerous straits, finally to burst forth safely into orgasm.

Let me end these thoughts on sadomasochism with the old question. Does hostility exist as an independent force ("drive," "instinct") or is it due to our being victimized—a result of suffering, pain, and frustration? The issue is blurred, I think, when the word "aggression" becomes synonymous with "hostility."[16] Hostility, along with rage, hatred, malice, revenge, and harm, connotes nothing less than the desire to hurt an object. It is, then, motivated, planned, desired, and willed and exists as fantasy, in the form of scripts. (The fancy speculation on aggression using animal behavior is meaningless unless it can be shown that animals are not just aggressive but also act from hatred when they attack or kill.)

The word "aggression" sometimes has the connotation of hostility. But the dictionary shows it can also be used for activity that does not have within it malevolent intent: "healthy self-assertiveness or a drive to accomplishment or to mastery esp. of skills . . . marked by driving forceful energy."[17] This aspect of the word is present in such words as readiness, boldness, determination, enterprising, energetic, self-confident, vigorous, active, variable, adaptable, forcefulness, confidence, resolute, and intrusive. None of these implies desire to harm an object. But if "aggression" contains too many implications of hostility, then another word—perhaps "assertiveness"—might do for those realms of activity and forcefulness not motivated by anger and hatred.

It does not seem, then, that we must accept as logical the announcement that a destructive instinct, a biologically determined force, is present in all living creatures, inevitably impelling them to destroy. Till better data appear, I join those who think that rage, hatred, and desire for destruction are learned and defensive behaviors. These impulses may draw their strength from biologic forces that energize activity, but the desire to harm is, I think, an added feature. The fact that it is universal in our species does not make it instinctual.

8

Exhibitionism

BELLE WAS DOMINATED by her exhibitionism. Because she had been unable since earliest childhood to put aside her sense of being observed, she rarely felt herself to be genuine. Except when she was alone (and not always then), her head was filled with fantasies that men were watching her. This was happening, she imagined, for both happy and malign reasons: either she was admired and therefore was dominating her audience with her loveliness and sexual attractiveness, or the observers were judging her appearance in ways that would humiliate her.

Simultaneously feeling these opposing themes produced her excitement. No wonder she had for so long believed herself oversexed. She was, in fact, chronically excited, spending all day performing in her sadomasochistic, exhibitionistic role.

Beneath that was her fear no one would look. If they did not, it would mean that they were not interested, that they did not care, and that she would once again have to confront her expectation of being abandoned. And abandonment was certainly not exciting, not erotic. This fear of being unnoticed, therefore, drove her to call attention to herself at any price; if the sex show failed, she fell back, as we know, on making a pest of herself. But so much performing was tiring. False behavior demands its price: chronic guilt, loneliness, loss of hope, a sense of being unreal. To make matters worse, knowing and at the same time having to disavow knowing her falseness, she constantly exaggerated—dramatized—to rectify the feeling that no one (especially herself) believed her.

So she usually felt awkward, almost foolish up there on stage in the real world. Only in her daydreams, with the unattended knowledge that she controlled the script, could she comfortably enjoy herself. Only then could she play the dangers in advance and live them in her mind where they need never be experienced in reality. In other words, simulated risk, an essential element in Belle's exhibitionism, was a part of her excitement. We have seen the risk mechanism at work in the ways that the Director and the watching men were portrayed: she was in continuous danger of humiliation because they were so cruelly male. This fantasy spilled over into the innumerable public acts that made up an ordinary day. She was fully or subliminally concerned that each garment be chosen to show to advantage her hair, face, figure, movements. Too often she was sure that, all external evidence to the contrary, some detail was awry. Then not only would her physical appearance disgust men who saw her, but they would catch her out in the even greater humiliation of having tried to look perfect and having failed.

Yet for all this, Belle never looked bizarre, as exhibitionists can. Rather, she seemed casually stylish, feminine, lively, and comfortable in her body—until she lay on the couch. Then, during storms of exhibitionism, the flailing, histrionic, wriggling, miserable performance was enacted.

She was in analysis over a year before I got the first blast; it was many months more before she exposed me to the full dimensions of this behavior. Then not until the last year or so of treatment did it die away (except for a few episodes lasting only moments, in response to treatment ending).

A complete run-through went like this: instead of lying down, she sat on the couch. But before that, she signaled what was coming by wearing a soft, silky, light, delicate skirt that flowed at her slightest movement. In time she might sit or lie down. In either case, I would gradually become aware that first her knees and then an inch or more of thigh were twinkling at me while at the same time she chattered away. The subject could be anything, potentially important or inconsequential; it made no difference. Sooner or later (sooner as I got wiser), I would recall that the previous hour had been filled with masochism, for instance, with her insisting I could no longer stand her. At first in a frenzy with these fantasies, she would return the next hour calm, quiet, talking briskly and lightheartedly as her skirt slowly and casually floated up her thighs.

Perhaps the piece of insight work that most contributed to her dropping this display of her bottom was the analysis of her anality, her bringing to consciousness the scripts—masochistic or exhibitionistic—related to her buttocks, anus, and rectum. No one thing made this behavior disappear. It went, as did so much else, when, toward the end of treatment, she began to own herself. At the same time came more trust, allowing her to give up her secrets, of which the skirt trick was one. Once we were both in on this, it became silly to her, and then she admitted to herself that she knew I had never been excited by her bottom.[1] I think we finally got the enema apparatus out of her insides, the prying eyes off her bottom, and the others' intrusiveness out of her mind. At least she stopped substituting me—and, I think, anyone else —for her mother's and the Caretaker's assigned parts in the drama.

Many of us in infancy are the objects of our parents' proud and narcissistic pleasure. We find ourselves on display, clothed and nude, admired for nothing more than that we exist in an anatomic form that thrills one or both of them; heady stuff, but not enough on which to build a personality. But for children who grow up to be the grand exhibitors, that may be the best they have. To some degree that was true for Belle. Her mother, histrionically preoccupied with her own physical beauty, saw her child—if I have read it right—as mostly an extension of Mother's body, a female deserving attention and credit for having come out anatomically the same as Mother. If a mother is so extremely and bizarrely involved in femininity and if she encourages it in her daughter, then the daughter will develop the appearances our culture defines as femininity. This I consider an aspect of primary femininity, and emphasize that this aspect is more the result of positive reinforcement of behavior than of the more complex, psychodynamic mental activities that we summarize in the term "identification." (That mothers may encourage some behaviors they consider feminine and discourage others, or encourage their daughters to appear feminine but at the same time put them down for being potential rivals, are examples of the many complexities in this process.)

Belle's first memories are a mixture of sadomasochistic and exhibitionistic elements: being set out nude in the sun and feeling embarrassed; smearing the walls with food and being humiliated for it.* (Although these first memories are painful, her mother told her she was a happy baby. But Mother always took away while she gave: to the statement that Belle was happy was appended the story that the baby was intermittently marred by her skin turning a sickly, unpleasant color.)

The theme of being lovely yet simultaneously disgusting was constantly present in her relationship with me, reflected in an endless number of memories "proving" that this representation of herself was true. (We shall look at the gratifying side of this in the next chapter when we take up her "lovely.") And so, as one of her analytic rights, she went on and on about her disgustingness: she was sweating on the

---

*Only late in treatment did another style of early memories appear, and these never came through with crystal clarity; they were memories of happy, quiet, nontraumatic experiences with her father, such as remembering his legs and feet and feeling close and content with him during walks in the woods. (He never appeared whole in these memories.)

couch; she was not in a ladylike position; her hair was ugly; a wrinkle was starting on her face; she knew she smelled even if she could not smell it herself; her outfit today was a mess, her sexual feelings were dirty and unbearable to me; her associations were not neat, clever, and organized as are a good patient's. I always felt—and she finally found this herself toward the end of treatment—that she knew these complaints were absurd, because they were exaggerated and because she had reason to believe (though not admit) that I was not disgusted. Still, by being silly she could believe she was, right then, disgusting me.

Thus two contradictory fantasy systems were at work. In one, derived from being Mother's doll, she was lovely. In the other, the result of her mother's and father's lack of attachment, she was unacceptable, and this was brutally confirmed by the enemas. This business was then played out on a stage in which she assigned people in the real world the roles she could prove they always filled, since she interpreted whatever they did as "really" meaning whatever she needed the meaning to be.

Belle occasionally came to my office without underpants, though she kept it a secret for a couple of years. She first told me of this trick of not wearing underpants after an hour in which she had reported a dream, in one part of which "I was driving down a very busy street; the car stalled in the left lane, and I had nothing on. Then I had to get out. I found a towel." Then part of another dream: "I was high up at a high point. I was inside a stone building and down below were a lot of people. There were a lot of bushes. There was a lip on the hill of earth where they were standing." Then part of another dream: "I was with a little girl. She was nude. She had a beautiful body. I felt very proud." During much of this hour, she was busy pulling her skirt down over her knee, which kept finding itself uncovered (owing, I could see, to her movements and the dress material). She seemed oblivious, but this activity, the dream material, and talk in recent hours of exposing herself (by which she had consciously only meant revealing her thoughts) let me finally say that there seemed to be something going on in her "about showing your body, about exhibiting yourself; but let me word it even more clearly, because perhaps there is even a sexual quality to it—about being bare-ass naked."

Next hour. She says that my having changed the term from the neutral "exhibiting" to the loaded "bare-ass" upset her, for, at that moment, she had in fact been bare-assed: no underpants. She says it was not just naughty to do this but dangerous and that she now feels terrible (mostly frightened) at the risk she skirted. Even worse, yesterday was a windy day. Suddenly, memories of sitting in a highchair without diapers; childhood dreams of being eaten by a goat. From then on, this aspect of the exhibitionism was in the analysis.

Months later, during another skirt-waving attack, she recalls lying in bed every night in puberty believing someone was peeking. She could hear rustling in the bushes. Despite this nightly problem, she never pulled down the shades or turned off the lights.

Shame. As a teen-ager, she had one of her most exciting sexual experiences; while going steady with one boy, she went off one evening, without apparent reason, with another. She did this in such a way that everyone in her crowd knew of it: her boyfriend, all the other boys, her girlfriends. The excitement was extreme; so was the shame. They made up a circuit: shame led to sexual excitement; sexual excitement was shameful; the shame then produced led to more sexual excitement; that proved she was oversexed, which was even more shameful; that led to more excitement.

Shame comes from being watched. (That is certainly rampant in the Director fantasy.) The first time her breasts were touched she was at a movie with a boyfriend. It was terribly erotic. I heard that story several times and thought nothing further of it. Then one day, she added another detail that explained why this had been stunningly exciting: in the row behind was a little old disreputable man who watched and kept giggling. The dirty-old-man had been a standard fixture in her sexual fantasies since puberty; he participated in the Director fantasy either as the ring of watching men, who might be portrayed as dirty-old-men, or at times as the tramp who stimulated her in place of the stallion.

As another example to show how exhibitionism invaded Belle's life, let us take one of the problems that brought her to analysis. Although she could quickly and effortlessly have orgasms with masturbation, she did not have them in intercourse as the result of intercourse, only as the result of fantasy and by using the man's soft penis—after he had come—on which to masturbate. Yet foreplay always excited her, as did the early stages of intercourse. She was therefore mystified that she could be so excited, so ever-ready for sex, so filled with erotic fantasies, and yet be unable to have an orgasm while doing what she most wanted sexually: having intercourse with a man whose erect penis and excited presence penetrated her. Early in the analysis, she knew nothing of fantasies, psychodynamics, conflict, or other such analytic talk. She told herself she just had something wrong, such as an anatomic or physiologic defect, since she always found that her excitement turned off after reaching a peak a few minutes after intercourse began. The flaw, she thought, was in her body (also in the impotent penis), not in her mind.

The first stage in detecting the meaning of her "frigidity" was a clear description of her sexual behavior. Since Belle was so vulnerable to humiliation, that task took many hours. She would tell a detail, become vague, drop it, pick it up a few hours later, circle it again, and so on. After months, I learned that she did get excited, where the excitement occurred anatomically, what consciously excited her, when the excitement cut off, what loss of excitement felt like as the shift occurred, and what she did to salvage any pleasure from the mess. During this time she was becoming an analytic patient, which in part means she was starting to be interested in observing herself. (This process is tricky with someone like Belle who, being exhibitionistic, is already so loaded with self-observation; the art in treatment is to mobilize another, previously unknown, observing part of herself, one that is "connected" to her real self rather than one that serves her exhibitionism.)

It helped us to find that, during intercourse, she was excited and getting more so until she *noticed* that she was excited. This meant that another "part" of her mind—another fantasy system, another script— had been plugged in, as if she were of two minds, each with different, contradictory motives, that took turns being conscious. At that instant, excitement stopped.

In time, we learned about her different fantasy systems; they were represented in one element or another of the Director daydream. The one we are looking at now goes like this: on noting herself being excited, she switches to a new mode—the exhibitionistic—a familiar state wherein she imagines herself seen by a watching audience. That lets loose a shower of micro-fantasies (that is, they are not spun out one by one, with the characters filled in and acting their parts, but rather, sparkle together like fireworks). Imagined audiences: hellfire preachers, Peeping Toms in the bushes, the boys of her adolescence, the Caretaker, the dirty-old-man who watched her pet in the movies, the men in the Director fantasy, the Director, the people who saw her bare bottom when she was put out to sun as a small child, anyone, all of us: all now watching to see her excitement mount. If, there in bed with that real man, she goes out of control, she will lose her self-respect. So she takes over control; she becomes the writer-director of all her scenes—the master.

So long as she loses her excitement. And she can manage that because she tries hard enough, started early enough, is inventive enough, and has the proper intent. But she has to not know she is doing this if it is to work. Otherwise, she would have to admit she could lose control, is vulnerable, needs to use magic. Her triumph—turning off—is bought at the price of her losing sensual pleasure. She has taken back the control from the parts of herself that had their own motives (minds of their own). No wonder she resisted insight.

When she saw all that, she was freed up and could add details. She now (during the analytic hour) recalled that at the moment she notices she is observing herself, she also notices she is not in a state of feminine loveliness. Her hair is untidy, she may be sweating, her face will not be set in tranquil prettiness. The whole thing is so unladylike. She will not humiliate herself further in front of the audience. So she rearranges herself, starts playing to the audience, and substitutes simulated excitement. The danger is over.

Whatever the cost, and it was high, staying in control—anticipating trauma—meant she could never again be abandoned, never be shocked by being caught unawares. Someone was now built in who took care of her, always there, observing silently, dependably.

Something is unfinished in this explanation. How does sensing the audience inhibit her excitement when in her daydreams humiliation is vital? To the imagined audience—her own creature and therefore no true risk—we must add the man in bed with her. It is his real presence and her knowledge that she cannot control him (her unrestraint could disgust him) that turns her off. So she waits until he has been disarmed—is finished and inattentive—to have her unsatisfying orgasm. (Most people do not get excited doing with real people the cruelties they most want but only imagine. That may be a difference between those who are perverse and those who are not: the perverse, when really doing what they think about, can still remain excited.)

If this idea is correct—that unplanned loss of control is traumatically humiliating, not just a contrived and therefore riskless simulation—it explains the following. One day during an analytic hour Belle was immersed in an exhibitionism scene, sitting on the couch, nattering, while her skirt flowed up her thighs. As always (until it ended late in analysis) she was burying me in noise so as to not feel her own excitement. Suddenly she noticed a hole, exposed as the skirt rose, in her stocking. The excitement stopped; she was seized by humiliation. I believe the sequence of feelings occurred in the following way. Because she secretly trusted me not to be excited by her behavior, she could indulge it as safely as in a daydream: the skirt hikes up, and she pretends she is an innocent girl unwittingly the object of a voyeur's (sadist's) attention. That part was planned, the pieces in place and she in control. It was more exciting than just daydreaming, for it was staged in the real world. She could be assured, however, that the risks were small, that I would not stop being her analyst by becoming excited. But the hole in the stocking had not been planned. It was an unexpected, uncontrolled, sudden danger. With the hole, she was no longer a lovely lady.* (Instead she became anxious, which motivated her to more analytic work.)

Another set of Belle's erotic scripts that are dependent on exhibitionistic impulses (though they draw, as always, on other modes as well) are her mirror scenes. These began with breast development.

As one of many manifestations of a pubertal upsurge of sexual excitability, such as increase in masturbation, fear of Peeping Toms, interest in dating boys, and the congealing of the idea that she was the inevitable victim of brute male masculinity, she turned on to women's breasts. She hinted at this early in treatment, heralding it with vague remarks that she feared, without knowing why, being homosexual. Months later, feeling safer one hour, she said that the previous evening she had been looking at a boyfriend's girlie magazine and had "admired" the girls' figures. Squirming, she amplified that to being "interested," and then elaborated that into erotic interest. This was not just competition with her own figure, though that was important, but an erotic desire to look at those breasts. When, as if to test the water, she mentioned it again, she began to reveal the mirror procedure. Since adolescence, when alone, she would undress and look at her growing breasts. This excited her, but she did not know why. (Nor, at first, did I; without knowing her fantasies, we can either suffer in ignorance or "explain" with words like "narcissism" or "latent homosexuality.")

First step: get a precise description. An episode started when she saw her breasts *in the mirror;* looking directly on her breasts never was exciting. Then a lot of analytic work made conscious the fact that the mirror allowed her to imagine she was looking at another woman, who was nonetheless also herself.†

Much later we learned that the person looking in the mirror, although literally herself, was also, in a different but simultaneous fantasy, an unknown man who, seeing the breasts, became excited. And even later, on attending closely, she found the man to be one of the dirty-old-men types, which led of course to her father. With these scripts finally conscious, her erotic fantasies shifted; no longer could she

---

*I do not interpret her response to the stocking hole as castration anxiety, penis envy, introjected bad objects, attacks by or on or with a bad breast, etc. Rather, I let the hole represent trauma, humiliation, threats to feminine identity, potential disturbances in interpersonal relationships, transference reactions, etc.

†She commonly transmuted herself in her dreams. For instance, she might dream of someone whose physical features were completely different from hers but who was labeled as herself. Or, she would be observing herself, a visual image in which she actually looked like herself but was divided in the sense that she, the dreamer, was observing herself doing whatever she was doing —a common but far from universal kind of splitting in dreams.

be excited by sadomasochistic, exhibitionistic humiliation displays. Instead, as we have seen, she began variations on the theme of an innocent young woman being taught to find and appreciate her sexual excitement by an older, loving, nonperverse, potent, masculine man who was sometimes represented openly as being the young woman's father (though not literally Belle's father), sometimes as some other fatherly type.

This fantasy was powerfully supported by an actual event that had happened to her at puberty. Her music teacher, a man in his thirties, had in his music room a copy of a painting of Rubens-like nude women. On surprising Belle one day staring at the painting, he said, "You'll soon look like these women, and you'll grow up to have large breasts like your mother. I bet you can't wait." That would have been provocative enough. But then he sat down and told her to sit next to him. When she, puzzled, did so, he put her hand on his genitals so that she experienced for the first time a man's erection. She was terrified, jumped up, and abruptly left, ending all contact with him but telling no one her reason. Only gradually, as years passed, did she untangle the thread of sexual excitement from the snarl of feelings consciously sensed, in the actual moment with him, as fear. Once removed from the danger, she could play with it and allow it to energize her excitement. So this man, who had been *in loco parentis* but existed more safely now as a memory, contributed to the ambivalent quality of the Director as a nasty-kindly mentor.

For two years after this episode, she turned in on herself, rarely went out except to school or on errands, and confined herself to reading more and more. She filled herself with romantic novels, using these stories to invent her own daydreams of amorous adventure.

The erotic storm that grew in her at puberty was focused with unbearable intensity by this moment of seduction, kept hot by the biologic surges of early adolescence, and unassuaged because she thought masturbation would ruin her for motherhood. So, unable—in the rare times she did masturbate—to permit orgasm, and living in the presence of her stiff, desirable stepfather and sex-dazed mother, Belle had quite a problem. Had she been adolescent in a culture where all her peers, boys and girls, could freely enjoy each other sexually, she might have been coaxed out of her isolated daydream. Or had she been less masochistic, less able to sit alone and make pleasure from her suffering, she might still have managed an adolescent erotic life gratifying enough to lower the heat. But she was the wrong person in the wrong place at the wrong time. And when she finally began circulating again with her friends, she brought to her social relationships such jangled nervousness that she managed to keep herself from almost everything she wanted in regard to sex and love. Instead, she had to settle mostly for the Director daydream—"baroque," as she puts it.

In talking of those days, she underlines how awkwardly she dealt with a typical problem of adolescent girls: how shall I manage the challenge that they treat me as a sex target? She said, "I know that both boys and girls go through intense experiences because of their genital growth and the secondary sex characteristics. But the girls have a special burden; they have to become aware of—create themselves as—sex objects, and if you were going to be popular and wanted, you had to feel this was natural and enjoy it. The point is that the girl *believes* boys are noticing her development. She may be pleased or afraid or excited or all, but—at least where I came from—you did not imagine questions about it." At this point, she thought of the myriad experiences many girls recall, of being rubbed, jostled, and squeezed by strange men, of penises flashed in buses and on beaches, of grossly provocative sexual remarks, of stares. She sees these now not only as rude attacks against which a girl is given no adequate defenses but also as a covert but accepted part of society's dynamics—accepted by both sexes, each with its own style of acceptance—for educating boys and girls, teaching them how to play their assigned erotic roles.

You wait endlessly and finally angrily. You are being observed in a special way: your breasts, your legs. You have to get used to the separate parts being there, treated as if they are different from you. And you have to come to feel that that is correct, not crazy. Your body is changing, but no one lets you get away with just that. They keep watching the changing, not just the body. Your changing is being watched by males with kind of a proprietary, anticipatory . . . I mean, the kid *senses,* is told by the social setup, that her body will be at someone else's disposal one day. And if you don't get the experience of *acknowledged* shared physical intimacy with a loved man—your father, for instance—where tenderness is a transaction and a very two-way event, then you're *really alone.*

So I felt my excitement wasn't appropriate. I thought it was a male prerogative: women who felt it were inferior, women who exploited men's sexual excitement were superior. But still, I kept being excited; so the fantasy served as a masochistic punishment for having stolen what I thought was rightfully only for males: sexual excitement. Is that the kind of end products our culture wants for its social education of the sexes? Anyway, I think of Susanna and the Elders and I can't get too twentieth-century about it. It's a pretty old phenomenon. Maybe we're wired to feel excited to show ourselves, to passively wait for an approach. Maybe we're hormonally organized like animals. But that doesn't reduce the impact of what the men do to us.

In her teens, we recall, in order further to heighten the play-acting–reality blurring, after undressing she draped herself in filmy shawls and photographed herself. When her breasts had fully developed, she turned herself on by pushing them up with her hands so they would look even bigger. This was set off when, by chance before a mirror, either the light, the angle, or her posture made her seem to have especially large breasts; that quick vision was enough to ignite the excitement.* (Once again, her experience, before it was analyzed, seemed automatic: "I just looked in the mirror and got excited; I don't know why.")

She reveals that a year or so later in adolescence she would find a secret place, a room where she could lock the door and dress as femininely as she could imagine, in frilly clothes, fancy underwear, makeup, and jewelry, moving about "as if I were on exhibit as a sexual thing." The excitement, set off by putting herself on display, was enhanced by the tactile experience of silk brushing her breasts. Her mother was in her.

Some years into the analysis, we were working on the resistance we now called "chattering." I had gradually become aware—one sometimes is exposed to a resistance many times before sensing its form—that Belle had episodes of fast, vigorous, yet empty talk; I had been alert and listening one moment and in the next feeling anesthetized. I never fall asleep with patients, catching signals like this quickly enough, but if ever a patient could have knocked me out, it was she.[2] (The desire to fall unconscious—"fall asleep" is too gentle—always disappeared as soon as I became aware of the state, replaced by curiosity at what she was communicating.) I began to underline this symptom by asking what she was feeling or what she thought I was feeling, sometimes other questions—whatever seemed appropriate.

Now she might catch it herself, ending a long, empty spatter of words with "I must be boring you," or "What am I talking about?"; and if I called it chattering, she was not insulted. Then one day she focused on a story mentioned vaguely for years. After she and her mother were reunited, after the years of intermittent abandonment, she would sit in the afternoon with her preoccupied mother, who lolled abed, posed as if on stage. Mother would talk and talk, in a fascinating way, about the

---

*Despite all the excitement generated, there were long stretches when she did not masturbate but only daydreamed. For all these years of excitement in adolescence, she never had an orgasm. Her first occurred—spontaneously, suddenly, unexpectedly, and without accompanying daydream—with the first man with whom she had intercourse. Then there were no more orgasms of that sort for years, until her sexuality shifted during analysis. Instead, now frigid with men, she fell back on her daydreaming skills, turned to the Director, his stallion, and his ring of men, and had her instantaneous masturbatory orgasms after the man was finished.

sexual and social lives of everyone she knew. Belle loved this, because it was her only lively contact with her mother and because the stories were filled with marvelous erotic romance, like the child's favorite novels but more compelling since her mother offered them as documentaries rather than fiction. The child knew she was allowed to be with her mother only as an audience, not as a person in her own right. If she had not been just admiring—enthralled—she would not have served Mother's narcissism and would have had to leave, to suffer the ultimate trauma, abandonment. So she sat and listened. And the knowledge that most of these tales were fabrications and distortions had to be driven out of awareness: not a single question or quizzical look to arouse Mother's suspicion. Belle must never know her own mind about Mother's tricks. (Learning this helped us understand better why for years she did not dare see me as a liar and then could know she thought it but was terrified to tell me, then could tell me in order to test whether I would throw her out, then could shower me with accusations, then —after years—could judge me realistically.)

During these visits to Mother's bed, Belle attended only to keeping Mother immobile. For those delicious hours, so long as she was wary, she could be with that voice and with the body that spilled out on the bed.

So Mother talked, announcing her femininity, beauty, and desirability to men. (She did not expect to have anything else, being notorious to the rest of the family as an incompetent, immature glob of femininity.) Belle's part was to be a dazzled audience, to confirm the glories of that wanton flesh, to hear of the men unstrung by it.

Mother would finally lose interest. That was the point at which Belle would begin chattering: "It was in order to remain longer *after* she had finished, to remain in contact, a last-ditch stand to make contact with someone who would not. It was an effort to remain in the room when she was *through* with me."

So now Belle talked, and though Mother rarely spoke back, the girl was allowed to remain, talking away about anything. The trick, she found, was that, although she could not have full contact with her mother, she could remain in the room if she kept talking. She might be a pest, but if she stuck to Mother's limits—incessant talk with nothing said and nothing demanded—she could stay longer with this beautiful, feminine, voluptuous, overindulged, humanized bosom.

And the child, alerted years before—she had spent her infancy with that same body and by age six was ready to be turned on by her classmate's bottom—was now susceptible to looking at Mother as the men did. Theirs was an experience for Belle to covet and therefore with which to identify, for they were allowed to possess Mother. No wonder, when Belle saw her own enlarged breasts in the mirror, she did not simply see them as her own, which would have been unerotic, but rather —the mass of experiences, memories, and fantasies activated—instantly moved into the role of, the experience of, became identified with (what are the right words?), the men Mother had said were the lucky beneficiaries of her bounteousness.[3]

But that is not exactly how she consciously experienced it. She never felt she was the man but rather the woman with the grand breasts, who was the object of the man's passion. The girl, hungry since infancy for her mother—this teasing, desirable, uncertainly available carnal delight —re-experienced her lifelong traumas, frustrations, hopes, abandonments, gratifications, fears, and disappointments; and that became the terribly complicated affect we call desire, when hope, the end of passive and defenseless victimhood, control over others, success, mastery, and triumph were added. Now that *she* controlled the action in sexual excitement, pleasure would be the outcome. Her whole life was summarized in that mirrored bustiness. (As Freud suggested, the ultimate person to be seduced in a woman's exhibitionism is her mother. In a fantasied reversal of roles, one's feminine body is to seduce mother as mother's seduced the infant–little girl.)

It is often noted that women with "hysterical personality"[4] are an exaggerated version of our culture's definition of femininity (and that this will change when women become free). A quality that is often part of this personality type is pseudo-stupidity,[5] which takes two forms (occasionally merged): wide-eyed, cute innocence (the sweet young thing) or flat-out stupidity (the dumb blonde). Both are massive defenses with which a woman smothers her awareness of the world, her impulses, and her insights. The results of this inhibition may devastate her: "I never have trouble acting screwed up; what I can't be is to be myself," said Belle. But if she exudes erotism, a special exhibitionistic quality is created that, if she is young, inflames men. (The same act, persisting into the middle years, makes aging a horror for these women.) The game is worth the price when it attracts men, for then it promises—for the moment—to bring her the loving closeness she needs. (However, analysts have long known that the object desired is not men but mother; this sex-goddess state, despite spectacular appearances to the contrary, is barely heterosexual, barely erotic.)

Belle, being smart, did well with her pseudo-stupid role. We have already seen examples, such as her saying to an analyst, "I won't tell you this dream because you're not interested in my dreams." This went on for years, many times an hour. Having a mother who is pseudo-stupid helps a girl become that way herself, but I think the technique is easy enough to invent even without a model close at hand, especially if the behavior is either reinforced by punishment or encouraged with a few amenities such as were granted a woman in the days of Victorian femininity. If it was established that she was stupid, she could suffer the humiliation (which itself had its values) compensated by the belief that her stupidity stirred others to protect her.

It was understood in the family that Belle's mother could not be competent, but, the insult secured, her mother then (in Belle's opinion) was allowed to be forever gratified. The child, however, was not assigned the role of Mother's little pudding. Although she was told (and was expected to conform to the tale) that she was like her mother, it was also decided from infancy that she was not to be as pretty. So she was taught (and it became an identity theme) that she would never be as appealing to men as her mother and would never attract the best men or marry well. She always knew no catastrophes would come to her as long as she accepted the assigned role. Cleverly, she learned stupidity.

As automatized as such maneuvers become, it still takes vigilance, even if unconscious, to remain stupid if one is not naturally that way. It was our task to reveal the mechanism.[6] After years of analysis, Belle became conscious that she was playing at being stupid, was constructing her stupidity just stupidly enough that I would recognize that it was not well made. But I had to pass two tests: first, I must not be destroyed by her trephining, and second, I had to discover the mechanism.*

She did not reveal much about her father's contribution to her exhibitionism. She recalls that when she was four or five, her father enjoyed noting how she was dressed, even to the details of the print of the cloth or the manner in which the dresses were sewn; in doing this, he emphasized how feminine she looked. In addition, he gave her strong confirmation by photographing her in her dresses; she has seen these pictures in the family album. They reinforce the impression of a loving and erotic bond between them, its very intensity at that age making her even more susceptible to his leaving the family in the next year or so. Her memories of this period are not only of his admiring her clothes but also of times when they were alone together, as when going on walks.

Taking a person apart in an analysis gives a distorted picture that is even more pronounced if one fragments the results in a written report. I can never make Belle seem whole, but I can at least stress—once more

---

*Hidden in such maneuvers is unconscious revenge, for in testing us all while inflicting her trick, she could find us stupid either if we responded with irritation or if we failed to recognize the trick. One of the pleasures, then, that energizes such behavior is secret (unconscious?) sarcasm.

—that in spite of the material reported here she was not weird, not strange, not eccentric. But one aspect of her was so loony that it struck me as little short of delusional; and coming out of a person who was otherwise natural-appearing and feminine, it was even more startling. This was the big show: sitting up on the couch, she would pose herself in pin-up-girl fashion, leaning against the adjoining bookcase with back arched, legs drawn up in knee-chest position, skirt fallen so that her thighs and part of her buttocks showed (but with the genital area always "casually" covered by clothing and posture). At the times when she let on she was aware of what she was doing, she was not embarrassed or humiliated but said that she knew if she carried the act any further, I would not be able to stand it but would fling off my rigid control and leap at her.

In judging her odd for momentarily believing her legs would stun me, I am not forgetting that this reciprocity between the voyeuristic men and the women who offer anatomic segments for fetishistic distortion is "normal" in our society. It is expected, pleasurable for both parties, usual; it is the subpornography that lightens our everyday lives—so long as we are not conscious of the hidden ancient angers that excite both participants.

The oddness was in her *doing* it in front of me. The ambience of the analytic situation does not encourage most people to do more than fantasize or at most surreptitiously and momentarily emphasize a bit of anatomy. Of course, it was not strange that she should have had these impulses. What was puzzling was the intensity, the exaggerated posing, and—most unexpected—her willingness to be seen behaving grotesquely, she who was so concerned about humiliation. She had not suddenly just become herself, lost her inhibitions, broken through; rather, her need to dramatize had shifted, and she was now simply crazy.

A manic fling, it passed as soon as she recognized the underlying affect—despair: something had made her feel I was going to abandon her. The fear was unspoken for many minutes, visible only in the behavior. Perhaps I had begun the hour with a schedule change. Without yet knowing why, she would start climbing up the couch and on into this exhibition, thus keeping hidden from herself that the fear—genuine enough—was the result of manufactured scripts ("he hates me"; "he's so good but he's reached the end of his patience").

Suppose a child's doll were actually alive. The doll would, at certain moments, get the most extreme and loving attention and then, without warning, would be tossed aside. Nothing the doll could do by its own efforts would attract the child who owned it, its "mother," who would only turn to it again when she wished and as part of a game that had no lasting significance. I can imagine the doll developing a crazy magnification of its own value mixed inextricably with the feeling of being only a fetish. Greenacre talks of "focal symbiosis," wherein a mother focuses on an aspect rather than the whole of her infant.[7] Belle, I believe, is the product of that dreadful, tantalizing process. Perhaps it accounts for her conviction at certain moments that her legs and bottom were quite irresistible. Despite her knowledge that, stripped of their fetishistic aura, legs are just legs and that there are millions of other pairs of comparable shape, she could still genuinely feel that she could blast me out of my senses with the view.

Once the script was openly stated, she calmed down enough to examine what had actually been arranged and then saw the possibility that I meant what I said rather than that I was secretly giving her the message that the treatment would end but did not have—as she would say—the guts to be honest about it.

The last of these episodes came in an hour when, for the first time, the idea popped out of her that her mother's behavior, even appearance, was often disreputable—a thought that had earlier been too awful to admit, for it would have signified what was then unbearable: a split in the symbiosis she held together in fantasy, no dependable linkage having been present between them in reality. Her next thought was of the dirty-old-man of her excitement. So now, on this last time she had to treat me to her show, it became clear that one of its main functions was to reverse roles: she was not the child victimized into unsatisfiable excitement by her mother's display of fancy underwear and concealed-unconcealed flesh. Instead, she, like her mother, was in charge of the performance; I was the assigned victim. Perhaps the performance became extreme—beyond the subtle exhibitions she usually staged—because she remembered (unconsciously) the intensity of her own excitement with her mother and because she was also her mother grotesquely using Belle. But if her mother could do this with enthusiasm and without reproach, Belle could also do it without guilt or feeling foolish. This last was the essence of what made the performance seem so strange to me and what made it so hard to reduce with analysis.

In the next hour, she realized for the first time what I had taken for granted since early in analysis and had pointed out and interpreted untold times since: one reason she wanted treatment was the tension that accompanied her constant sense of looking on at herself as if she were an audience judging her performance. She was forever looking at herself in mirrors and in shop windows; in college, mathematics was dull but anthropology interesting, because she could, as it were, see herself reflected in the latter; she could never have intense sexual excitement in intercourse because she was always watching herself.

Let me summarize what I know of her exhibitionism. Belle was the only child of a woman who felt herself to be a luscious bite, whose only purpose was to give men pleasure; if Mother did that, she would be taken care of and never have to function as an adult. On giving birth to a girl, brought from deep within her and mirroring her femaleness, this woman used the infant as a living doll, of her body but still a separate creature to be taken up or discarded at whim. This unfortunate mother-infant relationship was not interrupted by a strong and masculine father who might have pushed his wife to better contact with her infant or substituted himself in place of this haphazard connection.

The counterpoint to the glorious voluptuousness was Mother's ability to concentrate only briefly on Belle, as when telling the child of her sexual marvels. For the rest, she was not there; Belle's expectation of abandonment, its dreadful tracery laced through the analysis, was made even fiercer by the display of enticements, exhibitions always beyond her reach. When the girl wanted to snuggle with her mother or even reach out and touch her, this was not allowed. So she sat looking, separated, free to devour but only with her eyes.

It seems to me that this mother could use her daughter only to confirm her own marvelous femininity, which, complying with the identity themes placed in Mother by her own mother and aunts, was defined not only by female tissues and a feminine appearance but also by marriage and motherhood. But these were roles for Mother, applied like makeup rather than experienced as identity's flesh and bones. One genre of Mother's tales incessantly reported how Belle had grown within and come out of Mother's body, to be fed on Mother's milk. Rather than making her feel close to and loved by her mother, these stories disgusted the child, who felt she was commanded to be the emissary of Mother's flesh to the outside world, yet was denied the gratification of enough contact. Disgust: in swallowing Mother, Belle had also to accept Mother's right to abandon the baby at any moment. It is hard to be eternally, unalterably joined by one's insides—tissues-to-tissues joined—to a mother so succulent but so bad. Where is there escape—except by knowledge?

If skin-to-skin contact is disrupted, if trunk and face and arms feel deprived, an infant must turn to the less immediate techniques of using its eyes (its ears too, but eyes, in seeing mother's anatomy, promise to deliver more). I believe Belle's later imaginings of the voyeuristic men —more precisely, of their excitement—had their origin in her own hungry need to look at her mother's body, which Mother said was available to the men. The result, which some label "splitting," is that she contained the two identity themes of the watcher and the watched.

In time, her father played his part. Exactly how is not clear, but it seems she turned to him for the closeness her mother could not provide and found him responsive; the evidence for this is the series of early memories of being alone with him and of his admiring her feminine clothes. Unfortunately, he failed as a substitute, first because of his being delineated in the family as a failure and second by his all-too-real failure: he was vague when there. And then he left.

By the time Belle was six, the mechanisms were in place. Though the forms of her sexual scripts were modified over the years to include new information and contingencies, when she saw her little schoolmate's underwear and the buttocks swelling beyond the cloth's edges, she was fully both the looker and the one looked at. Genital excitement flared up.* Now she knew consciously that she could excite others with her bottom, just as her mother and this girl had excited her. And so began the games in which she dressed up in the most feminine clothes, with diaphanous draperies, jewelry, makeup, sexy poses and wiggles, excited at being the girl who was looked at and, in a different way, excited by the fantasy in which the man looks at the girl.

Perhaps Belle gives us clues about the perversion "narcissism."[8] Rather than explaining it only in the language of fixation at an infantile stage of development ("narcissistic stage"), we may see the capacity to become sexually excited on contemplating one's own body as the surface manifestation of a script like Belle's, wherein she is (1) herself looking at (2) her own breasts imagined as being on another woman's body (3) which would be exciting to a looking man. I doubt whether we could understand that perversion, or any perversion, or any sexual excitement in humans, without discovering the scripts.

NOTE

I want to make visible my failure to discuss "narcissism" at length, either as a presence—a demonstrable thing with a history from infancy to the present—or as a metapsychologic tool that could order my data and ideas. I do this wittingly, not from ignorance of the importance of the theoretic issues to analysts. When one wants to move from clinical dross to the underlying laws of behavior, it is tempting to speak of "narcissistic mortification," "narcissistic reverie," "narcissistic rage,"

*It really is not so simple: we do not know why she not only was affected by the sight of the other girl but also was consciously, genitally excited. Is there a biologic precocity—capacity—in certain girls and not in others?

and the like. But what would be the form of mortification or reverie or rage when their "narcissism" is extracted?

Although I find "narcissism" a good word to summarize such states as observable styles of behavior or attitudes toward external objects— its clinical meaning—the concept is so broad when used as a fundament in analytic theorizing that I really do not know what it means or in which of its protean meanings it is being used by an author. Like "cathexis" or "libido," "narcissism" becomes in effect—at bottom— synonymous with *"élan vital"* or comparable mystical generalizations that supposedly define the state of being alive (cf. "phlogiston"). "Narcissism" has too many meanings[9] until it is defined with extreme precision, at which time I find it has lost its meaning, because each definition depends on other words (such as "cathexis") that have not been defined without using undefined words such as "narcissism."

9

Lovely

BELLE WAS DRIVEN, as we saw in regard to her exhibitionism, by her preoccupation with being lovely. What caught my attention was that "lovely" was not, for her, an adjective describing behavior that revealed a sense of herself but rather was a noun, a specific "substance" within, that was drawn on when necessary and could be depleted by too many withdrawals or with age. Her "lovely" was a commodity. On rising in the morning, she had to put on her "lovely"; she could only hope as the day unfolded that if she had "lovely" then she was lovely.

Her mother, of course, had lots of "lovely," had had it since childhood, had never earned it, and could not lose it no matter what happened in the way of physical or mental deterioration. This was a source of the greatest envy for Belle, who felt she had to work constantly to keep up her own depletable reserves. Being Mother's daughter entitled her to a certain amount of "lovely," but Mother made it clear that Belle had not been assigned the same amount by fate, could never acquire it by effort, would have it only as a part of physical attributes (external appearance and internal organs), and would have a "lovely" that—at best—was contaminated. Mother and women like her might sweat, but their sweat was "lovely"; such women, perhaps, had bowel movements, but of course their bowel movements were somehow "lovely"; when "lovely" women made love, every movement was lovely, while Belle was always in danger of fucking.

What contributed to "lovely"? At birth Belle was unequivocally assigned to the female sex.* This was a piece of good luck, for all the women in her mother's family openly liked femaleness; it was purely and simply to Belle's credit. Mother was happy to have borne a daugh-

*This seems obvious and beyond needing mention, but when we recall the effects of this assignment, we immediately see that it is a necessary first step in creating a female core gender identity.

ter. With father and his relatives perceived as inferiors by mother's family, an infant male would be at jeopardy simply because he was male. In Belle's case, with an ineffectual father and no brothers, no maleness was present to contradict the evidence of female value. That became a lifelong theme: her femaleness was fine.*

The problem was that she was a flawed girl and woman. The family did not say this was due to femaleness, however, but rather that it was the product of her being her mother's child. Although such solid acceptance of the baby's sex does not preclude feelings of inadequacy, we should not be tempted by analytic theory to extrapolate these feelings of defect as necessarily the result of penis envy. I am not implying that little girls, including Belle, do not experience penis envy. The evidence that they do is clear. What I am saying, rather, to restate my theory of primary femininity, is that penis envy may not be the earliest stage in the development of femininity, as Freud said, but may come after an unalterable sense of femaleness (core gender identity) has already been created.

A subcategory of "lovely" was "darling." This rarely appeared, for Belle had not been trained by others to be darling and neither saw herself as that nor tried very much to accomplish it. She was occasionally tempted in that direction, however, as a device to cover over shittiness. (Being dirty and being lovely were themes that for years lay there in her, contradictory and immiscible.) To be darling is not quite the same as to be lovely: "darling" has more child in it and less feminine woman. One is darling if one mispronounces a word just right.

But you cannot keep mispronouncing the same words over and over, and that, in effect, was the limit of her darlinghood. Besides, she knew that she belonged, rather, to the category of pest. Although you won't be loved, there is no way you can be abandoned if you are a pest, for you have already burrowed under the person's skin, safe in there if you don't mind discomfort and being scratched at. They cannot ignore you, they cannot abandon you.

The simple fact was that Belle secretly felt lovely. But that raises complicated questions. Did she *really* feel that way or was she just trying to? What are identity, self, narcissism, learning, imitation, acting, impersonation, imposture, internalization, incorporation, introjection, identification, conditioning, true self versus false self, character structure, tradition, and time-binding?

Femininity (in females and males), I have maintained, is not, after one has considered biologic anlagen, just the product of conflict. It also

---

*As do other women, she could also describe her vagina as a "sewer." I do not believe, however, that this is evidence of a fundamental hatred and disgust with femaleness.

has elements that occur nonconflictually and nontraumatically, starting in the first year or so of life. It is more than the product of defensive maneuvers in childhood that allow a girl to accept bravely, masochistically, and with envy the grim fate of femaleness in final repudiation of the hope of being male. Therefore, when working with most women, I *expect* to find a "true self" who knows, accepts, does not question, is at ease with at least a part of herself as a woman who is female and feminine. It is not surprising, then, that my data (except in the most masculine women) show the existence of this female and feminine gender identity; an analyst with the opposite bias sees the same manifestations as the result of envy, anger, revenge, desolation.

Beneath her histrionic displays it was easy to feel Belle's conviction that the parts of her body that were anatomically and physiologically female were solid, dependable anchors, making the prognosis for treatment better than in those women who have no pride in femaleness. This admired biology was ever-present, a literal central core of her body that was safe and unalterable. She never, after a fit of masochism, fell into a state of complete despair, for the sense of femaleness was always a home to which she could return if frightened or unhappy. And to confirm its validity, a sexual experience, whether with another person or masturbatory, was not fully satisfying unless that center was touched. One reason she finally had fully satisfying orgasms, experienced deep in her vagina, was that after some years of treatment, she had explored the sensate and psychic dimensions of this core, discovered it had been preserved secretly in her, saw that even the enemas had not destroyed it, and had let this center of her being be manifested in her feelings and associations with me. When I did not harm it—after she had tested in every way whether I would or not—that part of her was no longer split off, walled away for protection from the outside world. She was now safe to experience it, to know it as part of herself, and therefore to let it exist when she was sexually excited.

Unfortunately, the women of her family could not let her alone with that. Because of their own problems with males, the stories they inculcated in the child had complications beyond simple self-esteem. Some of these have been noted: your mother is a strange one, and since you are her daughter, you will also be strange; the worth of being female is not to be considered the same as that of being a woman; if you ever get married, you will not marry well; you are truly a female, and that is fine, but some females, like Mother, are more appealing.

Competition with Mother was significant only in the arenas of femaleness and femininity; and her mother was too terrific to beat: "Mother often bragged about her periods, telling me her menopause would come at a later age than mine." "My mother wanted to own, to control, my insides but she didn't want to take responsibility for me." A dream: "A PBX [telephone] switchboard. Because of a strike, I was supposed to help out. Lights were going on all over the board and I couldn't do anything. When I tried to plug in, I either just couldn't get in or else in place of a hole there was just a blind indentation" (a nice way to describe an exciting, unhuman mother one cannot plug into). The next day, another dream: "There were two nuns and my mother playing, and none of them knew how to play [that is, mother's two breasts are, like nuns', without milk; the breasts are nones, no good for mothering—though she knows she was breast-fed; her mother bragged endlessly of that munificence]. No one [none, nun] paid attention to me or acknowledged me. They didn't remember who I am. Then I was eating medicine off a bell [breast-shaped] . . . Ma Bell. That's in the telephone company's ad." Yesterday's dream, of the PBX wherein she cannot plug into mother, and today's addition, that I, the doctor, make treatment to be "eating medicine off a bell" (early in treatment, she had often phoned, trying to force me to be direct and talkative), starving her need for love as did her mother long ago. Dream: "I'm in a low room. My mother is moving out. There are many plugs in one socket. So it's overloaded and unsafe. Then they're all unplugged except one." Associations to uteri, to hysterectomies. She is connected to her mother only by the prized femaleness—and that can be cut off. Dream: "My mother had cancer. She called me on the phone and sounded courageous. Then I was in the hospital visiting her. She was on the bed. She had turned completely into a hollow breast with a cancer on the edge. She tipped over."

In brief, then, she got a solid start into femininity in the encouragement she received for being female, but too many unpleasant messages were also transmitted on the same subject.

Her "lovely" was those characteristics the people in charge of her defined as "lovely," which they in turn had been taught. Obviously, this learning is cultural.* Whatever part biologic factors play, they are almost always overcome by these social-interpersonal forces. The process goes more smoothly when, from birth on, the attributes defined by the family as "lovely" are introduced to the infant in a gratifying manner and the attributes not wanted are efficiently discouraged.

If everyone surrounding the little girl is thrilled when she does some-

_____

*Some of the argument among disciplines could be avoided if one traced the paths of communication of such learning from the multiple sources in the community—human and manufactured—into the individual who accepts and automatizes them and back out to others whom the individual influences, eventually, via some of these others, to return to the cultural sources for dissemination.

thing "lovely" or when she looks "lovely," she will repeat that behavior, and in time, if not discouraged, it will become automatic. I do not know what inner processes occur that make a single act change to one the child builds in as part of a permanent repertoire any more than I know how "identification" works; scripts carry the message, but they do not fully explain motivation.

Learning the outward forms of femininity does not go on only in early life; obviously it persists indefinitely, with reinforcements coming more and more from outside the family. We also do not need too simple-minded a picture. In real life, innocuous words like "reinforce," "reward," "discourage," or "punish" are complicated events: rewards are mixed with options, cautions, threats, and punishments. For instance, the act of spanking a child may contain multiple messages of reward and punishment, advice and warning, predictions and observations: a father preoccupied with his own erotic feelings toward his daughter may announce them and encourage hers when beating her for being what he calls oversexed. *All* his messages probably get through, including his secrets.

Although I know no controlled research to confirm the following, I think one could show that if, from earliest childhood on, a mother and father powerfully encourage behavior they consider feminine, that behavior will appear and, unless they try to blot it out, will become a permanent part of their child's behavior. (That is true whether the child is female or male.[1]) And the fewer contrary attitudes they manifest, the purer will be the state of these appearances. But they are appearances; to give them more dimension requires that the girl move these attitudes somehow into her fantasy life and use them to help her solve the traumas, frustrations, and conflicts that must arise. At first parents and then others teach a girl what is expected of her regarding clothes, choice of vocabulary, ways of sitting and walking, subjects of interest, games to be played, companions to associate with, styles of erotic behavior, themes for daydreaming—an unending flow of suggestions, commands, disapprovals, enthusiasms. This all seems so obvious that I do not understand why it is not included in most psychoanalytic descriptions of the development of femininity.

Just when and how appearances change from imitation to identity is hard to conceptualize, though not too hard for the practiced eye to discern. Take, for instance, the popular earth-mother number: although it can be a fine performance, we can see behind it a woman uneasy about her femininity. (This pose is also a great way to avoid the more prosaic admission that one is getting fat.) It is equivalent to cock-strutting in macho men.

One pays a high price for the privilege of being a living doll. Here is part of one of Belle's dreams: "You had a picture of me. It was me as a cute, chubby child, a very little girl, with ribbons and dolls; but all the stuff just hanging down disorganized. The picture was supposed to represent your attitude about me, which was that I am very lovable and that was the only part of me that you wanted to think about." Reruns of Shirley Temple movies had had a big pull in her childhood; the most delicious parts were the waif routines. A main task of treatment, therefore, was to see what more substantial qualities were present in addition to her acts. Was her "lovely" only a front or was it all there was?

When a woman shows us one of these awful façades, we must look to see if she nonetheless has hidden away qualities more substantial than those of a doll; our evaluation, for better or worse, is influenced not only by our theory and training but by our personalities. To get through the bad spells, it does not hurt to be optimistic. One day, before she had found her fuller sense of self, Belle was arguing her case: "I'm lovable because, when I look at my driver's license, I see a picture of a woman that's me. It doesn't look like me; but that's all right because anybody who saw her would think, 'How lovable she is.' " For a therapist of my ilk, it pays at such times not to fall into despair. On the other hand, if we can determine that that is all there is—and have confidence in our capacity to evaluate accurately—then the form of treatment used should not be analysis, which cannot create what does not already exist.

And one must be patient, to bear the repetitions of emptiness. Another dream: "I was kissing a lovable baby. Its skin was lacelike. It actually looked like the holes that are punched in piano rolls. It was to disappear in time; nothing would be left."

I suppose the biggest advantage of "lovely" is that it makes one tempting. If she could only manage it—if only smells are a bouquet, skin stays smooth and unblemished, hair gossamer, figure firm yet soft, conversation a tinkling delight—then this whole precious morsel would be swallowed by someone good enough to keep her forever safely, softly, silently inside.

She came in one day dressed deliciously, an impression designed to be clearly different from other appearances and underlined by a new dress. She kneeled on the couch in order to go on display and proceeded through a number of associations, including dream elements having to do with eating and a shade of red that is the color of "inside organs." She was so edible that I wondered to her if the couch was not functioning as a table on which she was serving herself up. The suggestion gave her an acute erotic attack, for which she was ripe; from the start of the hour, her clothes and position had indicated that the affect, although not yet conscious, was close by. (Incidentally, after much reading on the metapsychology of affects, I still cannot see how one can question the existence of unconscious affects.) In addition to responding erotically, she said, "I don't feel right now as if I'm going to be exploited but I *do* feel like I am a meal that's going to be eaten up." The kneeling position, she said, let her offer herself up as "a bounteous, Renoir woman."

The following day, in order to recover from this episode, she came in with a hole in the knee of her stocking. She would never before have knowingly put on such a stocking,* but she had today; the hole had not developed after she left home. As usual, she was not conscious of the fantasies that underlay her choice of the day's outfit until informed by her associations. To her, the hole signified her sordidness, and, typically for her, she had to act out her feelings and fantasies by a real alteration of appearance before she could translate back to thoughts and feelings. She said that after yesterday's hour, she had a "really disgusting fantasy of having anal intercourse and of feces being smeared all over the place," an unheard-of fantasy for her. I said it sounded as if, with this fantasy and with the "sordid" stocking, she was preparing today's episode, which, of course, had to be stated dramatically to undo yesterday's delectable-morsel scene.

The suggestion unleashed her; in a manner that had rarely been possible up to that time, and for a longer stretch than ever before, she spoke to me directly, honestly, without dramatizing, and with historical material not mentioned before. Crying softly (not the drizzly whimper she usually affected), she told of the many occasions when she had known her mother was not beautiful, voluptuous, and seductive but simply ugly, in certain physical parts and in spirit. She went on: "I needed to invent a way as a child to make it possible for me to have a future as a woman. People were telling me—my mother, of course, all the time—that being a wife and being a mother was marvelous and exciting and that sex was wonderful."

As we know, her mother had endlessly filled the girl's head with stories of romantic and sexual exploits with Mother the irresistible heroine. But Belle had another version, latent, about the nature of sex. I have mentioned how she heard from a girlfriend, around age nine, the anatomic facts of intercourse, news that stirred both primary and later feminine identity themes. She first said no, telling her friend that boys would never do such a thing; even if they tried, it was too astonishing

*We have seen how she responded earlier to doing that by mistake.

and awful an act for a woman to permit. At any rate, she said, *she* would not allow it. But when her friend insisted it really happened, the child knew it was true (touching earlier, long-unconscious knowledge) and became frightened. Fear was the affect that remained through childhood, and it was still there, she said during the analytic hour, mixed with the good feelings that came later. But when one is small there is the threat to one's body, especially its insides, and just as severe is the shame: "Someone pushes inside of you, and you are supposed to come to like it! But I knew that would be impossible. I knew of no way that I could ever get rid of those bad feelings, and there was nothing about what sex seemed like that could ever make it pleasant, much less exciting. It was not just the penis in there but other things I did not know, perhaps dirtiness, certainly more even than that." The intimate, urinous, naughty, mysterious part of boys' bodies was going to be inside her, her valued, vulnerable vagina, with which she was already becoming familiar: it had been described and she had long since been poking around in there. It was an allowed subject of conversation, a part not only female but, for her family, feminine. It had been represented to her as not only precious but also delicate and unsure.

> The kids [young girls] know it's a rape and not pleasure. I knew as soon as I heard that it was nothing like when you're tickling your clitoris. And almost the worst part of it was that they had the right to do that because they marry you. It makes no difference about your body and whether it belongs to you or not. It doesn't belong to you. Marriage gives them the right, and you're supposed to love it and think that it feels marvelous. After that, the little boys just never looked the same to me. Before, they just looked like little boys who were boys, no better than I was, just grubby or nice little creatures. But now it made no difference if they were grubby or nice, good-looking or not, rich or poor or whatever. That was all aside from the point.

They knew; she knew; and she knew they knew she knew that they had the fundamental right—legally, biologically, and from God—to do that to her interior and that she had no right to prevent it. What made it all even more fantastic was that universe of adult women who obviously indulged, who had managed to traverse this rite of passage, and who —probably genuinely—got fine, if not incredible, sensations from the act. (She read a lot.)

"In order to survive, I had to teach myself that I liked it." Here her body helped out.* She found, soon enough, that the sensations from

---

*Of course, in the sense now being used, her body is no more than an extension of her mind (as in the concept "body ego"). We still would want to know why the erotic sensations arising in her body, as childhood progressed into puberty, were acknowledged to be intensely pleasurable; that is more a function of "mind" than an inevitable, unalterable response of the body.

clitoral tickling spread inside, created erotic tension, one aspect of which was a need to have that inside stimulated, and pressed her, despite her limited knowledge about the act of intercourse, to invent scripts to account for and cater to these sensations. Obviously, the development of this erotic capacity went a long way toward solving the question how one can bear to take in that alien organ.

So the daydreams had a function beyond erotism: they made it possible for her to accept the idea of intercourse, for only intercourse —as she had been well informed—would affirm her femaleness and femininity. Without the ability to perform sexually, she would never be a wife and a mother and therefore—by the standards of her family, to which she was committed—a woman.

A well-formed sense of femaleness is present by age two-and-a-half or three in most girls[2] and is one of the fundaments of personality from then on. To repeat: a woman's sense of integrity (meaning completeness, intactness) is based on her parents' attitudes toward her anatomy, not just on penis envy or on the belief that she is castrated. That core of gender identity, once established, is impervious to damage from neurosis and even psychosis. Then the girl must deal with such pressures as the discovery of male genitals, envy for the functions male genitals enjoy, and the related but not identical powers and responsibilities males are granted by our society. We see Belle struggling with these issues, doing the best she can. My version of this struggle says that her sense of femaleness was intact and served as a bulwark against traumas and conflicts that tended to spoil later aspects of her femininity. Is it not obvious that there are many women, in many cultures, who from the beginning of life neither question nor hate being female but like that state and would not give it up?

Her sense of integrity as a female led to her shock in childhood that sexual intercourse would occur regardless of her fear. The Director fantasy, then, helped her bear that inescapable law of man and God. Yes, she had to submit to the males, but she maintained the control, and they ultimately were the ones left frustrated by their failure to destroy her being. At most, they could only have her body—that old, familiar lament heard down the centuries. Analytic theorists make a mistake, I think, when they look on this as being necessarily rationalization, a pathetic story created by women whose fundament is mere envy.

In her sexual scripts, it was understood that her suffering was the result of her being oversexed, that is, filled with femaleness and femininity. The males, never that strong (that cursed, that blessed), therefore had the sneaky advantage. Depriving her of what would finally completely fulfill her as a female, a masculine and loving man, they could turn her potential strength (femaleness) into weakness.

In Freud's theory of masculinity and femininity, castration is a central feature; the male fears it can happen, the female mourns that it did. The idea should be enlarged. Men do not just fear the body wound to those precious parts. Our genitals represent our identity as males and as masculine. Castration then would mean we were cut off from our being, ourself. But by castration, Freud meant the same thing for both sexes: male organs. I think that is incomplete. Each sex suffers its own distinct threat. Just as the loss of a penis means for a man the loss of a penis, so for a woman, whatever else it might be, the loss of a breast is the loss of a breast, the loss of an ovary is the loss of an ovary, and the loss of a uterus is the loss of a uterus. At a deeper level than the fantasy that she was a person who was robbed of a penis is, I think, a woman's fear she might be or was robbed of her femininity.

Example: although Belle was chronically aroused from childhood on, she rarely masturbated and even then invariably kept her genitals from intense reaction, not to mention orgasm. She felt that her sense of sinning could not have stopped her. What did was a fantasy—she says she was told this when little—that "doing that" would damage her organs and prevent her ever having babies. It was only when, as an adult, she knew there could be no such dire consequences that she proceeded to full excitement and orgasm. And even then, she could never quite shake the dread that she was inflicting irreparable harm.

Example: a woman does not like the appearance of her breasts, although her boyfriends think they are great. Her mother has been constantly at her, disparaging her physical features, including her breasts, since childhood. Why is that not as much a cause of shame as penis envy?

One day when Belle is being, she says, stubborn, she reports a dream: "My leg was amputated and was being replaced by a man's leg, but the operation wasn't working. It started to turn black around the kneecap, which meant it was going bad." In another part of the dream, a teen-age girl "was having surgery on her ovary. There was some question whether it had to be removed, and yet it was dangerous to put surgical instruments inside her. The doctors didn't know much about what the condition was. I preferred they would just look in and then close her up without really operating. But they wanted to rip it out, without even knowing what they were doing." She wonders if this has something to do with analysis. She has read that analysts think women believe themselves castrated males, and, she says, she fears I will give her an interpretation that says she really wants a penis. The dream, among other things, is a warning that that kind of interpretation would not take but would turn gangrenous.*

This keeps coming up: "I was up many times during the night. In the dream it was four in the morning, and in reality it was also four A.M. Someone was at the door. He was formally dressed, and his name was something like Mr. Collodi or Collidi. (I don't know anyone with that name.) He was a carpet layer; he was a sweet man but ineffectual. He presumed I needed him. Even though it was four o'clock in the morning, he wasn't scary. I treated him as if I didn't need him, but somehow there was the feeling that I did. That name sounds something like the name of the man who wrote *Pinocchio.*"†

Yesterday, she made love with a boyfriend and was unusually unexcited, literally dried out. She didn't move, hardly felt alive. She reports another dream: "I was in a house, in the family room. There was a food shortage everywhere, and there were instructions written down and tacked up as to how to get food. So I followed the instructions and saw there were a bunch of little human bodies that had been frozen. The instructions were that these frozen corpses were to be licked. It was disgusting." The previous day, having no sexual excitement, she had no desire to go down on her boyfriend. Then, as if this thought were unconnected with any of the others, she breaks in on herself and says, "I am trying not to give you any lies today." That is just the mood I have been sensing; no exaggerating, posturing, tear-drizzling, masochistic picking on me, or the rest of her repertoire in these earlier years of treatment.

She had not wanted her lover to undress her, thinking, "I'll do it myself," that essential advertisement for her life. I remind her of the ineffectual carpet layer in the dream who was needed nonetheless. "Carpet layer," she says, "has something to do with sex and pubic hair and being a layer."

I ask if her feeling during intercourse yesterday was not only dry but wooden. "Yes" (surprised). She adds, "Isn't there something in the story about Pinocchio being tempted not to be real?" Pinocchio is wooden; only if he does not tell lies and is a good boy will he become human. His father, an Italian woodcarver (typical of the inferior old men who excite her), is like me or like the other men in mythology and fairy tales who awaken maidens. And I show up at four A.M., for I am the (her) dream man. Always prying.

*It had other meanings for her equal in importance to the one above but apart from the theme dissected out in this chapter. For instance, she was warning me not to analyze further lest I (she) discover the conflict she had that questioned her core conviction of being female and feminine. The conflict was not *in* the conviction but rather was *about* it.
†That author's pen name was Collodi.

I hardly need to remind her—she was thinking it—that the dramatic part of Pinocchio's struggle with truth and reality is that if he lies, his nose grows longer. Because of her need to dramatize, exaggerate, and otherwise exhibit, she knows (fully now, after a few years of analysis) that she lies all the time.* And the punishment could be to lose her femaleness and femininity, to become a wooden, phallus-nosed imitation of a person.

When Pinocchio is not his true self, he is naughty. She now begins, for the first time, to give examples of her naughtiness (thus illuminating the sadism that underlies her masochism, finally experiencing the connection). When she was little and made noise on the piano, she would be ordered to stop, and so she would have to give it one last bang; she carved valuable furniture with eating utensils, knowing it got people angry. "I do that to you all the time, just like when I was little. Oh! I dreamed about furniture last night: a little girl had put all the good furniture into the shower where it got soaked, and it was destroyed." She laughs.

The key words in this discussion have been "female" and "femininity," their meanings worked out in relation to her "lovely." She never doubted, at any level of awareness I found, the intactness of her femaleness, and when anatomic bisexuality appeared in her thoughts, it represented punishment (as with Pinocchio's nose). Nonetheless, her "lovely" was not an uncontaminated psychic structure; it also had defensive aspects in its construction and was used defensively. Her preoccupation with her appearance and her sadomasochism were examples of this. There is no question that sometimes she laid it on pretty thick and did so in order to convince herself that being a woman was as good as being a man, but she did this when she was envious of or enraged at a man because she felt humiliated.† One can envy an attribute of another without wanting to be that other in entirety; she wanted men's power, but she was not looking for a penis. I do not believe that her pride in her femaleness was just a reaction formation against wishes to be a male.

Appearances can mask their opposites; it is easy, with exhibitionistic women, to talk of "the body as a phallus." Certainly men and women have such experiences, but at times that explanation may be an incomplete, if not glib, interpretation for a woman's displaying her body in

*At first, it would be inaccurate to say that she was lying, for she was not conscious how her acting roles served to falsify her truth; but by this point in treatment, she could scarcely make a phony move without feeling it.

†A feminine woman may use her body to create in men the sort of tantalized frustration men produce in her. She will do this partly for revenge, not necessarily because she wants a penis. Penis tantalizes; female body tantalizes. But that need not always mean that female body equals penis.

revealing clothes. Owing, perhaps, to the regression that comes with age, I have finally decided that if it looks like steak, sizzles like steak, smells like steak, and tastes like steak, I shall think it believes itself to be a steak. If Belle says she is a delectable female and expresses pride in her female attributes; always looks feminine and never masculine; dreams incessantly of being pregnant or giving birth, of babies and children, of cupboards, cooking, and ovens, of mothers with their children, of making, buying, and trying on clothes, of menstrual periods, vestibules, flowers, grassy lawns, mirrors, carpets, shops, curtains, kitchens, household appliances, lace, linen, silk, cotton, textures, patterns, colors, sizes, functions, styles, fields, earth, soil to be fertilized or planted; and if she is excited by men and not women, why not conclude that she believes herself to be a female and a woman, not just a castrated male?

Belle suffered endlessly from her anger at males and envy at their happier lot, without hope that she could move from her inferior position and ashamed that she mismanaged these issues. Yet she discovered that knowing men to be sadists (she did not make that up), she was using that knowledge to read sadism into all our acts. And that is propaganda, whether used for social causes or for masturbation.

Women, too, are sadists; she ignored that. Humans, whether by nature or nurture, are often villains. Big news.

PART 3

Theories
of the Mind

10

Microdots

HAD THE ANALYSIS gone on and on, Belle and I could have found even more roots of her erotic daydream. Still, in the time we had, we learned enough to be able to recover memories of how and why she built it as she did. She and I are clear that what she experienced before treatment as simply a surge of excitement was in fact an intricate, highly condensed, carefully constructed fable in which, in an instant, she relived the major affectional and erotic events of her life from infancy on. As with a chemical analysis, we broke a compound—the daydream—into its component parts and binding forces: its meanings.

But that leaves unsolved lofty old philosophic problems: What is my mind? Who or what makes my decisions? If Belle, at the moment of excitement, did not feel she had created it, was not aware of the years spent in constructing a workable excitement, then who or what residing within her did invent it? If that could be answered, we would move our discussion of sexual excitement to a broader and more significant level.

But I cannot answer it. And in reviewing the literature or discussing the issues with colleagues, I am still left unsure. However, there are several ideas worth our attention. This chapter and the one that follows review the issues.

During World War II, the Nazis devised a system for hiding messages: the microdot, "a photograph the size of a printed period that reproduced with perfect clarity a standard-sized typewritten letter."* Most human

*"At first the microdot process involved two steps: A first photograph of an espionage message resulted in an image the size of a postage stamp; the second, made through a reversed microscope, brought it down to less than 0.05 inches in diameter. This negative was developed. Then the spy pressed a hypodermic needle, whose point had been clipped off and its rounded edge sharpened, into the emulsion like a cookie cutter and lifted out the microdot. Finally, the agent inserted it into a cover-text over a period and cemented it with collodion there." D. Kahn, *The Code-Breakers* (New York: Macmillan Co., 1966), p. 525.

behavior—the functioning of the mind—works the same way; Freud described something like this long ago.[1] In a process comparable to the miniaturization that allows stupendous amounts of information to be stored, arranged, rearranged, and transmitted within so small an apparatus as the brain, we—our minds—use psychic mechanisms that work at high speed to compress great masses of data into amazingly small "space" in a purposeful, organized way. One might even look on the mind as the movement of these very efficient microdots: their content, the rules and mechanisms of their functioning, and their teleology—their motivation.

Sexual excitement is a microdot. Microdots are fantasies; the term "microdot" is useful because it suggests certain functions and purposes of fantasies, efficiency above all. "Microdot," more than "fantasy," implies all at the same instant: an ability to condense masses of data; to be retrieved instantly into consciousness for action, affects, and inspiration; to be moved around weightlessly and slipped into situations in which it brings about desired results. It is efficient. But the conscious experience of instantaneousness hides logical, motivated (even if unconscious) planning.[2]

Microdotting not only implies condensation, which is the squeezing of a mass into a smaller space. It is, much more, a process in which a measureless, random amount of mental debris is scanned and suitable elements chosen to be then organized into a coherent product—a dream, a thought, an erotic impulse. "Microdot" signifies a process that is present in all mental activity (after earliest infancy) and is concerned not only with primordial wish fulfillment but even with intellectual activities far removed from what Freud called "primary process."[3] It is not only narcissistic but is necessary for communication between people. Microdotting is, I speculate, a universal quality of thought. I stress again that the process of condensing is guided with shrewdness and at times with genuine creativity. It is never (except in deteriorated mental states) just a smashing together of elements into a compaction of junk, but rather is moved by clear-cut—even if invisible—motives ("motivational systems"[4]) of complexity and vigor. It is an act of intellect, will, foresight, and synthesis, not just primal impulse seeking discharge.

In addition to their obvious meanings, words like the following also have aspects that imply fantasy and microdots: memory, feeling, attitude, conviction, belief, thought, word, language, syntax, inner (internalized) objects, introjects, identifications, object, self, identity, ego, superego, id, idea, hallucination, wish, motive, conflict, dream element, transference, impulse, body sensation, body parts, meaning, symptom, character structure, ambivalence, defense, concept, fetish, symbol, context, experience, reality, complex (as in oedipal), customs, morals, trust, truth; in brief, everything one might call "mental." Fantasy (inextricably mixed, always, with affect) is in the content of all mental life;[5] and it is observable via our reports of our inner life. But there are also mechanisms ("dynamics"), which may also be motives, that shape and move fantasies (for example, keep them out of consciousness), and these cannot be observed.[6]

I want to underline my awareness that not everything is fantasy: for instance, beneath fantasy is inner-driven brain physiology (such as REM mechanisms), outside-originating but now inner-driven brain physiology (conditioned responses, imprinting—if that or something like it exists in humans*), outside-originating stimuli that release inherited behavior (such as rooting reflexes in infant feeding), sensations (hearing, proprioception).[7] These, I think, are grains of reality upon which precipitate, from infancy on, the fantasies that in time aggregate into microdots. Fantasy, as Freud indicated, is the mental experience created, by means of these inherited and learned mechanisms, to control biologic drives and to control the effects of external events on that biology. Its purpose could be to defend us from—to rationalize, explain, deny, distort—reality, but I cannot guess how the capacity to fantasize comes out of the original chaos.[8]

Everyone knows of the microdots of sexual excitement: a genteel, clean woman in a quiet marriage of low erotic intensity is stabbed with excitement at the look and smell of a physically disreputable man of clearly lower class; a twelve-year-old boy puts on his sister's clothes, never before having cross-dressed, and has an instantaneous, spontaneous orgasm, his first; a forty-year-old woman, well experienced in sexual activity, is with a new man, who, without warning, gives her a vicious slap on the buttocks, causing her to experience simultaneously rage, humiliation, and fierce genital excitement; a man looks at a woman with a certain hair style and becomes nauseated; a philosopher (male or female) looks at an erect penis and starts to write a political tract; a woman looks across a room at an unknown man and decides she will marry him. The number of examples is endless.

Past experiences, words, syntax, body sensations—all mental experiences—exist in us in the form of memories. But they are not just literal replicas of the past. They are more, for they are condensed masses of information, organized around particular themes.[9, 10]

At the core of motivated behavior (behavior that is not purely reflex-

*I suspect that a lot of what is called conditioned response or imprinting in humans is actually microdotting. On the other hand, the primal focus on which a microdot may then begin forming could be a conditioned or imprinted response (fetal, or postnatal infantile).

ive, such as random nervous-tissue firing or simple conditioning) is fantasy. Each mental act implies fantasy, even the most precise memory, even the memory so precise that it comes back with hallucinatory realness.* Most of the time, we serve up fantasy in the form of microdots rather than running the fantasy out as a lengthy, conscious script.

If we were cryptanalysts studying code, we would want to know who was the person motivated to send the message, what was the motivation, what techniques were used to get the message into code, what form the message took when encoded, what was the message, who was the enemy to be tricked, who was the friend who should have received the message, and what action was to result from the information received. These same steps, obviously, apply to our microdots, the main difference being that the whole process and its participants are contained within one head. That throws an additional burden on us, one I cannot fathom, to determine who, in you, in me, are the characters—the personalities—involved in this cryptography. What are their motives? How do they manage to exist inside the same mind and yet be of such different minds? Do they, as implied above, exist as discrete personalities or in other forms? And how are they kept separate? Once again, then, I am struggling with the process called splitting, the condition in which two or more fantasy systems are active at one time.[11]

When, for instance, one talks of the ego deforming itself, one is referring to a collection of fantasies being modified. The ego has not split; rather, contradicting fantasies are being lived. There is no ego; it is only a concept. But we can experience a fantasy, or multiple fantasies. Comparably, the analytic concept of multidetermination can be seen as a collection of scripts at different levels of consciousness, all serving to motivate a piece of behavior.

The following illustrates again the way that multiple scripts can appear clinically. Toward the end of an analytic hour that has allowed a woman to feel freer in expressing herself, she says, "I just feel quiet. That's all. [Silence] I feel soft all over. [Silence] There's a sexual feeling between my legs, but it's a loving one. It's way up. [Silence] It's so far away that I can hardly feel it. [Silence] It's a throb, and I know it is very strong even though it is so far away that I hardly feel it. [Silence] My stomach is afraid. [Silence] Listen to my dead voice. But there's also sadness in my throat and my chest. [Silence] And my arms and my hands are holding me. [Silence] And loving my flesh. [Silence] My head is angry. [Silence]

*For even when we remember exactly, it must be explained why we chose to remember exactly rather than selectively; or put differently, exact remembering is only one selection out of all the possible ways of remembering.

My toes are free, wiggling, like a child having a good time. [Silence] And me: I'm holding it all down."

Examine this question: When I sleep, who is the dreamer? Neurophysiology cannot tell us, nor, for all its richness, can Freud's metapsychology. Dividing the mind into ego, superego, and id has occupied many analysts, but even attempts to break these concepts into subspecies (such as the ego-ideal aspect of the superego, or the unconscious part of the ego that is contiguous with the id and powered by instinctual energy) have not moved our explanations much.

At one time (before he invented the concept of the id) Freud would have said the Unconscious *(Ucs.)* is the dreamer. But who is that? As Rosenblatt and Thickstun remind us:

> The idea that there are unconscious mental processes is a necessary part of psychoanalytic theory. The idea that some unconscious processes can more readily become conscious than others is also most useful. If the term "preconscious" were limited to describing unconscious processes that can readily become conscious, then it could be a useful term. However, the terms unconscious, preconscious, and conscious, when used to describe systems of the human mind, are not useful, and should be abandoned as they were by Freud in 1923.[12]

And so, to improve our understanding—to make the fit closer between the observable, clinical world and theory—we turned to such ways of organizing data as "identity" or "self," or to studying inner objects (the forms external objects take when represented inside), or to the more precise observations and dissections of interpersonal relationships and (though hardly yet touching psychoanalytic thinking) a study of scripts.

Microdotting is great. Why, then, have the slower, lumbering, conscious, problem-solving thinking? Probably because we need both for survival, though too much reliance on either may be dangerous. We can see that microdotting can be life-saving; barring disruption by brain damage or other mental illness, it is always available when we need instantaneous decision-making. And all through the ordinary days as well, it is stunningly adroit, rapid as a reflex. (That measures the difference between man and lower animals; both can react in an instant, yet the rat cannot assemble much of his past personal history right then, while each microdot for us is a scan of all we have ever known.) But it is vulnerable, since the same quick selecting leads to disaster when panic is put into the mix of facts and motives to be computed. Confronted with certain dangers, only experienced ("mature") people can switch over from the "automatic," "reflex" process of cognition to slower and now more effective forms of choosing, such as contemplation.

Looking at the way we put together and use microdots brings up that old fundament of morality: Am I responsible for my acts? When? (I do not want to be told, as the computer scientist affirms, that I never am; that "I" may only be a complex thing that has built into its mechanism, among other qualities, a part that insists it exists, insists it chooses.) And can I be both responsible and unknowing at the same time; can I be two people, each acting with different information? Or three? Or a dozen? When are my impulses fully the result of biology beyond the reach of my choice, when partly, and when do I have lots of choice unencumbered by any imperatives but that of choice? The goal of education—including the learning I do when being analyzed—is to give me new options, the choice to act (or not act), when before I felt compelled. Having the information available in uncoded form (that is, becoming conscious of it) lets me act more effectively: penicillin often beats prayer.

Perhaps mental life is nothing but a river of microdots, the consciously experienced moment selected from the whole and arranged to present a point of view. If the selection shows that all is rationalization, illusion, then we analysts need allege only that the illusion of having more conscious choice is preferable to the illusions called ignorance or innocence.

Here are some more microdots: words, language, music, a gesture, a blocked thought, inspiration (as with creativity), a facial expression, a joke, a symbol, love at first sight. The one studied herein is sexual excitement. A man looks at a woman and gets an erection: microdot; fantastic. A man looks at a photograph of a woman and gets an erection: fantastic. A man looks at a woman and doesn't get an erection: fantastic. A man looks at a woman in a dress and gets an erection: fantastic. A man . . . a nude woman, etc. A man . . . a dress hanging in a closet, etc. A man . . . a piece of music, etc. A man . . . a sunset, a corpse, a shoe, a nipple, an ankle, another male, a sigh, a groan, white skin, dark skin, tattooed skin, beating, being beaten, looking, being looked at, anus, mouth, eye, ear, nose, and throat. Fantastic. Dot. Dot. Dot.

Words. Ordinary language functions by evocation, making use of multiple meanings. Mathematical language is a successful effort to reduce meanings, ideally, to one; art, an essential of which is ambiguity, is a successful effort to increase the number of meanings, called poetry when the vehicle of the ambiguity is words. A number (when used in calculating, not a lucky number or a star athlete's identifying label) has the least evocative force; then come words in ordinary language; then symbols used in such interpersonal communications as religion, patriotic propaganda, art, or metaphysics; then autistic language (dreams, psychosis), where so many meanings are possible that one is lost without a guide.

The more meanings crammed into a small space (such as a word), the more impact—acute tension followed by acute release—on the recipient (such as a reader), so long as his "apparatus" picks up, as instantaneously and subliminally as the sender created the microdot, awareness of its thickly packed meanings. That impact is not communicated if the message (density of meanings) is beyond the capacity of the receiver to comprehend (as when he is from a different culture, or does not have artistic training or sensibility, or is too young or otherwise inexperienced).*

Sometimes—always in a creative act—the sender and the receiver are inside the same person, as in the "eureka" experience of discovery or instantaneous dislike for another person.

Every word in a sentence is a microdot; the excess meanings slop over so much it is a miracle we even begin to understand each other. How differently you will understand the writing in this book from what I think I am saying. The problem is how to make my script, each word and sentence, overlap yours with enough shared that the communicating is worth the effort. What is the right word to be chosen at this very point, so that, if used just here and in just this context, you will understand me?

Music. Even more profusely than words, music stirs up connotations, fantasies, stories, memories, so efficiently that affects can be produced —manipulated—with almost no effort. One discovers, on listening to music, what a storehouse of scripts lies just below the surface, swollen with daydreams' sleazy sentiments. It is downright obscene; music is virtually a pornography of affects.

One can get a hint of the microdotting function in music when listening to alien music that has almost no familiar connotations. (If it literally has none, we probably hear it as noise, not music.) Training in "appreciation" is really the teaching of connotations. Put the notes together a certain way and everyone in town is sad, sucking on yearn-

*This would include the audience of a revolutionary artist that does not yet have the "equipment" to hear his message; those first people who do get it, the avant-garde, do so because they already have enough experience to form the subliminal pool of information necessary to respond instantaneously to the new microdots.

ing. The rhythms, chords, and progressions of the music, once we have learned our society's connotations, microdot our moods.

The melody is a story (or at least the beginning of a story; orchestration can change the script, even to reversing its original meaning). For instance, there may be a build-up of conflict, as with the uncertainties of romance and with the resolution at the end (success in love, bittersweet finales, loss, death) and complications, uncertainties, suggestions of several possible conclusions signaled along the way.

Gestalt. Here we have a microdot that orders our perceptions so that a complex situation acquires meaning. Instead of accepting gestalten as true entities, we should look for the detailed scripts for which the diffuse experience we call a gestalt is the algebraic sum, the final conscious experience.

Fetishes. These can either be inanimate objects or body parts, and for them to work erotically, the fantasies must not be consciously known. Whatever story lines are developed, their connection with the unconscious fantasies is disguised, so that the fetish exists as if alone in the universe, unconnected with the rest of material reality, separated from its usual functions, not a part of the whole, as if a unique, untouched object. The fetishist has ringed his fetish with a protective barrier meant to be impenetrable, lest the unconscious origins of the fetish be discovered.

Speculation: the fetish and its isolation in psychologic and material space represent (microdot) the fetishist's efforts to isolate his mother and depict her as no longer being in contact with him (no longer threatening to merge with him and thus destroy his identity as a separate person). If the sense of being separate is the crucial part, then the fetish may also represent the fetishist, safe behind his surrounding barrier. With that, when all the isolation has been scripted and staged, he can succumb to the temptation to merge again with his mother. Then, for instance, he can put on her clothes (transvestism), feel that he is inside her skin, and at the same time—especially because of the sharp, precise delineating power of an erection—still be a separate creature while inside her skin.

The garment that excites the transvestite is, thus, a microdot: (1) phallic women exist: the transvestite, with his penis under the woman's clothes, is living proof; (2) the garment stands for a whole woman—mother—one can be close to, a cure for separation anxiety; (3) inside the garment, the fetishist is a woman, (4) but one with a penis, (5) and therefore still also a male, (6) free to pick up his masculinity again when he chooses, (7) safe from women's threats to harm his maleness and masculinity or to abandon him; (8) he can then, in the same instance, be both (imagine himself to be) separate from and at one with mother, (9) and so be superior to anyone who is only a female or only a male; (10) with all these mental acrobatics, he runs no real risks, (11) and yet ends up with a storm of pleasures that are engrossing, dependable, repeatable, (12) for a fetish, unlike humans, is totally cooperative, nonjudgmental, uncomplaining, and, when cast off, does not retaliate. All that, I suggest, can be crammed into one erection.

Passion. Here is an example: love is blind. People believe that because it is unsafe not to. It serves to protect knowledge that must remain unconscious, allowing us to persist in habitual behavior without suffering the inhibitions of insight. Object choice, whether for the purpose of love or hate, is not blind but exquisitely clear-sighted, even clever enough to subscribe to such hogwash as "love is blind." For a function of microdots is to communicate falsehood to ourselves (and at times to others). More creative uses to which the process could be put—revelation, inspiration—are less often found.

Body Parts. Read these and let them resonate; you will sense the microdots: face, hand, mouth, knee, breasts, penis, fingernail, anus, hair, calf, kidney, vulva, thyroid, stomach, eye, brain. They are friends, strangers, enemies, villains, victims, victors.

Postures and facial expressions are microdots; when these physical states become habitual, the tissues permanently change so that the fantasy becomes character structure becomes musculoskeletal structure. What a history we read: the lovely girls and the strong bright boys turn gross and savage with age.

And also body positions. Belle, as she moves through these next associations, unravels a microdot. She sometimes squats to masturbate. "I don't know why. It just makes the orgasm come in a few seconds. Before I even have time to think. I just spread my legs far apart. I guess that really exposes my genitals . . . that sounds like I have some reason for doing that . . . [Silence.] Because someone is looking. Then someone can see. A man is looking. He's off at a distance; he isn't going to get close. He won't touch, just look. He's teasing; that's the excitement. If he wasn't there, or if he moved close and wanted me, or if he was kind and loving, I wouldn't be excited at all.

"When I was little, I was squatting all the time. I mean, there are lots of snapshots of me squatting. In one, I am about three, with my father. You can see my genitals." Associations to urinating as a child, boys standing to pee while the girls, embarrassed, go off into the bushes.

Actions. These can be habitual, such as the way one gesticulates (or does not) when talking, giggles nervously, knots one's eyebrows all day as if in pain, lifts one's pinkie to express delicacy while eating like a pig, thrusts out the chest or hunches the shoulders to emphasize or minimize breasts; or engages in disruptive, nonhabitual behavior like tics or parapraxes.

But if all that mental activity described above can be subsumed under "microdot," is not the word so imprecise as to be useless? I think not quite. In using the term, I am not thereby suggesting that a microdot is either a newly found theoretic or clinical entity. It is, I need to repeat, simply a figure of speech that adds connotations to such closely related words as "fantasy" and "script." These latter do not make us think, as does "microdot," of a *mass* of memories, scripts, themes, fantasies, affects, all tremendously packed and purposefully organized.

Other metaphors such as "the tip of the iceberg" also imply that mental elements have more bulk than appears,* but these others do not also imply the desire to shape the mass for narcissistic purposes or that the shaping is so logical, so carefully and efficiently guided.

I have only described microdots; I cannot explain how they work.[13] That "how" will be most important. The "hard" theorist would like to know what energies, structures, transformations, vectors, natural laws, or neurophysiologic underpinnings produce a result like a microdot.[14]

But I want to move in a direction that in recent years has concerned psychoanalytic theorists and struggle with the question inherent in the microdot: Who is the agent who constructs these clever cognitions? Who makes microdots?

NOTE

Although affects are scarcely mentioned herein, they are a fundamental though noncognitive part of fantasies. Experiencing affects puts life into fantasies, establishing their meaning and value. I know nothing more about affects than what others have already said, but the omission of an extended discussion here does not indicate that I think them less significant than scripts, only that it would force one more round of mind-body ruminations. Perhaps affects are microdots to the extent

*How rich and vague sometimes is the language analysts must speak. How would we manage without metaphors: "elements," "bulk," "appears," even the designation "analysis."

that they are inseparable from their cognitive element—the fantasies. As Greenson says, "One can describe moods in terms of objects. They can be personified. The patient described above, for example, would not become angry, but would become his angry father. It seems to me that with moods, this is usually the case. Patients do not just become depressed, but they become the rejected little boy they once were in childhood. The anxious patient is not just a frightened adult but the scared little child of the past. Moods are not only derived from the internal representatives of external objects, but are often the representatives of one's own past state of mind; one's conception of oneself in the past. All of these considerations lead me to conclude that there is a very close connection between alternations in the cathexis of internal objects and moods. One's outlook on the world and one's conception of oneself are determined by the status of the various internalized objects."[15]

Also, affects are microdots in being *compound;* there are no pure affects, except, perhaps, in earliest infancy or profound regression, as in organic brain syndrome. Nor is an affect ever exactly the same the next time or any other time it occurs: there are, for instance, as many different forms—conscious experiences—of anxiety as there are times one feels anxiety in a lifetime.

11

Who Is Belle?

MY THERAPEUTIC PURPOSE as an analyst is not to cure symptoms. There are other techniques, quicker and more tidy, that compete well for that market. The strength of analysis is to help us find ourselves, to reveal the person we are when not hiding. To the extent that we do that uncovering, we know we are intact, are less likely to blame others, to be victims, to say "I can't" when we mean "I won't," to be enraged and bitter, or to fetishize others.

Since Belle did not have neurotic symptoms such as phobias, severe anxiety, or depressions, since the worst she suffered was a sense of the wastage of her life (which is more a dull ache than severe pain), and since she was curious enough to try to discover why, analysis was appropriate. The therapeutic question for her and me was, then: Who is Belle? But that is a metaphysical issue, too. Let us look at it.

Our Belle has two aspects. First, there is the person who experienced herself as Belle, whom I knew and responded to. But also there is the complex biologic machine that was given the label "Belle" at birth and that was the ultimate source of the group of functions known as Belle. This notorious "mind-body problem," discussed whenever scholars are concerned with the major issues in the realm of the mental, lay in wait for Freud from his earliest work to the end. And it lies in wait still.

Freud's magnificent struggle with this problem is best seen in his study of dreams. There is no need for one more review of that achievement. Let me turn only to an issue he left unsolved that has gradually moved to the center of philosophers' and analytic theorists' concern. Freud said the dream was the product of agencies, systems, independent minds within the mind, each pursuing its own needs. The new wave of analytic theorists, however, say there are no such agencies. Rather, we are biologic information-processing machines, preset by heredity and constitution and constantly primed by each day's extra- and intracorporeal input. In this chapter, I shall rummage through both of these collections of ideas, selecting from each in order to find a state of—I hope—enlightened uncertainty: that a someone who is really a something that is really a someone does the work.

Who Does the Dreaming; Who Runs the Show?

Microdotting—the metaphor for the process of creating the present instant by sorting many memories of real events, past fantasies, and affects, putting these all together so rapidly, and making them fit so exactly—is a way of naming the process that constructs a dream: that instant just before the manifest dream is dreamed. The intelligence, speed, efficiency, and slyness in getting what we want are a work of genius. Imagine having these powers consciously available in the daytime.[1] Who is the marvel who does this? Not I, certainly. I could not consciously make myself think so clearly, effectively, spectacularly, even if my life depended on it.

The search for our invisible genius, this conspirator, is everywhere in Freud and other analytic writers. A typical quotation reminds us how Freud tried to solve this by giving independent minds to the agencies ego, superego, and id: "The id sends part of this libido out into erotic object-cathexes, whereupon the ego, now grown stronger, tries to get hold of this object-libido and to force itself on the id as a love-object."[2]

Can we find a clearer way to describe how we work mentally? The data we have on Belle's excitement should help us. It, we saw, was fueled by what she experienced as multiple inner people and multiple scripts. She discovered in analysis that she had gradually put her daydream together, the steps in the process taken with some aspects occurring with her full awareness. Yet, the script completed, she had succeeded in not knowing her erotism was her own invention. We must, now as we struggle to understand her excitement, bear with the complexity of people's ability to be aware and not be aware in the same instant. "Who runs her show"—who runs ours—is not a problem for theorists only. It is the central moral question of our lives, obscured but not invisible in each moment of the day. When we cracked apart the instant—the microdot—of Belle's excitement, we found it was constructed of many artifacts: mysteries, illusions, safety factors, reversals of real traumas to phony victories, revenge against invented villains, fetishes. Once these were made visible—inspected by us in the analytic process—she could no longer maintain the impact, the wholeness, the realness of her daydream. Now she knew too much: why she needed *that* story, what were its parts, how and when those parts were chosen, and what functions the daydream served in repairing the past.

She knew then that it was a pack of lies that nonetheless had its truth: the erotic sensations that resulted. And the script of each lie, and each defensive maneuver that slanted the form of that script, was supported by motives, memories, and themes that in large part had been unconscious, unavailable to the Belle who was trying to fathom them.

We are again into the old problems: What do we mean by intentionality ("A notion both commonplace and unfathomable"[3]), by free will, responsibility, to know, to choose, motive, motivation, need, desire, wish? And so the question: Since this (any) cognitive act is purposive and motivated, *who* or *what* is the motivator? At this point, we face those imprecise words "self," "I," "identity." Who thinks (does the work of putting the thought together) when I think (experience that the thought has appeared "in my mind")? When I think, I neither sense nor otherwise catch subjectively the functioning—the dynamics, the action of the decision-making—or the creation of my thoughts, microdots, story lines, or manifest dreams.[4] With the dream, when I awake, I know I was the dreamer. But when asleep, I am only the major participant, as in the daytime, when events impinge on my receptivity without my feeling they are created by me. So if you tell me (if I myself believe) that I created the dream, I take your (my) word for it only because I like you. You have not proved it; that is not the way *I* experience it. I don't ever understand my dream in the first moment of awakening, but either my companion the dreamer (he/she/it) does or the whole theory is nonsense and the dream is random, unmotivated: central-nervous-system fireworks; no symbolism, no communication, no wish fulfillment, no plan, no awareness of past or future.

In the reverse position, found at times in psychosis, religion, philosophy, or information-processing theory, I may either feel I am inventing it all or that someone or something else is inventing it all, even inventing me. We shall get to that.

I dreamed the dream in that I witnessed it, but the "I" who is I did not dream the dream in the sense of manufacturing it. (This is what Colby—see Appendix A—calls an enigma of pronouns: these two uses of "I" refer to two different beings, a subjective versus an objective "I.") To my dreaming it they tell me (and I agree) that the following contributed: my past life; unresolved problems; chronic desires; the day's residue memories; somatic perceptions that rub against or even pierce the dream's walls; the brain, which shoots into the action the chemistry of the REM, as if these were like the messages of a full bladder (caution:

slippery analogy); and perceptions from the outside (and even here someone, something, decides which to let into the dream and which to deny entrée). But who runs the show when I am asleep, and when I am awake? Fantasies don't; desires don't; the id doesn't; instincts don't; narcissism doesn't; thoughts don't; affects don't; beliefs don't; primary processes don't. Is it no one? Nothing? Impersonal forces? The brain? Energies? Cathexes? What are the cathexes of the cathexes; who moves them around? What is a prescient cathexis? Who decides which affect is appropriate for this moment? Who decides now is the time for a spot of repression? Who decides that the arm will be paralyzed; if I, then I am malingering: guilty. But if *I* don't decide, I passively suffer a conversion reaction and remain innocent.

Ricoeur asks, "How do desires achieve speech?"[5] But of course we know, and he knows, that desires do not possess the functions necessary for speech; only people do.

Belle, cold and lonely as she lies in her memories,* holds herself in her arms and is a bit comforted; is "she" her arms or her torso? At another time one hand rubs the other, again to comfort her. But which hand is "her"? She looks in the mirror at her breasts and becomes sexually excited. Who looks; whose breasts; who is excited?

There are moments when I—as do you—glimpse a shadow of the answer. Usually I drop into sleep like a stone, but occasionally it takes a few moments. Then, in a hypnagogic state, I experience thinking becoming random thoughts becoming free associations becoming the earliest state of dreaming when I still know I have not yet left. Throughout these preliminaries, I am I. Then I go over the edge.

I awaken at the beach and realize that, asleep a moment before, I did not hear the surf. In a variant of this, I slide toward being awake; but still asleep—lightly—I sense not hearing the surf and so, instantly, now hear it.

At times, having awakened a few seconds later, I know that the moment before, all my muscles had fallen loose: I had just escaped from my body. (Physiologists pick this up in the laboratory with their jaw-muscle measurement.) At any rate, there is almost an awareness of the moment when, no longer the agent, I become, rather, the recipient of my thinking. Waking thought, too, can feel unwilled: free association, hallucination, inspiration.

We spend time at this border between the willed and the spontaneous when a word, a name, a memory, or the solution to a problem is on the tip of our tongue but does not come forth. Then also we feel ourselves

*Schafer warns us there are no memories; only "I remember."

partly the agent—we try to will ourselves to get it out—and partly the passive victim of an invisible part of ourselves that does not free the thought so that we again own it.

I do not usually (ever?[6]) experience myself in the process of forgetting, though I am sometimes conscious of turning aside from a thought or mood (by changing the subject, as in going to the movies or not concentrating on someone who is talking to me, or by avoiding in advance people or situations that will force me not to forget). But the exact moment that forgetting occurs must be one I do not notice; if I do notice, then I am not forgetting. So: who does the forgetting? The same with remembering. Who brings the thought up into my consciousness? The brain? Brains do not remember. They do (are) physiology: *I* remember. Do *I* remember? What does it mean, to remember? Is remembering the process that leads to the memory being available, or is it the subjective state wherein the product of that process is recognized? In the first connotation, my machinery is in action; in the second, it is *I* who remember.

For whatever it is worth, my *experience* is that I am the responsible agent of my body's movements (when they are not reflex), sometimes the agent of my thoughts, and almost never the agent of my dreams or emotions.

Can we catch this brilliant creature whose thought processes move within a split second, who can pull, from a cabinet of memories— events, vocabulary, syntaxes, styles, emotions, the whole mental content we summarize with the word "mind"—just those elements needed to construct a story?[7] This mind within my mind, this fellow without form, knows in advance of the manifest dream what he will use to portray his intent. And as the dream unfolds, this silent intelligence continuously monitors the story to modify it moment by moment as indicated.

What does that mean, "indicated"? Indications have to indicate themselves to someone or something that comprehends. Freud tried to give structure to this invisible process by talking first of a censor, or a psychic force, that does this or that, and then of an ego or superego. But he never discovered the mischief-maker; he just kept inventing names for it.

Do we all suffer multiple personalities?

Sometimes I think I almost glimpse it. If only we could take its picture; we need a cloud chamber for psychoanalysis. Perhaps hypnosis could help, or a renewed attack on dissociative phenomena such as trances. Subliminal awareness is another of the borderlands that touch on the problem area.[8] "Subliminal" implies that my sense of choice is blurred across an expanse that stretches from what I can make aware if I attend, to that which slips by below conscious perception but is nonetheless perceived.[9] For instance, with a tachistoscope, one can flash an image so fast that the observer is not conscious of having seen anything, and yet he will respond to the "unseen" image. That is the point—the instant—to be understood. Is it to be described in brain or in mind terms? How did the observer know what the image was? Was he aware of it? What is "to be aware"?

It may be appropriate here to ask, as Colby does (see Appendix A), what is the function of consciousness. We could consider it a mere epiphenomenon: no matter how loud or complex to us, the ocean's roar serves no function for the ocean. With what, Colby would ask, does consciousness provide us that could not be accomplished without consciousness? My answer is the same, I think, as Freud's. The value of consciousness is pleasure and pain, an effective motivating system: the present models for behavior, such as computers and their programs, will be closer approximations when they can itch as well as scratch.

We have such heavy problems with "to know," "to be aware," "to understand," "to sense," "to feel." In a state of concentration on other aspects of reality, as can occur in combat or in athletic events, one may not be aware of pain until the event is over. And then we not only feel the pain but realize we were feeling it all along. One of the commonest experiences in psychoanalysis is finally to remember fully. At that moment, we may say, "But I knew that all the time."

I try to puzzle out the problem whether I am in control of my thinking or whether that sense of willing is only an illusion. As I track back on a phenomenon that comfortably fits the term "mental," I eventually bump up against physiology. That happens especially when I theorize on the earliest processes of infancy (see Appendix B). There, one finds situations easily described in physiologic terms, but right at that point the vocabulary begins shifting to the mental. For instance, in the first months of life, along with the maturing of the central nervous system, something is slowly appearing that was not visible before: mind, soul, personality, ego, self, awareness, consciousness, identity, thought, fantasy, will. It is, of course, not a "something," any more than energy in the physical world is a "something." Nonetheless, it is clearly emerging from, absolutely connected with, a function of yet not the same as, and utterly dependent on a brain matrix. In those first months of infancy, there seems to have been a shift in hierarchies. At first the infant made its decisions in the absence of a mental act we could call "choice," but after a while, the vocabulary of will is the one needed. At bottom all is brain and its function, but that explanation is of little service when we are confronted with the subjective experience of choice.

A matter that especially makes a person believe that his behavior was motivated and cleverly defended is analysis. After a resistance has been worked through, a forbidden impulse of which I was not aware becomes conscious, and I sense not only the impulse and its goals but also the techniques I used to keep myself ("my conscious self") uninformed. As this awareness expands, previous behavior is more and more well informed and is felt now to have been well informed even then when it seemed to be out of awareness. I finally comprehend what was formerly only dimly seen: that I had my reasons—that I knew I had my reasons —for not knowing why I did such-and-such or failed to do such-and-such or why I did it only on the periphery of awareness, carefully deflecting attention to other, "more important" activities. The fog lifts, repression turns into suppression, and finally, with full visibility, at worst only to lying. Of course, repression is not the same as lying[10] (though Sartre rather thinks it is[11]); I only mean that in trying to achieve the same ignorance now, I would be lying, having lost, at least in this sector of life, the microdotting capacity called repression.

You see then that if, in erotic life, a microdot is a condensation of a carefully selected group of fantasies organized to tell a story that provokes excitement, we are faced with the question, How is such a complex, instantaneous, creative act done, and who does it? The way I have presented Belle's story has answered (too confidently): she did it. Analysis slowly took the microdot apart and showed us how her conscious choices (not only unconscious dynamics), her skillful creative work, led to the realized daydream. Belle wrote her script; Belle, the girl with consciousness, sense of identity, chooser of scripts, purveyor to herself of good and evil, not the Belle who is just a biologic information-processing machine.

One sign that a patient has joined the analytic process rather than being simply a physical presence on the couch is a change in the dreaming. A new kind of wishing is added: the desire to use dreams in order to communicate with oneself and with the analyst.[12] So here again may be a hint of a something that is as smart as a someone, who works for the someone—the patient—just as the patient would. We can say that "someone" ("I," "you," "he") is just a sloppy way of conceptualizing an aggregate of somethings, one of which is the state of awareness labeled "I." That means, though, that I am a function, not a person; and I am not ready for that yet. That is a displacement more painful than those caused by Freud's pantheon of shakers: Copernicus, Darwin, and Freud. But the neurophysiologists, ethologists, cyberneticists, and computer philosophers are pushing us into that corner. They are telling us that we, dreams, consciousness, and all, are an "it," or even less—just the rumbling of a subterranean machine.

Perhaps, then, there is no "I" or "self" anywhere; perhaps I am an "it," or worse, just the emanation of functions, an algebraic sum of forces, each of which is without choice but all of which add together to create a neurophysiologically driven, instinct-driven, reflex-driven, logic-driven slug, one of whose qualities—pretty, like the color of a butterfly's wings—has the appearance of free will, gives the illusion of being "I." That is one way to handle the problem; yet because the illusion that I am I is differently constructed from the illusion that he is he, I have the illusion that I exist as myself.

Someday a neurophysiologist will present the story of another Belle and show that every bit of it depended on cell function, synapses, and communication nets. As he tampers with her brain hardware—and as that hardware modifies itself—he will change (someday, not quite yet) every detail of her script and even give her new characters and plots by direct chemical and electrical inputs to the brain, without her having brought them there through life experience. What will he think of the concept of free will? He will surely know it was her illusion.*

Let me review philosophic and analytic arguments that underlie the attempt to answer "Who is Belle?" and to indicate why the struggle has been important to analysis from the start.

Sartre discusses the difference between a lie, in which I hide the truth from another, and *mauvaise foi*—"bad faith" (self-deception[13])— wherein I hide the truth from myself, a process analysts label "defense" or "defense mechanisms."†

---

*But what about his scientific work, which will now illuminate the darkness of our understanding of brain function? Was his research not also the product of his illusion that he wanted to do the work? Could he have done it without that illusion?

†In using the concept of defense, we refer to mental mechanisms that try to protect one from both external and internal dangers. I think, however, that the mechanisms at work beyond our awareness aim only to protect us from our own—intrapsychic—beliefs, expectations, desires, truths. (The outside world is handled well enough by our consciously keeping our mouths shut, except when, as with projection, we cannot tell inside from outside.) It sometimes seems as if the history of mankind is the unfolding of the story of deception—of ourselves and others—that deception was not only the force behind the events as they happened but also behind their subsequent reporting. The essential psychologic feature that separates humans from the other organisms is our capacity for trickery, a product of the growth and evolution of the brain: the self-preservative drive in animals has evolved into the drive—often more important in our species than life itself —to deceive. If hiding one's motives has become the fundament of human existence, then—as I think can be demonstrated—we are stuck, when we try to cure this malignant state, with techniques already contaminated with deception: language, art, humor. We seek the truth by artifice. Our only other hope is the scientific method—techniques of objective confirmation that try to undercut even the researcher's own biases. But even that seems doomed, for the technologic applications may kill us all.

It follows first that the one to whom the lie is told and the one who lies are one and the same person, which means that I must know in my capacity as deceiver the truth which is hidden from me in my capacity as the one deceived. Better yet I must know the truth very exactly *in order* to conceal it more carefully—and this not at two different moments, which at a pinch would allow us to reestablish a semblance of duality—but in the unitary structure of a single project. . . . [But] that which affects itself with bad faith must be conscious (of) its bad faith since the being of consciousness is consciousness of being. It appears then that I must be in good faith, at least to the extent that I am conscious of my bad faith. But then this whole psychic system is annihilated. We must agree in fact that if I deliberately and cynically attempt to lie to myself, I fail completely in this undertaking; the lie falls back and collapses beneath my look; it is ruined *from behind* by the very conciousness of lying to myself which pitilessly constitutes itself well within my project as its very condition.[14]

Yes. It does sound absurd. Yet I think it happens somewhat like that. The liar and the one lied to are the same person, or more precisely, can know they are the same.

Sartre gives us another example of the problem of using a system in which there are these multiple minds within:

If we reject the language and the materialistic mythology of psychoanalysis, we perceive that the censor in order to apply its activity with discernment must know what it is repressing. In fact if we abandon all the metaphors representing the repression as the impact of blind forces, we are compelled to admit that the censor must choose and in order to choose must be aware of so doing. How could it happen otherwise that the censor allows lawful sexual impulses to pass through, that it permits needs (hunger, thirst, sleep) to be expressed in clear consciousness? And how are we to explain that it can relax its surveillance, that it can even be deceived by the disguises of the instinct? But it is not sufficient that it discern the condemned drives; it must also apprehend them *as to be repressed,* which implies in it at the very least an awareness of its activity. In a word, how could the censor discern the impulses needing to be repressed without being conscious of discerning them? How can we conceive of a knowledge which is ignorant of itself? To know is to know that one knows, said Alain. Let us say rather: All knowing is consciousness of knowing. Thus the resistance of the patient implies on the level of the censor an awareness of the thing repressed as such, a comprehension of the end toward which the questions of the psychoanalyst are leading, and an act of synthetic connection by which it compares the *truth* of the repressed complex to the psychoanalytic hypothesis which aims at it. These various operations in their turn imply that the censor is conscious (of) itself. But what type of self-consciousness can the censor have? It must be the consciousness (of) being conscious of the drive to be repressed, but precisely *in order not to be conscious of it.* What does this mean if not that the censor is in bad faith?[15]

Perhaps the solution to the Russellian paradox "I am a liar"* lies less in philosophic diligence and more in psychology. That is, the word "I" in that statement actually refers to only one of the several "I's" residing in the same body. One of them lies while another tells the truth. That is not complicated; is it not the way we experience our conscience? A woman invented "I am a liar" as a belief, a microdot of identity, in early childhood.[16] It served as an announcement of surrender to her frozen, accusing mother; a sarcasm that secretly attacked mother; a propitiation of her conscience; and a sadomasochistic maneuver that, with the slightest twist in wording, inflection, context, or facial expression, would make all who knew her fascinated, confused, loving, despairing, hopeful, irritated, rejecting. The patient had all these options, in differing degrees and states of awareness, in one ball of affect (microdot) at the same instant. That paradox is the source of a rogue's charm.

Belle tricked Belle. The Belle who was tricked was meanwhile tricking (the "inner object" or fantasy that represents) her mother in her mind. And that inner representation of Mother was also hidden inside the Director, who Belle now knows is a trick. And on and on and on: endless permutations; and all are tricks. Yet the final product is no trick: capillary engorgement, vaginal transudation, clitoral erection, tachycardia, humiliation, anger, and someday, perhaps, pregnancy and an infant.

There could be practical reasons for persisting in these questions. It is often noted that there are powerful forces in us, not available to our will, that can turn the world around. Think of the strengths, physical and mental, we mobilize when in extreme danger, in a trance, under hypnosis, or otherwise "possessed": feats of memory or mathematical calculation; scientific or artistic inspiration; voodoo deaths or miraculous cures; bleeding from the palms on Good Friday; walking on red-hot coals. There may be no such thing as free will, but if I could perform these acts when I chose, you might admit that that was a damn good imitation of will. Would I not then have more power over external reality?

That hope seems a good reason to find who is the dreamer. (But I dare not say it is a *moral* reason: if we all had such powers our world might come to an end.)

---

*If I am a liar when I say I am, then I am telling the truth and so am not a liar.

Personology

Being a clinician, Freud never could shake off the problem of the multiple voices—personages—all present and speaking at different levels of consciousness within the same person. And of course, he did not want to. No practicing analyst fails to sense those voices. As Ricoeur says in his examination of *The Ego and the Id:*

> The agencies of the second topography are not so much places as roles in a personology. Ego, id, and superego are variations on the personal pronoun or grammatical subject; what is involved is the relation of the personal to the anonymous and the suprapersonal in the individual's coming-to-be.[17]

Yet when Freud says that "the ego is not master in its own house"[18] we now ask, Who is the master, then? What house? Who created the neurosis and who took over the house?

Many of today's best theorists scorn Freud's personology, which exudes the sinful anthropomorphizing, his finding of mini-minds within, working independently of each other, going about their business for their own reasons. I cannot claim not to have been warned when I agree with Freud that the mind is thus populated, that when we dream at night, the people inside come out and play. Their names, however, are not *the* conscious, *the* preconscious, *the* unconscious; or the ego, the superego, the id; or the libido; or the death instinct; or the primary process; or the secondary process. Nor are they "agencies" and "processes," for these also do not decide, think, want, demand, say, feel, or need.[19] (Analytic theory would do better to restrict itself here to its vocabulary of inner objects.)

We know they are there because we find their tracks in the scripts of our daydreams, unconscious fantasies, object choices, and daily behaviors. The problem, I keep insisting, is that the writer-director does not appear. When, for instance, I ask, "Who is the dreamer?" the fact that I cannot answer should suggest there may be no "who." But if dreams are motivated, then *something*[20] is the thing that does the work. Ricoeur says:

> Freud's theory of the ego is at once very liberating with respect to the illusions of consciousness and very disappointing in its inability to give the *I* of *I think* some sort of meaning. . . . Psychoanalysis would be mythology, the worst of all, if it would consist in making the unconscious think.[21]

That is, make it an "I." For his "unconscious" does not think.[22] Though it does.[23]

Ricoeur goes on:

> The expressive force of the word "id"—even more than that of the term "unconscious"—guards us from the naive realism of giving the unconscious a consciousness, of reduplicating consciousness in consciousness. The unconscious is id and nothing but id.

No. Even Freud corrected that, in *The Ego and the Id.*

Yet there *are* these inner creatures, their tales spun out, often several at the same instant and somehow managing to not know of or at least to not acknowledge each other's presence. They act as if they were separate fragments, "splinters of mind," unaware of the others who are simultaneously playing out their own scenes. Experiencing these many characters is surely blatant anthropomorphism, seen most clearly in multiple personality or in psychosis, in which the other part-selves are allowed equal consciousness so that, at best, the part called "I" is no longer ascendant but only one among many.

Anthropomorphizing bothers most of our best theorists these days.[24] For instance, says Schafer, the trouble with Freud's use of "energic-functional conceptualizations" (such as cathexis) is that "although the language is less dramatic, the mind remains an assembly of minds working together and at cross purposes."[25] That is it, exactly. But while for Schafer this is a fatal flaw, for me "an assembly of minds" is a naturalistic description that any theory must work with, not ignore or deny.

Schafer accurately points to techniques we use to disclaim action, to deny our own responsibility. One of these, he says, is the word "mind" as in "I must have been out of my mind" or "I am of two minds about it." There are times, however, when the subjective experience really is that there are different minds at work within oneself, as, for example, in the voice of conscience or the co-consciousness of multiple personalities. Schafer's complaint here is my affirmation.

This comes up again when, disagreeing with Lewin, he says, "Mind is not, as he . . . suggests, a room or a suite of two rooms; and there is no man or maniken looking in or looking on, or guarding doorways against entities at once mechanical and furtive in their actions."[26] Yet there is someone on guard, though I agree mind is not a room. (It is, rather, this instant's complex of fantasies.*) Which is not to argue with Schafer's fine comment: "Mind is something we do; it is neither something we have nor something we are or are not related to or in possession of."[27] The difference in perspective is between being subject or object: I can experience myself as being of two minds (or at least, two

*Schafer would more accurately say "this instant's complex fantasizing."

impulses or two scripts); an observer sees that "mind" as what I do.

Using multiple levels of fantasy systems (another way of talking of multiple people within, mini-minds, anthropomorphizing, or scripts), we can look at a concept like "resistance" and be on ground familiar to analysts: the patient consciously wants to speak, a bit less consciously thinks it may not be safe, and on down into different levels of consciousness in which the analyst is seen as father, mother, husband, siblings, children, and who knows what else. There is a separate script available for each role assigned. (Schafer describes these multiple levels as "a family of actions, each in its own mode rather than . . . one action carried on . . . with mixed emotions."[28]) In the same instant, the patient takes on different roles to play in all these scripts. This may be complicated, but it can—sometimes—be demonstrated.

What, then, is conflict?[29] Conflict is not forces or structures in disagreement (though forces—drives—propel the action), for forces or structures cannot have the sense to disagree with each other. Rather, conflict takes the form of people within (including the multiple people who stand for me), simultaneously living out scripts, each separate from and often incompatible with the others, each reaching for different goals, trying to satisfy different wishes. Ultimately, I think, it is different personalities, each an aspect of me.*

Psychoanalytic anthropomorphisms have several functions. In one type, we anthropomorphize our theories: for example, ego, a theoretic construct that is treated as if it were an inner self. In a second, as Schafer warns us, we anthropomorphize as a semantic device for reducing responsibility, as when we say, "My mind told me to." But the third type is a clinical fact: people, in sensing themselves, know, more or less consciously, that they are made up of rather separate aspects that can feel like separate people acting autonomously.[30] But we should not anthropomorphize so as to sound scientific, as when we talk of a cathexis that makes decisions.[31] The following, full of sound and fury, will be scientific to some, but to me it is a shambles of undefined terms, untestable assumptions, and alleged dynamics so global in explanatory power that—as the adherents of this language use these concepts—it could describe everything from the development of the superego to embarrassment that one's fly is open. And what anthropomorphizing.†

> Anxiety appears in conjunction with the oral sadism as an expression of the ego's helplessness when faced with self-destructive instinctual urgings. These promptings arise from the rage experienced as a direct result

---

*The more familiar analytic language here is "inner representation," "identifications," "introjects."

†The authors are herein describing a writer's ideas, not necessarily subscribing to them.

of the libido being unsatisfied. The ego splits the impulses so that they defend against each other, giving rise to the superego. Once this split occurs, fear of self-extermination is projected onto external objects as a wish to destroy the unsatisfying object. All of these developments continue until the end of the anal-sadistic stage. Since the superego has been formed solely on partial incorporations into the psyche of early preverbal and preconceptual impulse images, object relations are confused and partially directed toward fantasy objects during the anal-sadistic stage. Significantly, the individual's own impulses, not parental demands, are instrumental in superego formation.[32]

Fairbairn is another who has struggled with metapsychology, bound on the one hand by a need to adhere to structural theory and on the other by an even greater need to break free to mini-minds (anthropomorphs) that match subjective experience. Working with the same clinical impressions we all have, he tries to think through the issues raised by people's sense of being divided within. Taking a clue from Freud's revolutionary shift in theory—the concept of splitting of the ego—he moves in directions similar to Melanie Klein's:

> Some measure of splitting of the ego is invariably present at the deepest mental level—or (to express the same thing in terms borrowed from Melanie Klein) *the basic position in the psyche is invariably a schizoid position.* . . . There are probably few "normal" people who have never at any time in their lives experienced an unnatural state of calm and detachment in face of some serious crisis, or a transient sense of "looking on at oneself" in some embarrassing or paralysing situation; and probably most people have had some experience of that strange confusion of past and present, or of phantasy and reality, known as "déjà vu." . . . there is one universal phenomenon, however, which proves quite conclusively that everyone without exception is schizoid [ego-split] at the deepest levels—viz. the dream; for, as Freud's researches have shown, the dreamer himself is commonly represented in the dream by two or more separate figures. . . . the universal phenomenon of "the super-ego" as described by Freud must also be interpreted as implying the presence of a split in the ego; for, in so far as "the super-ego" is regarded as an ego-structure capable of distinction from "the ego" as such, its very existence *ipso facto* provides evidence that a schizoid position [splitting of the ego] has been established.[33]

His description of a patient who uses intellectualizing shows again the business of splitting oneself into several partial selves:

> The explanation of this phenomenon would appear to be that the ego (or, as I should prefer to say, *the central ego*) does not participate in the phantasies described except as a recording agent. When such a situation

arises, the central ego, so to speak, sits back in the dress-circle and describes the dramas enacted upon the stage of inner reality without any effective participation in them. At the same time it derives considerable narcissistic satisfaction from being the recorder of remarkable events and identifying itself with the analyst as observer while asserting a superiority over the analyst as mere observer by reason of the fact that it is not merely observing, but also furnishing the material for observation.[34]

In other words, fantasies.

In his—to me—desperate attempt to convert the humble stuff of fantasies into grander theoretic structures, Fairbairn invents: the pristine whole unitary ego, the central ego, the internal saboteur, the libidinal ego, the antilibidinal ego, the rejecting object, the internal exciting object (the internal saboteur as "an aggressive, persecutory ego").[35] This is strained.[36] Transactional analysts have tried to do the same, though keeping their labels ("games people play") close to conscious experience: "I'm only trying to help you," "Look how hard I've tried," and so on.

Does Psychic Energy Think?

If we talk metapsychologically about repression, we have to bring in an energy somehow shifted about to defend weak spots in the line so that access of thoughts to consciousness is stopped. Then we need the agencies—ego, id, and superego—that draw on the reserves of energy in order to lock the process in place. I cannot absolutely disprove that there is a palpable "psychic energy" that "cathects" around "psychic structure," blinking on and off like a Christmas tree. But even if such an energy system exists, "repression" does not decide what it will do unless you think repression has a memory, a point of view, a wish— all the attributes of a person. It sounds right to say, "He repressed that thought," but it should be embarrassing to be caught saying, "The thought was removed by repression and kept unconscious by a counter-cathexis."

Is this hair-splitting? I think not. First, the present style, metapsychology, while giving a pseudoscientific ring to theory, has produced no substance greater than more theory.[37] Second, by remaining clinical, searching for observations, and then developing ways to deal reliably with the observations, we may unveil the parts of ourselves that move behavior.

Gill has often said this, most recently as follows:

What psychoanalysis needs is systematic research on the psychoanalytic situation in which the variables studied are those of clinical psychological psychoanalysis. I am of the opinion that the backwardness of such research is in significant measure due to our metapsychology. On the one hand, metapsychology permits psuedoexplanations in the natural-science realm to shut off investigation in the realm of meaning. On the other hand, the effort to shoehorn psychoanalytic data into the mold of natural-science investigation has been so unsuccessful that researchers and would-be researchers are demoralized. The field is now largely content with metapsychological speculation, on the one hand, and impressionistic clinical accounts, on the other, on the ground that psychoanalysis cannot be systematically investigated. I believe that a disentangling of metapsychology and psychoanalytic psychology and the carrying out of research in terms of concepts of human meaning would radically change psychoanalytic research and bring psychoanalysis to its rightful place among the sciences.[38]

When I use this clinical mode with its "self," "identity," and "scripts" elements, I find that independent streams of thinking, in the strict sense of "thinking," are always present at any moment. The one that is conscious is the algebraic sum of the others. Even when the conscious thought is muddled, it is the resultant (barring gross brain disease) of a number of simultaneous (nonconscious) thoughts being contradictory, overlapping, or tangential to each other. But each of these component thoughts is in itself (if we could listen) clear, logical, coherent, and purposeful.

Psychoanalysts are in a predicament. On the one hand we believe most behavior is motivated, consciously, preconsciously, and unconsciously. On the other, the nonconscious motivations do not speak out, either to ourselves or to others. Since motivation and meaning cannot reside in forces, attributes, or structures, a system that uses the latter vocabulary for explanation will always miss the essential nature of motivation and meaning, that motivation is *by someone* and has meaning for that someone.* "Psychic energy" can no more have motives or discern meanings than can electricity or light or protons.

Here is an example of how "science" is injected into what otherwise would be a clear description and valuable discovery. Freud is talking of "the affectionate current" that develops in the child in regard to its "primary object-choice":

---

*In the sense that analysts use the word "motivation," the question of "who" cannot be avoided. We are not talking of motivation as, in some metaphysical sense, one might in saying that red blood cells are "motivated" to carry oxygen in order to keep tissues alive. Nor, I think, are we into the teleology expressed when one says that God or Nature or life or Eros or *élan vital* intelligently guides the processes of evolution. Our word "motivation" connotes a mental act, a choice in which possibilities are weighed and an algebraic sum achieved, for the purpose of gratifying a need.

These affectionate fixations of the child persist throughout childhood, and continually carry along with them erotism, which is consequently diverted from its sexual aims. Then at the age of puberty they are joined by the powerful "sensual" current which no longer mistakes its aims. It never fails, apparently, to follow the earlier paths and to cathect the objects of the primary infantile choice with quotas of libido that are now far stronger.[39]

This does not describe a child with motives, who sees a world that has meaning. Instead the child has been reduced to a hunk of machinery impelled by an energy labeled "libido." When Freud talks of "the powerful 'sensual' current," "current" is one of those innumerable metaphors that help us communicate. In fact "the current" is not a movement of anything as in a flow of water or electricity. What we are really referring to are subjective experiences, more or less poetically rendered as "current."

But Freud slips across the metaphor's space, and if we do not pay attention, the metaphor "current" is converted into the physical energic state "current" (itself a metaphor from flowing water). Yet all he really was saying was that with the increase in sexual desire at puberty one turns back, and more intensely, to the people erotized in early life. A fine discovery; but who needs cathexis?

Freud goes on:

Here, however, it runs up against the obstacles that have been erected in the meantime by the barrier against incest; consequently it will make efforts to pass on from these objects which are unsuitable in reality, and find a way as soon as possible to other, extraneous objects with which a real sexual life may be carried on.

Motivation and meaning have been removed from the child and put into "it," the current. Now currents have motives, read the world from their own perspective, find meaning in objects, and propel the child who is possessed by the "currents" into behavior. "Well," you say, "one must not take such expressions literally; Freud so often noted he was working with metaphors. These are just reflections of writing style necessary for starting discourse on difficult subjects." Yes and no. We can quote dozens of his remarks to illustrate both moods: that a something, such as psychic energy, is a thing, or that it is only a way of speaking. But if you take the trouble,[40] you can show that he believed these were not just metaphors but facts of physics and physiology existing in the organism.

Despite these disagreements with Freud, I hope nonetheless it is not confusing to agree with him that we live psychically as if we contained many people. The raw experience called "current" is actually the affects with their inner people moving through scenarios. They populate that child's fantasies, conscious and unconscious, representing real, remembered people and also those who are usually labeled "I" but who stand for different versions of that complicated, algebraic sum we experience as "I."

A few sentences later, Freud says:

> The libido turns away from reality, it is taken over by imaginative activity (the process of introversion), strengthens the images of the first sexual objects and becomes fixated to them.

How busy "libido" is; it certainly has a mind of its own.

And in a moment we read of "the masturbatory activity carried out by the sensual current": a sensual current that masturbates?

Ricoeur states the problem Freud was forever attacking with his metapsychology but never solved:

> What is the status of representation or ideas in relation to the notions of instinct, aim of instinct, and affect? How can an interpretation of meaning through meaning be integrated with the economics of cathexis, withdrawal of cathexis, anticathexis? At first glance, there seems to be an antinomy between an explanation governed by the principles of the metapsychology and an interpretation that necessarily moves among meanings and not among forces, among representations or ideas and not among instincts. As I see it, the whole problem of the Freudian epistemology may be centralized in a single question: How can the economic explanation be *involved* in an interpretation dealing with meanings; and conversely, how can interpretation be an *aspect* of the economic explanation? It is easier to fall back on a disjunction: either an explanation in terms of energy, or an understanding in terms of phenomenology. It must be recognized, however, that Freudianism exists only on the basis of its refusal of that disjunction.[41]

We shall never make it with a pseudophysics (metaphysics) of psychic energy;[42] rather, psychoanalysis is the study of, the search for, meaning.[43] It does not believe only in behavior motivated by the reflexes of biology or of conditioning. Rather, the arena in which it operates is that of meaning, motivation, mind, levels of choice. (Psychoanalysis is the subjective study of subjectivity struggling to become the objective study of subjectivity.) But we also search for origins: the prize for Freud was to fuse biology to meaning.

So he kept squeezing his physics. It did not work; Ricoeur notes:

> It must be admitted that this quasi-physical conception of the psychical apparatus was never completely eliminated from Freudian theory; how-

ever, I think the development of Freudian theory may be looked upon as the gradual reduction of the notion of psychical apparatus—in the sense of "a machine which in a moment would run of itself"—to a topography in which space is no longer a place within the world but a scene of action where roles and masks enter into debate; this space will become a space of ciphering and deciphering.[44]

With the concept of signal anxiety, Freud committed himself to meaning. Yet he never let go of an energy explanation. Here is as close as he came:

[Once] the function of anxiety as a signal announcing a situation of danger . . . comes into prominence, the question of what the material is out of which anxiety is made loses interest. . . .[45]

Information Processing

Why don't I admit there is no "who" in "Who is the dreamer"? No one has ever experienced such a "who," and as some of our best thinkers have shown, Freud's theories are so shot through with faulty anthropomorphisms that only unregenerate metapsychologists could cling to the logical impossibility of a force or process or structure that also has its own mind. Ryle gives us fair warning:

The more the child tries to put his finger on what "I" stands for, the less does he succeed in doing so. He can catch only its coat-tails; it itself is always and obdurately a pace ahead of its coat-tails. Like the shadow of one's own head, it will not wait to be jumped on. And yet it is never very far ahead; indeed, sometimes it seems not to be ahead of the pursuer at all. It evades capture by lodging itself inside the very muscles of the pursuer. It is too near even to be within arm's reach.[46]

Some say that we should recognize that "who" is actually a number of "whats" in action. But it can be unfortunate—and is surely premature—if computer experts convince us that what we consider subjective experience is equally well stated in terms of a machine that is processing information, for that can lead to a manner of speech—"I don't exist; I am just a figment of my imagination"—that leaves out the subjective experience of subjectivity. (It is also correct but insufficient to say that a cell or a flower or a baby is an information-processing machine.) In the following quotation, for instance, it seems that Peterfreund would have us believe that descriptions of subjective experiences such as "demanding attention" or "unconscious force" are poor renditions of the true state of the experiences, better put in terms of information transfer. Although the language of information transfer is fine—helpful, increasing our understanding—it does not yet capture the subjective.

To speak of unconscious thoughts or fantasies is also acceptable as a *façon de parler* in theoretical discussions. Here the situation is no different from a computer scientist speaking of an input device "demanding attention" from central control: "demanding attention" is an anthropomorphization used only for the purpose of communication. The computer scientist can spell out in terms of circuit designs and demonstrate with actual electronic devices how signals are interchanged between the input device and central control, the situation crudely described as "demanding attention." Similarly, "unconscious thoughts" and "unconscious feelings" are acceptable terms if it is recognized that they are but crude descriptions of certain physical processes or information-processing programs which ultimately must be rigorously specified, just as the computer scientist must rigorously specify what he means by an input device "demanding attention."[47]

It may be that the immediacy of subjectivity blurs my understanding: I am impressed by remembering events from earlier in life in which I now know I knew more than I knew. I now know not only that I closed a door then—at age six—but that I had a good reason, which I now recognize, for closing that door. I simply would not have closed the door had it not been for that reason, but if you had asked me then why I closed the door, I could not have told you, for the reason was *unconscious.* To describe all that as if I were a computer is to leave out part of my experience. You leave out what I feel, what I felt, what I failed to feel, and what I felt as the result of failing to feel. "To not feel" is not the same as "to fail to feel," for the first describes a complete absence of feeling and the second is an attempt to put into words a peculiarly different state of having been *unable* to feel.

But, says Peterfreund:

In an information-systems frame of reference one need not postulate the idea of an anthropomorphic "doer" which cleverly and imaginatively actively distorts, condenses, displaces, reverses, and so on. The clinical relationships that are offered as evidence for such postulated mechanisms or functions are merely appearances that emerge when any limited body of information is processed by a sophisticated system which has available to it a larger body of relevant information.[48]

I think this position can be sharpened if Peterfreund accounts for the fact—the subjectively felt state—that at times there *are* "doers" inside who, one senses dimly or sharply, direct us. Though they can be described in terms of information systems (terribly crudely, however), they are not "merely appearances."

Then too, information is not information without a something that responds to the information as if it were information, not random noise. In the human machine, that most complicated of information receivers, the tremendously complex receiver is a *person*—a fantasy generator, a microdotter, a script-writer. No other receivers, animate or inanimate, deal with—manufacture and respond to—fantasies. Fantasy immensely increases the complexity of the apparatus being studied, and so far as I know, no information theorists have faced the issues raised by fantasy. A computer that fantasizes and does so because of its own wishes will be on its way toward humanness. And to fantasize is not to mouth the words as do parrots or phonograph records.

Once again Gill helps us:

> I believe the lure of information theory for psychoanalysts is that it seems to offer an escape from metapsychology, which they find offensive because it does not deal with meanings; but they have been misled by the fact that the terms information and communication connote meaning only in their nontechnical sense. It is my view that the application of such theory to psychoanalysis has so far been characterized by a nontechnical rather than a technical version of information theory, that the application is no more than a restatement of psychoanalytic propositions in technical-sounding terms like "feedback" and "match and mismatch," and that the psychoanalytic propositions have not been clarified any further by the new language. Indeed, the information-theory language is usually so general and abstract that it obscures the specific psychoanalytic insights.[49]

A wish is not just a thought; it is a sensation, machine-measurable, that can range from subliminal to explosive. When one experiences a wish, he feels it—somehow, somewhere—in his body. The same is true of fantasies, which are how the wish expresses need and hope. Until computers can engorge their selves with desire, they will never wish. Without fantasy, motivated by yearning, they do not adequately simulate people.

I think I discern two camps in regard to the way the mind works. In one—let us call it the "clinical"—are those theorists most influenced by the reports we give of our subjective states: that we can experience ourselves as having multiple selves, more or less isolated each from the others. Critics say such anthropomorphizing gives credence to what is really only illusion or metaphor.

The other—the "information-systems" position—measures the mind, including of course the subjective experience of minds within the mind, as a conglomerate of signals sent and received. I find both positions helpful and not necessarily at odds. We just need to be sure we direct the appropriate questions to the appropriate perspective, that we know when to ask "Who is Belle?" and when to ask "What is Belle?"

I Yawn: Therefore I Am?

Here is an example, of a sort familiar to all analysts, of the way one of the different "people" within manifests itself. A woman is in analysis because she has felt cut off from everyone for years. Although she can act involved for brief periods, she cannot sustain it. So she feels angry at acquaintances when she can blame them, guilty and angry at herself when she does not blame her problems on others, frightened she will not unfreeze; and she demands to be taken care of in the treatment rather than analyzed (in other words, she is in a pseudoschizoid state with good prognosis).

After several months of analysis, she yawns during an analytic hour, without comment. A couple of days later she yawns again, at which time I say, "You yawned," and she says, "Yes." No further associations. The next day, she yawns, and *she* says, "I yawned." No further associations. The following week, on again yawning, she says, "I yawned again; maybe it's getting to be a habit. I wonder why I did." A few days later she yawns again and this time remarks, "I guess I must be bored about something." I say, "What?" She says, "I don't know; I have no idea. I have nothing to be bored about; in fact, you know that what I was just talking about is terribly important to me." She had been going on at great length about her suffering because she has, for five years, felt imprisoned by her inability to sense herself in genuine contact with other people, and about her despair that life is slipping away and her future in jeopardy. As she talked, I had floated along, gently vague, shifting—on becoming aware of the floating mood—to sharp alertness just before she yawned. Awareness cued me to ask myself what she was doing to cause this mood in me. With that, I knew instantly that despite her apparently important and earnest associations, she really was not interesting. And if she did not interest me, I knew she did not interest herself. So I began to know why she yawned.

She went on, talking of her surprise, mild but real, that this yawning was occurring in the analysis, it not being a "habit" of hers on the outside. And she expanded at length on her puzzlement at the discrepancy between the importance of what she was discussing and the casualness she experienced while yawning. Then, in mid-sentence, she yawned again. She followed this with a laugh, a bit rueful but mostly amused. And at that moment she clicked into full focus, that is, she felt completely in contact with me. It was a sensation she had not had for years. She was joyous but still puzzled, not knowing why she was having these experiences and yet feeling as if an explanation was on the tip of her tongue.

Her next hour follows a weekend, during which, she reports, "I've been yawning all the time; I can hardly stop." She chuckles, but is also irritated at not knowing why she is yawning. The yawns just come out of her, she says. She can scarcely stifle them; they seem to have a will of their own. And she has discovered that at the time she is yawning she is not "just bored" but has a conscious feeling at the moment of boredom that the experience is discrepant from what she should feel. So she now not only has yawns but yawns that insist on coming out of her on their own—and so frequently that she cannot blame them on a physiologic process. Also, she is conscious while yawning that her mood is different from what it was just before she yawned. Something was coming toward consciousness in her, something that felt at first alien and inconsequential—"only a yawn"—but that now is beginning to seem like a thing with a mind of its own. I say, "Don't you yawn when you are boring yourself?" She says, "Yes, I do feel bored, but that does not make sense because, each time, I know I am talking about something important." I ask her if, at the moment she is talking, she *feels* it is important, and after a silence, she says, "No, it does not feel important; it feels as if I'm not talking about the right thing. But that doesn't make sense; I don't know what the right thing would be if it wasn't what I was talking about." And we go on to other subjects, the hour ending with her sensing that she has slipped away from the complete contact with me she had had while we talked of her yawning.

The next time she yawned, the parts fell in place. She observed that *she* yawned: the yawn no longer just came spontaneously up from her body but rather was she, *herself,* being bored with herself while she was seeming to impart important information.* Now she knew *she* had been avoiding the associations that would have had her talking directly with me, with appropriate feelings and language. Before, she would have told herself the subject was too trivial to be noted,† perhaps the fish swimming in the tank in a corner of the room, insignificant as compared with the greater issues about which she had been gabbing. But now, unpleasant and frightening as it was, she knew that my fish at that moment were more important than the future of the world.

And thus the split in her, the experience of herself as the passive victim of her yawn, had shifted to an awareness that there was a part of her, at first unconscious, that was in better contact than she was and that was telling her she was a bore. That part, "the true self,"‡ is

*Self-deception? *Mauvaise foi?*
†Self-deception?
‡This term is filled with as many questions as answers, but we can make do with it for now.

necessary for the success of analysis. The more available it is, the more the analyst can bring it to consciousness, the better the treatment progresses. Is not this mundane bit of analytic work more properly described in terms of another person, who is still herself, at work within ("mini-mind") rather than with labels (not descriptions) such as "cathexes," "ego," "the unconscious," or even what it is: information processing?

Who did the yawning? I think it was the patient, not just a thing to be described as an information processor. A part of her—a part that, once insight arrived, could easily be recognized by her as being and having been herself—was bored. It was bored with the part of her, experienced by her as herself, that was avoiding contact with me. And the part that yawned was motivated to yawn, was communicating its beliefs and motivations to the part of her that was conscious, the one talking to me. That silent, still unconscious part, though invisible, had access to her memories, her fantasies, her hopes for the future ("I must not yawn my life away"), my functions as analyst and rescuer, the English language, and how many minutes into the hour we had gone. It was impatient, sad, angry, worried, hopeful, bored. It was concerned for her future. It prognosticated on the treatment process. It could even write a treatise on resistance, though that might only be published as a dream. What other word except "person" or "mind" do we have for whatever does all this?

The route to an answer lies in determining when a "who," as we track down its origins, becomes a "what." A "what," at this stage of our ignorance, is best pictured as a program: genetically preset; primed by prenatal biologic forces (such as hormones) plus postnatal experiences (such as conditioning, imprinting); established and simultaneously modified in the epigenetic unfolding of development (such as oral, anal, phallic stages) and in the growing capacity to fantasize, that is, to read meaning into outer and inner sensations and perceptions, the most complex form of which is scripting. (In Appendix A, my colleagues Basch and Colby, who are more informed and original in their thinking than I, have tried to guide me on these hard issues.)

But at some level of this hierarchy, as I also noted when commenting on the development of the infant's mind, we observe that the program has taken on attributes of what we call a person, a creature that can be described in terms of intention, meaning, and fantasy.

Perhaps we can say that everything—animate and inanimate, matter and energy—has intention, if intention is synonymous with a thing abiding by natural laws. A proton, a salt crystal, and a car have intention. Do they strive, yearn, wish? What are the differences between the intention of a chemical constituent of a cell and the cell, between the cell and the organ of which it is a part, the organ and the organism without its central nervous system, lower animals and humans? All have or have not intentions, depending on how one defines intention: at any rate, they make efforts to accrete, avoid, assist.

Granting intention to all (which may reduce the meaning of the word to zero, if we are left with the rule that everything that exists has intention), then where, in the hierarchy, do we introduce meaning? Probably only in animals, where it contributes to their having a far greater range of responses than, say, cells or rocks.

But beyond that is the crucial issue, fantasy, especially that aspect of fantasy we call "wish." I cannot understand information theory and the relationship of a computer to a brain (much less to that brain function called "mind") as long as experts in these fields do not fit fantasies and wishes into their models.

We still go on living convinced at bottom that we make our own choices. No one, not even a madman, knows he is just a machine. No scientist really believes in the determinism he reveals in his laboratory. Which leads to a thought that is flagrantly controversial.

In these gentle and liberal times, it is the style in some circles to call off the moralists and to see us all as victims, freed from the accusation of sin because our behavior is determined: choice is an illusion. But take the battering father. We know it was predetermined he would batter his child, in part because he too was battered when little. Yet even at the hottest point of his rage, when he lifts his arm to bash in his baby's skull, there is a moment when, were he not indulging himself, he would hold back his hand. Most parents take advantage of their children because the poor things are little.

And if, at a moment in analysis, the patient decides not to say something, or to choose different words, or to change the inflections, is that not a moral choice? Rhetorical question: Is all resistance unconscious? Does he not know what he is doing? I am not saying there are not unconscious forces that press us to our actions, but rather that we should look more closely and see that the expanses of consciousness and choice are wider than most analysts publicly admit.

When the passive and distant father of a transsexual boy sits down —again and again—in front of the television, prepared to soak his brain in beer, he knows he could refrain. And when told that his feminine son's future may in part depend on his coming to a conference or attempting his own treatment, his public statement that he is too busy or does not believe in psychiatry seems to have its own conscious, moral motivations. Unless we invent a new society—which we seem in the process of doing—fathers and mothers should not abandon their children. Yet responsibility for children's welfare cannot be legislated. If we could force these fathers to spend time with their sons, perhaps pathology worse than femininity would result.

There are those who have demonstrated that we cannot have free will and determinism simultaneously, and others who have shown that, with a bit of finagling, we can. For the present, at least, I have decided to pretend that everything is totally determined right up to the instant when we act. (Decide to act? choose to act? need to act?) Then, at that moment—I choose to believe—whether we act or not is a moral issue (barring gross organic brain disease, fierce external coercion, a truly unconscious process, or other irresistible forces). If that is so, parents actually do bear a heavy responsibility for the personalities their children create. (So, of course, do the children.)

In other words, though it may nowadays be in bad taste, it may nonetheless be scientifically accurate to go back to—even assign responsibility to—parents for what they do to their children.

PART 4

Conclusions

12

Treatment and Research

Techniques

WHEN A RESEARCHER wants to report the morphology of newly discovered bacteria, we do not expect him to describe how his microscope is constructed or what the constituents of the stain are. All that has long since been discovered, described, and routinized. And if one needs to invent a new language, or new words for a now familiar language, as mathematicians do, the symbols must have the same meaning for everyone or we cannot perform the needed operations. Who would dare expect the same of psychoanalysis? How seriously, then, are we to take the reports of analysts, whose minds are the microscopes used to view the data and whose reports are the fixing and staining materials that give permanence to the clinical moment?

I have not concentrated on that problem in this book but have, I hope, shown enough of myself at work that a reader can see the data-collecting process. It is clear, for instance, that I am not as likely as some colleagues to attempt to penetrate infantile amnesia and am not comfortable with reconstructions of that era.[1] Although I believe such data are crucial, I suspect our tool—analysis—is not yet as strong in finding the facts as in illuminating our fantasies about those earliest times.

Would Belle have gotten better sooner and more completely had I been able to deal with her experiences in her mother's uterus? If I could have, would that not have changed my "explanations" regarding her sexual excitement? Have I relied too heavily on later material, forced to do so by incorrect technique? What is proper technique?

Of course, the same style of question should go for other explanatory systems: what distortions come from my failure to use a Jungian, behaviorist, Catholic, existential, communist, Hindu, mathematical, neurophysiologic, general-systems, information-theory, structuralist, Rosicrucian, or dietary pathway to the truth about sexual excitement?

After several years, I got genuinely, uncomplicatedly exasperated with Belle one day and told her so, with appropriate affect. Other analysts have reported comparable experiences. Was that an unnecessary, antianalytic addition to the treatment, a mistake, an indulgence powered by countertransference alone? Was the opening up of the analysis that resulted an artifact, a transference phenomenon, a flight into health, a seduction of the patient, a permanent deflection of treatment from its proper course, more of a closing down than an opening up, a sure sign that this was not an analysis? I am not being rhetorical; no one knows the answers to those questions.

What is an unneeded or harmful artifact? Freud said that a scientific interest, a research interest, worked against analysis. What about a concern for fees? The analyst's impending divorce? Analysts who knit, smoke, eat, sleep, who never use parameters, who need a vacation, prefer golf to analytic practice, want to be president of the Analytic Society, have emphysema, dislike their office furnishings, put diplomas (paintings, books, nothing) on their walls? What is psychoanalysis? Is being oneself an artifact; is not being oneself an artifact?

Should I be more curious, less curious? Is my curiosity a mistake? W. R. Bion says we should practice without remembering. That is provocative; how do we determine if it is correct?

Shall I be a mirror to my patients? Shall I be as uninvolved as a surgeon? Do I work best without motivations? Should I be kind? How much? When is humor right, and when is it inappropriate? Should my interpretations come forth more in response to a patient's present emotional status or to the verbal content? Who is a good analyst; how do *you* know?[2] In regard to the unresolved problem of defining proper analytic technique, the following may not be exaggerated: whatever I (you) do is wrong; on the other hand, I (you) could have done worse. After seventy years of fussing about what analysis is, we have little consensus. If it took the discovery of psychoanalysis to make possible a first analyst, then, judging from the way "proper" analysis has often been portrayed in the literature, Freud was the first nonanalyst in history.

I am strongly influenced in my analytic work by Freud's belief regarding psychotic people: "In some corner of their mind (as they put it) there was a normal person hidden, who, like a detached spectator, watched the hubbub of illness go past him."[3] Expecting this to be true for almost everyone, not just those who are psychotic, I take it for granted that somewhere inside, our patients—like the rest of us—usually know what they are doing. (I do not believe this is generally accepted by analysts.[4] Yet if patients really believed the accusations they throw at us under the influence of their transference neurosis, they would get up and never return.) I suspect also that there is still another "self" who, too often, crouches inside the clear-eyed soul and does not intend to change.

Scripts

Once we knew Belle's sexual fantasy, we could have predicted how she would deal with me in the analysis. (No wonder people hide the exact details of their scripts; daydreams uncover us in ways even night dreams cannot.)

But until I knew the scripts, I could not understand what she was doing to me, and as long as one of her scripts was that I knew her scripts, she would not (consciously) understand what I did not know. Our only hope was to find their exact forms and then their meanings. Here are some of the erotic playlets that could be going on simultaneously at any moment in her analysis:

She and I are performing in a sexual drama, in which I—frozen and phallic—observe her as she humiliates herself by lying before me, saying what comes to her mind.

As does the Director, I sit behind her, sexually excited because I get turned on when humiliating women.

No analysis is actually in progress; there are only the two of us pretending—and both knowing it is simply pretense.

The analytic moment is actually a masturbatory act, in which she—aroused—is debating whether she should now openly masturbate.

As she lies there, she is a delectable morsel that I will devour with my eyes, if not my mouth.

My comments, looks, and presence are penetrations, having in them elements of sexual intercourse, enemas, invasions. Some days these are raping intrusions, at other times gentle persuasions. Their purpose may be simple penetration or more complicated attacks in which I will seize her insides, steal and then possess them.

Because I pick on her—by interpreting, not answering questions, not succumbing to her "lovely"—she has the right to drive me crazy with her chattering, pseudo-stupidity, vagueness, confusing anecdotes, whining and drizzling, hopelessness, accusations, indirectness, falsifications, "subtle" insults. Besides, she is in no true danger, because I really know everything she knows, thinks, and does, no matter how disguised.

These scenarios portray the manifest content of Belle's erotic fantasy; they are, however, disguises for an underlying, essential, secret (that is, conscious) script: no matter what happens, no matter how manifestly bad he is, the Director is steadfast. He constantly pays attention; he persists. Only late in the analysis did we discover that this fantasy, always present at some level, made her secretly comfortable with me. It was the ultimate resistance, however, for it served to indicate to her that treatment was not necessary, was only a game that (she imagined) we both played for fun, was only a scaffold on which to hang scenery. This hidden, comforting script, then, proved that analysis was unnecessary and that the only crucial element was that I, being the Director, would never abandon her, no matter what I seemed to be doing. Living out that role, she became a willing, even eager participant in the analysis, in no real danger from it because it was only a game. Therefore, interpretations, reconstructions, even insights genuinely attained, were never quite fundamental for her; everything we said, everything that hurt, everything that excited her, was just lines spoken in our play. All that counted, till we dealt with this belief, was that I not abandon her.[5]

An even more comforting defense against abandonment and its emptiness is excitement. To be chronically excited, therefore, was to have in herself a presence that informed her she need never be abandoned again. She had her daydream. Hers; no one could take it away. And the emotions manufactured by a daydream were not as insubstantial as cotton candy, for they moved to high excitement and real orgasm.

Yet at another level she had simultaneously a different belief. This was the fundamental one we all learn and either accept or deny: I may indeed be abandoned, for I *know* abandonment, having confronted its terror in infancy before I had defenses to mitigate its brute force. The success of the analysis, therefore, depended on her awareness that she needed insight.* Perhaps every analysis struggles with the patient's willingness to learn and accept the knowledge "I have and can again be abandoned," or to deny it with falsifications—defenses. That denial work is done by scripts.

What is there in abandonment that is so awful it must not be repeated? The only reportable experiences that can suggest the terror we think infants feel are extreme panic states (as in battle or the phobic states that can follow), nightmares, and paranoid psychoses. No one doubts these states can be unbearable. If that is what infants suffer, we should expect them (us) to gather their wits about them as quickly as possible to prevent further agony.

*I suppose people receive back what they put into their analyses.

Belle's parental figures appeared in her daydream in the following ways. Her real father was represented by the dirty-old-men (her mother, too, in more shadowy form), either when they took the place of the stallion or as aspects of the watching audience. Her stepfather was in the cold, ungiving Director. Her mother was in the Director as the giver of orders, as the penetrator from a distance (who does not use his own body for the penetration), and as someone longed for but for whom one must wait. Her mother was both Belle as the excited victim of the sexual assaults and the ambience that permeated the whole fantasy: If all this does not happen, I shall be abandoned. And all these different characters at one time or another were perceived and responded to in me.

To this list of scripts and themes we could add many more; some are reported in earlier chapters. The important point, however, is the principle that people are to be understood by their scripts and that we cannot find meaning if we slip over into concepts, metaphors, and pseudophysical explanations. Belle was sexually excited when she thought I was the Director putting her through the long-familiar paces she had written into her own scenario. She did not get excited because the id commanded the ego while the superego slept, and she did not get excited because the cathexis of the internal representation was deneutralized. She did not get excited because of the pleasure principle, the repetition compulsion, the libido, fixation, orality or anality, instinct, bisexuality, the Oedipus complex, internalization, erotogenicity, secondary narcissism, the primary process, the unconscious, neuronal inertia, the sum of excitation, Eros or Thanatos, bound or neutralized or defused energy, damming of the libido, facilitation, imagoes, or all the machinery that hums and chatters through "the psychic apparatus." *She got excited because of fantasies,* and in those fantasies were characters whose dimensions were drawn from Belle's past experiences, outer and inner.

Secrets

In trying to understand erotic daydreams, I became more than usually aware of something obvious: secrets are a major resistance in psychoanalysis. I suppose all analysts know this, first, because we have protected ourselves with them in our own analyses, and second, because our patients continually do the same. Yet this problem is little discussed in the analytic literature, even when an author is examining the structure of resistances or psychoanalytic technique. (And why not talk of secrets rather than the less accurate "conscious withholding"?)

There is special value in hiding one's thoughts from the analyst: one retains conscious control over the information, though at the risk of an unconscious impulse spilling over to give, at the least, a hint of what is hidden. However raunchy it made her feel, Belle's sexual excitement, from earliest days on, was her own. By keeping it her secret that no one else could know about, she made sure it was forever there. With their enemas, they could get into her rectum but not into her mind. Why give it up to an analyst? In counteracting this resistance, our advantage as analysts lies in our patients' free associations and in our interpretations, especially if we use such material to show patients why we can be trusted. But Belle constantly played scenes in which she assigned me the role of sadist. That done, she had "proved" it was crazy to trust me. Here is a description of sadism in which we can see the Director—the Analyst:

> The sadist literally makes of his partner a predominantly external orga-
> nism: there is no room for the subtleties of thought, and no way of
> keeping thought separate from what one feels and expresses, when he is
> convulsed with pain. The mind "comes out in the open" in the screams
> and pleadings of the body. There is no longer anything private or aloof:
> the victim is reduced to the barest terms of the body; all indwelling
> values, all cultivated sensitivity, all the graceful forms of thought and
> talent, all that man earns and learns as a cultural animal are reduced
> whimperingly and totally to the terms of the tortured flesh. When the
> sadist torturer "breaks" his victim he means that he has been able to
> bring the inner self of the other to full view and control.[6]

Once we learn in earliest childhood to have secrets, we have begun our defense against having our minds made external, visible, fully available. To separate and individuate, a child must develop privacy. Soon, the problem gets complicated by our need to keep certain ideas from ourselves, not just from others. One of the emphases in this study is that, to understand behavior, we need to know not only the processes that keep information unconscious but those that keep us "uninformed" of what we consciously aware. Secrets—those we keep from others and those we keep from ourselves—are a good part of our solution to this challenge. And so, when our conscience nonetheless demands honesty of us, we are as likely to squeak with fright as does the victim before the sadist.

Of course our patients see us as torturers, for we too, like sadists, instruct them that they are to keep nothing "private or aloof" from us. It is our task, then, to demonstrate that one can bring one's hidden, even unrecognized, self to full view under benign circumstances. What our patients have to recognize—and we to show—is that our purpose, unlike that of the sadist, is not to control.

People who undergo a second analysis endlessly report on the information consciously withheld from the first analyst. Perhaps we can conclude that that is a risk for all analyses, and we might even warn those analysts who pride themselves on having uncovered material hidden in the first analysis that secrets they were not told may be found in a third analysis, the one that follows their efforts.

The study of secrets may have been a victim of Freud's marvelous work on unconscious forces, primary process, psychodynamics, and etiology. What has happened, I think, is that we have decided to feel that examining preconscious and conscious dynamics is beneath our dignity, to be left to pedants in academic psychology, sociology, anthropology, and psychiatry. Probably, this omission should delay our claim to having constructed a general theory of human behavior. Rangell has recently reminded us of this, stressing how ubiquitous is dishonesty, which he label: "C of I" (Compromise of Integrity).[7] Although I do not agree with him that underlining such behavior marks the next revolution in psychoanalysis,[8] he is right that it is high time we stopped ascribing so much of behavior to unconscious forces alone.

It may even be that in the way analysis has disregarded preconscious and conscious awareness, we have an example of secretiveness: almost all our waking hours as analysts are spent in acting with others as if we believed in the value of not always speaking our minds and in responding to those others as if they operated comparably. Obviously, this does not preclude an awareness of dynamically unconscious forces; my point is only that if analysts are aware most of the time that preconscious and conscious activities—that choice and secrecy—are significant, we ought not to treat this knowledge as a secret to be left out of our theory and practice.

Changes Due to Treatment

In the last year and a half of treatment, an increasing number of changes occurred inside Belle and in the transference. Here are examples.

A dream in which rain falls, fertilizing the earth.

A new idea about the innumerable memories of little boys teasing her and her thinking she was no good, wherein she now felt that this was the way little boys and little girls often are just before puberty. She no longer claimed that this behavior was a proof of her inadequacy and was done only to her, not to other females.

The Director daydream lost *all* its power to excite her. In its place she used stories in which men specifically portrayed as normal treated either her or another young woman (sometimes girl) in a kindly, fatherly way. She was no longer scripted as humiliated, a fool, or on display.

On no longer needing a Director, she no longer needed a falsified version of her stepfather. From a frozen caricature of masculinity, he was restored to neurotic—that is, human—dignity. She also knew now that her anger at him had been jealousy, energized by his having stolen away Mother's cockeyed concentration on Belle.

Hysterical, tantrumlike scenes formerly played out with acquaintances stopped permanently.

I no longer felt she was trying to drive me crazy with her woodpecker rapping on my skull.

The grand scenes in which she displayed her bottom on the couch ended.

Her sexual relations changed, so that she was now able, freely and with erotic feeling, to behave as she had never before permitted herself. She had orgasms with intercourse, not just with masturbation or after the man was finished. The erotic capacity of her genitals shifted so that now, with intercourse, both clitoris and vagina were fully involved, with a spread of climactic excitement into her pelvis, through her whole body. Masturbation, now guiltless, was less gratifying than intercourse: she needed another person.

Intercourse from behind lost its excitement because she no longer enjoyed its sense of disengagement from another human. Much more, she needed—was strong enough to dare to need—a face-to-face relationship with its greater promise that she could be fully in contact with, more loving with, her partner.

She gave up the hope that she could wring love, attention, apologies, or change from her dead parents, and found she could bear being without that hope. Once one has the insight that the past cannot rescue the present, there is no more need for depression; instead, one feels sadness, or loneliness, or the like. This freed her to try to find with real people in the real world what she had formerly all too easily given herself by daydreams alone.

The dreams of disasters—bombings, wars, uncontrolled fires, runaway cars, tidal waves, and the like—stopped.

She gave up drizzling and whining and was instead able to weep and become angry.

On the day she discovered how to cry in my presence, she learned, "It's too late to hope to reunite with my mother; instead, I should be reuniting with myself.

"It's funny: I'm no longer ashamed of this treatment."
Friendly people finally appeared, and regularly, in dreams.

> The nightmare that I have been having all of my life is gone. That is not a big change; it's just that I had a nightmare, and it is done. I knew it when I was a child. I could never pinpoint it; I would just wake up every morning knowing it was there. Most of all, it was my badness; I never woke up feeling that I was not bad. Sometimes it was that my mother wasn't there. Some days I had it more than others, and some days I didn't hardly even feel it. But it was always there. So, what's happened is only slightly different in the ways that I feel; it is just that it isn't there any more. It was always so far underneath, and I had so many ways to not know about it. So when it finally has disappeared, it does not make a big splash. But it's gone; it's not just diminished. I no longer need the magic tricks—masochism, daydreams—that I used to use to deal with it, such as using those tricks to intensify it.

She discovered, and then told me, that she was greedy, immediately after which, in the same hour, she said, "I realize now that I'll be able to finish my treatment; I know that it will end. To get insight is to feed yourself; you serve yourself up to yourself; you learn who you are, and you accept this.

"I had a dream in which there was an elevator; this dream was different from all the other dreams I have had about elevators. In all of those, they go up and down and wander and I have no control over them. This one went straight up and down; it was strong and reliable."

Where before she would dream of losing things, now she began to dream of finding things.

"I can really feel for the first time my hatred of males. I just couldn't catch it before."

Friendly animals began appearing in her dreams.

Resistances that used to last for several days now lasted only a few moments.

Closed doors in dreams became open doors.

Anecdotes told many times were told one more time, finally became clear, made sense to me, and dropped out of the analysis.

She responded directly to my interpretations rather than changing the subject.

After years of inspecting her genitals, she finally looked and got everything straight in her head; she was now able to recognize the separate structures and later to visualize them in memory without getting the parts misplaced or blurred.

Horses appeared in her dreams more frequently, and now they were benign:

There was a huge field. It was really lovely, a great vista. I had been there, but when it had been smaller. A horse was coming along behind me. I was afraid. I was trying not to walk too fast to make the horse suspicious and so I tried to lead it away from the field, but that didn't work. Then I was going through a field which is a meadow, and the horse keeps moving behind me. Then it passes me, and I look and it looked pleasant. And as I looked, it was getting to look more and more human, and actually smiled; and as it went past, I saw that its rear wasn't like a regular horse's rear end but had some kind of a spiral appearance [later in the hour reported as resembling the vaginal wall]. Then there were other horses, more of them like this one. And as this went on, they turned into girls with long faces, and it is possible that they had just been playing at being horses and at being male horses. The girls went over to an area where there were play bars, like children play on; and they were doing tricks.

She was finally able to be fully in contact with me, and I did not feel she was changing the subject, boring me with chatter, reporting dream after dream in order to smother me in details. Rather, every word could be to the point: I could see and feel what she was experiencing and was not even conscious till later that we had been in contact.

She finished up her relationship with her inner mother after again remembering—and admitting it in an episode of gasping crying—that she had known when little that her mother could be physically ugly, that she hated her mother, and that she had paid too great a price for accepting her mother's blackmail (such as having to defend herself vigilantly against her own awareness that her mother could be ugly). The most difficult task in separating from her mother's memory she accomplished on admitting—saying it out loud, to me, with no equivocating language—that her mother had been a liar.

She found that little boys can be cute, had warm feelings when she looked at them, and was no longer sarcastic or frightened around them.

I begin appearing at times in dreams in the guise of a nice boy, her associations leading her to discover maternal feelings toward me.

Men were now judged each on his own merits rather than as all being in some ineffable way the same.

Dream: "There was a swamp that had to be drained, and I was really surprised that it was so easy. There was a machine, a filter that took care of the sludge, and clean water went through."

Dream: "I went down to the laundry room. It looked as if all the machines there were broken. But then I realized that they weren't; they were just machines that I didn't know how to use properly."

She looked directly at me more, on coming into the room and on leaving.

She could finally sprawl on the couch without concern for her "lovely."

Dream: "A fireman. He quietly but firmly did not allow me to ride on his engine" (chuckle).

Dream: "I dreamed about the fish in your tank. They could imitate each other, but they could not imitate death. I know what that means: a dead fish is a dead fish." Reality is reality; disasters that are really disasters are really disasters. But the rest is exaggeration and histrionics.

She lost her fear of taking trips.

"I'm glad to be free. Although I am the kind of woman who should be married, I'm glad at this point in my life to be free. For the first time, I feel I don't have to take on the responsibility and bother of a husband. And besides that, even though it makes no sense to me, I feel I'm not obligated to you."

She learned to use her dreams to digest the previous day's analytic activities; to have one part of her inform another part, in the dream story itself; to answer, in the dream's language, questions she and I had raised during analytic hours. Dreams became motivated efforts to extend the amount of time we had for working together to decipher her behavior; they were created partly to serve as the agents of her wish to know herself.

"You're the opposite of the Director."

I was about to go away, and, for the first time in her life, she expected the person leaving her to return.

Dream: "There was a new area, some kind of earth expanse It could have been a maze, but it wasn't. We had been lost before in the past, but now everything would be pinpointed on a map and not be confusing. Like showing where the hedges and the sidewalks were. This was a new experience."

Dream: "There is a truck driver. He's supposed to teach me math. I'm supposed to go with him, but I wanted to change my clothes first. Then there was another part to the dream: I could look directly down the hill and see where the road was going and where I was going to be going. I was calling it a shortcut, but it really wasn't a shortcut at all. It was just a proper way to go."

For years, parking structures had appeared in Belle's dreams. For instance: "I had a dream. It was something about an underground parking structure." Time after time, these places were dropped into the hour to lie there, inert. Immediately after the work in which everything shifted with the discussion of her traumatic anal experiences, I went away for a couple of weeks. On the first hour of my return, Belle looked different from ever before. Not only was she more stylishly (though not extravagantly) dressed, but her hair and the set of her face made her look more put together, more lively and charming, without histrionics or teasing. When she came in, she looked at me with more directness and less show than ever before. She reported a dream that telegraphed this new, benign directness: "A girl said it was OK for me to be there, and I liked being there and felt anonymous [that is, not on display]. Then there was another room, in which I had to stand up in front of a lot of people. I realized that I could talk to them all without having to stand up in a formal way."

As the hour progressed, she stayed more open, letting her feelings, such as anger, be free without the usual disguises. Here are her associations: "I'm thinking all men are pigs . . . I feel less guarded right now . . . I know now that you can help me . . . I keep reinventing the world . . . I could see a way to live . . . I picture a parking structure . . . It has a big, black opening." And then we knew together, what I should have sensed years ago, that she was the parking structure.*

So I tell her, and she tells me, and I tell her; and we overlap each other's insights as we make our discovery: a parking structure is a building with no style, no furnishings, no interior richness. Its only function is to let people drive their cars in and then drive their cars out again, in and out of the structure without regard for it, maybe dropping some grease on its floor.

Now the image has converted to a conscious fantasy: "People use me as if I were only a parking structure." In this form, the masochism is clear, and we are free to work on the issue masochists foist on the world as being fate's decision, not their own: that they are truly being badly used, whereas in fact they have arranged to be badly used. There is evidence for both in most people; the two must be dissected out. There is a difference, for instance, between Belle's abandonments by her mother and father and her present style of reinventing those traumas in order to guarantee sexual excitement via her daydreams.

She now says that she felt good—lively—the whole time I was away: "Not like an inadequate genital but a vulva that is filled up and alive." She says, "It's because of the anal things we discussed before you went away. I do not feel any more that I have been dragged in here, or that I am always fooling you and teasing you." Her changed appearance at

*Of course, I could have known that before—did know it at an intellectual level—but the insight had never occurred to me as a genuine feeling. Until that happens, I do not interpret, presuming that if it feels awkward to me, it will sound inappropriate to the patient.

the start of the hour and her directness in dealing with me as the hour progressed signaled that she was ready to drop the garage metaphor; it never appeared again.

"Yes. I'm not a parking structure."

But Nothing Marvelous Happened: No Spectaculars, No Miracles, No Magic

This collation is shorter than the good news just reported, but it is no less significant.

Although the exhibitionism died down, it was still there. She still was alert to her "lovely," still felt on display when in public, but far less so than before and with only a touch of masochism.

Erotic daydreams were still important for her.

In case of doubt, she still protected herself with masochism, though again it was less severe.

She still overestimated (and underestimated?) men.

I have presumed that, in her inability to remember fully her real father, she continued his expulsion, still voting with the women of her family that he was worthless. Yet, in another compartment, she had kept a secret vote for him: he was the dirty-old-man who for years excited her erotism.

At the end of her analysis she was still likely to begin the process of communicating important messages by being a character in a staged scene, with me as another player. Only after I caught on and described to her the plot and our parts in it was she able to understand an interpretation.

An Addendum to the Treatment

To be sure that Belle's anonymity was preserved, I contacted her while writing this book and told her it would not be published without her complete approval. To do this, I asked if she would review every word of every draft. She has. Doing that became an addendum to the analysis, a new piece of work that focused on her responses to reading about Belle. In this way, I not only hoped that she would catch details that might otherwise reveal her identity but also that I would be ensured accuracy in all other respects. This process became for both of us a creative and surprising experience in which we could, from this new perspective, check each of our impressions, first of what had happened between us in the analytic process and second of what had happened in the unfolding of Belle's life from infancy on.

Not only were the fires of transference rekindled, but the book's reality in itself re-created a central theme of the erotic daydream. As you recall, the Director makes Belle reveal her excitement, as a display for an audience. And that, most literally, is what I do with this book. So not only was reality conspiring with fantasy, but she was in the dilemma of deciding what were her motivations in cooperating with me: to what extent would she give me permission, from the detached view that it was of use in the study of erotics, to tell her story, and to what extent would she do so simply because she was still under the daydream's spell. For surely it is unethical to get her permission if she is unduly influenced by a persisting, powerful transference effect. (It has been Belle's absolute right, till the moment the book is actually published, to stop the production simply by asking that that be done.) Only when we both felt this was worked through, when we knew it was depleted of erotic charge, were we at ease that I could proceed. I recommend this technique—of doing a piece of analysis with one's patient during the writing—to colleagues in a similar situation.

For Belle this experience was a valuable "review," in which, with full impact, she relived the analysis and was able to reconfirm the insights and changes that resulted. For me, it was, at the least, a test of reliability, in the sense that "reliability" is used by the experimental psychologist. Did the data re-emerge pretty much the same? Yes. Were there many or important corrections in the facts or perspectives? No. Nonetheless, it was an amusing and sobering experience for me to see where interpretations I *knew* were correct—they came out of me with that sense of spontaneous, enthused creativity that is the most fundamental confirming experience one can have—had been wrong. Wrong either in emphasis or in significance if not just flat-out wrong. (Of course, now I know, with the same enthused conviction, that *this time* my impressions are correct.) Not all of my truths, we discovered, were Belle's truths.

This experience I also recommend to colleagues.

13

Last Thoughts

ON BEGINNING this writing, I wanted to do several things: to trace back the manifest forms an erotic daydream took from the present to its childhood beginnings; to find the impulses motivating the daydream in its varied forms from childhood on; to find the psychologic origins of these impulses; to dissect these elements out of the far larger mass of data that makes up a psychoanalysis; to give enough visibility to what went on in the analysis that outsiders might sense the process, judge the accuracy of the reports of what happened, and so feel comfortable in coming to conclusions and in playing them off against those I reached; to present the data accurately, despite the absolute need to edit the living experiences into a written language and to protect the patient's anonymity; to write clearly in my own language; to extend my search for a methodology in psychoanalysis to help us move toward the accepted rules for a scientific enterprise; to increase our understanding of the dynamics of sexual excitement; to go after larger issues of psychology, such as the nature of meaning, wish, motivation, will, awareness, intention; to participate with colleagues in the effort to keep psychoanalysis lively, useful, creative, pertinent, honest, and a continuing source of new data and ideas.

Now, finishing, I know I did not make it. The problem of editing—to preserve confidentiality, to reduce the immense mass of material to a sensible size, to make clear what happened, to restrict the focus to only one theme—these necessary modifications reduced the realities of the treatment to a bundle of opinions.

However, I think that other analysts who make similar attempts will do better; in time, we shall develop techniques of observing and reporting that others will find reliable. Once we decide such techniques must be found and used, we shall progress—if analysis survives.

For using a psychoanalysis to gather data is the most potent approach ever devised for suggesting hypotheses in psychology; that has been clear since Freud's earliest work. If, then, this study of Belle's sexual excitement is seen as a hypothesis generator, I need make no more apologies. The way is clear for anyone, analyst or not, to confirm or deny the idea that everyone has a preferred erotic fantasy, which may be expressed as a daydream, as a style of behavior during sexual activity, or even in nonerotic, habitual ways of confronting the world. I have suggested that these modes can be translated into or are in themselves scripts—conscious, preconscious, and unconscious—that not only reveal the motives and meaning of behavior but in themselves create new motives and meaning in the lifelong process we call the self. On doing this translating, we find the dynamics of sexual excitement, which unfortunately express for most people the theme of harming one's erotic object in order to get revenge or otherwise undo painful experiences from infancy on.

I hope it is clear that I do not pretend to have found all the dynamics of excitement; we still need not only to test the hypotheses so far proposed but also to add new dynamics, discard others, and change the emphases of some that can be confirmed. Always around the corner, in another dream, another association, and another patient, will be an idea that opens up new understanding.

You have probably noticed that I did not deal with the question in what ways women are unlike men in erotic behavior. An example of a physiologic issue ignored herein: I presume that higher levels of androgens in males make for differences in gender and erotic behavior. Boys and men will in general have more physical power and motor assertiveness, especially during childhood, youth, and into middle age, as compared with females of the same age. Levels of androgens (or some subtler expression of androgen difference between the sexes) also contribute to the more imperious demand by biology on the erotic behavior of most young men as compared with most young women. Although erotic excitement and orgasm depend, in both sexes, on androgens, the styles of response may change with the levels of androgens present. And so, at these different stages of development, gender and erotic behavior pressured by the androgens will demand different defenses, or at least different degrees of the same defenses, in the two sexes.

When there are differences, are they due to cultural or biologic factors, or both; to research design; to biases built into the research even before it was designed? Do women practice perversions less than men; do women masturbate less than men; do fewer women masturbate than men? Do women take more time to be aroused; do women need more foreplay than men? Are women less responsive to pornography than men; is men's pornography more anatomic and direct in portraying erotic behavior and women's more filled with romance and tenderness; are men turned on more by visual experiences than women? Do women have an inherently greater capacity for orgasm than men? Are men more uneasy with heterosexual intimacy than women; are women, as a species, less hostile than men; do women need, or can they stand, or can they give more affection than men? Much has been published. Yet the discussion persists in scientific and political circles; we need more data: psychodynamic, cross-cultural, biologic.

It has seemed to me that the fundamental theme in Belle's life was the threat of abandonment. That, of course, is the life-and-death issue that confronts us all from the moment when, as a fertilized egg, we first latch on, and persists until we last let go. So it is easy enough to find that issue in everyone's sexuality. But the history of our attachments and abandonments is different for each of us, and in those differences the psychomicroscopist can find the origins of each person's erotism.

It is not enough to claim "abandonment" as a cause unless we describe what happened and at what times in the child's development, what intent the abandoner put into the abandonment, and what reparations were attempted. Belle, for instance, had both her parents present in her first years of life. The abandonments then were for hours and days, not months or years. And there are the micro-abandonments— the physically present mother who has no feeling for the infant, the mother distracted by depression or anxiety, the hard-working father who is never home when the child is awake, the mother of the female transsexual who is tantalizingly beyond reach, the parents who are disappointed in or hate the child for its sex or its physical appearance.

There have, of course, been people dealt with more cruelly than Belle; there are mothers more malicious than hers and intrusions more destructive than enemas. Obviously there are people more disturbed, more destructive, more hopeless, more ruined than Belle. As we return to the surface from our subterranean search, I want to stress again that outside the analytic situation Belle was normal enough for our society. If you met her, the woman in your presence would not remind you of the dissected-analyzed specimen laid out on these pages. She is no more odd than most of us.

And beneath her two fantasies—the Director and the underground —lie all of our themes: excitement versus repose, appetite versus satiation, awake versus asleep, being born versus before being born, dying versus after dying, lonely versus alone, enslaved versus free, alive versus dead.

In sizing up Belle here at the end, I think we do better to summarize her in terms of style more than—as I tended to do in these chapters—of pathology. This would mean, for instance, emphasizing the nonconflictual, nondefensive roots of her "lovely" and the generally benign state—physically and psychologically—of her anatomic insides. Her fascination since childhood with her own erotism had its origins in frustrations, traumas, and conflicts, but there was more to it than pain and its permutations. Belle's life-style reflected an acceptance of herself as a woman, of an identity she defined as being feminine in appearance (by her culture's standards), wanting to love and be loved by men, preferring—in love objects—male bodies and masculinity (as defined by her culture) to female bodies and femininity, with penis-in-vagina intercourse as the most emotionally and physically gratifying, with the hope of being a wife in a permanently monogamous relationship, with pregnancy anticipated with pleasure, motherhood expected as a privilege and joy. Entering analysis with these as essential definitions of her self, she never for one moment rejected them during the analysis; they were unchanged at the end of the analysis, and they did not ever change from then to now. Whoever wants to argue that they are not genuine for her, are brittle, are primarily defensive in nature, are the products only of vicissitudes of instinct or life, and can be encompassed in the theory provided by classical metapsychology (especially ego-id-superego or libidinal stages and fixations) had better know how to walk on water.

In wanting to study sexual excitement, I am lucky to have once had Belle as a patient. Some people's style is to be depressed, others suspicious, others optimistic, others anxious. Hers was to be sexual. So, although the dynamics of erotism may be the same in the different types of people, these mechanisms are probably more easily studied in someone like Belle, who enjoyed not only her sexuality but the process of looking at it.

Our culture's preoccupation with sexuality is, at best, an artifact produced by our present freedom to worry over all kinds of pleasures. But we know that hatred is much more important than love; love without hatred can take care of itself. Yet I am not alleging that hostility is all. My hypothesis, as I hope you have inferred, is not that the more hostile one is, the more excitement one will experience. And when analysis reduces patients' hatred (which probably is the primary driving force in neuroses), people do not find their pleasure diminished. Instead, erotic activities—excitement and gratification—get more tender. They do not become less forceful or less potent for being less frantic. For Belle, with her lifelong focus on femininity and erotism to express what meant most to her, the crucial issues of her existence were best condensed in an erotic daydream. Other people whose lives are focused on different melodramas may use nonsexual scripts to represent their aspirations. I presume that generals daydream on war, gluttons on food, insomniacs on sleep, and astronomers on stars. I would suggest that within these scripts, too, may be found the dynamics described herein for erotism, such as pseudo-risk, pseudo-mystery, the victim becoming triumphant, the caching of secrets, and fetishization.

Psychoanalysis is not in good repute these days; there are faster and often more effective techniques for removing symptoms, more hard-nosed theories to account for human behavior, and ways to increase awareness more filled with drama and the supernatural. Psychiatry appears to be on its way to finding treatments that can reduce the symptoms of psychic pain. But what endeavor other than psychoanalysis, what treatment, what study of humans, has at its core unending curiosity and skepticism, the absolute demand that the individual find his truth—cut loose from magic, from secrets, and from the erotization of victimhood? Analysis, with astonishing speed, went from revolution to respectability to outdated mythology. I do not think that a free society can easily bear the loss.

Appendix A

The problems with which I struggled in the chapter "Who Is Belle?" have been even more central to the work of M. F. Basch and K. M. Colby. They responded to my inquiries with discussions that extend and correct what I have written. Their ideas will be most valuable to the reader who has puzzled over these matters.

Dr. Basch writes:

DEAR DR. STOLLER:

The issues that you raise are (1) how can the mind-body problem be resolved and (2) what is the nature of self, i.e., what is the reference point for what we call "I." (3) Who or what is the dreamer of our dreams?

What are "mind" and "body"? They are two words. And contrary to accepted usage, words do not refer to "things" but to concepts that we human beings have formed.[1] So we should trace how the concepts of "mind" and "body" developed, rather than looking for what we can find that might match those words. (As we have already found, we can point to that which corresponds to our concepts "body" or "brain," but no thing answers to the label "mind.")

"Brain" and "mind," as we use them today, hark back to Descartes. Descartes introduced mechanism into science and, the brain excepted, did away with the animism that had held sway until then. Because of his religious convictions it was necessary (and prudent in those days) to emphasize that the Creator had made us different from the beasts by infusing into our bodies an immortal soul which gave us the power and the responsibility of reason that other animals lacked. Ever since Descartes's work scientists, and especially we physicians, have been content to look at the various organs of the body as fulfilling particular functions, as doing their jobs either adequately or poorly. We have studied the normal functioning of organs and tried to understand their malfunctions, and by comparing physiology and pathology to arrive at a total understanding of the part and its relation to the rest of the organism. No one "explains" uremia as a problem of the organ's nephritic function; we look for what's wrong with the kidney and don't attribute some mysterious essence to the organ that somehow gets it to work, or whose failure causes it to stop functioning or to function improperly.

The exception, of course, is the brain. What the Church called the immortal soul, what Descartes called reason, what Freud called the mental apparatus, what common usage calls mind, all are what Gilbert Ryle correctly termed "the ghost in the machine." We take it for granted that we possess a mind and a brain, not because this is self-evident, but because we are taught to take this for granted. It is a cultural given, that is, our language is constructed in such a way that this concept is conveyed automatically; to question it seems unnatural. Perhaps it is similar to a child who has grown up in a truly religious household and in later life finds it necessary to examine the concept of God objectively; though as a philosopher he might be very adept at doing this, he will probably always have a subjective feeling that he is doing something that is not right. So we, brought up to take mind and body as two separate entities, find it unnatural to think of mind as a function of the brain.

Ambrose Bierce put it elegantly in *The Devil's Dictionary:* "The brain is the organ that makes us think we think."

Only the mystical notion of an immortal soul necessitates the concept of spirit in the brain. "Mind" is a verbal noun; mind is minding.[2] However, "mind" is not "brain," similarly "urinating" is not "kidney"; one is a function of the other.[3]

These considerations lead into your question regarding the concept of self. The notion of an individual self as the initiator of action is a relatively recent development in thought. As I understand it, it began with the Greeks and depended on the invention of the article "the," which made objectification in thought possible. What do we subsume under the concept "self"? Bronowski[4] believed it was the sum total of experiences and the relations between them that made up what one called one's identity. I would be inclined to a narrower definition. The symbolic transformation of experience into an over-all goal-directed construct makes up what we call self. It is this pattern of patterns that is lost in a fugue state: people so afflicted haven't lost their skills—they can still write, drive a car, know how to get dressed, etc.—but they have lost their identity because they have lost their goals and the memory of the roots of their aims.

All goal-directed behavior that is not simply tropism or reflex involves a perception of self, or, more correctly, self is a collective noun that subsumes the lasting record of the interrelated goal-directed activities in which the organism has been engaged. Self is not known directly, but is revealed in part by the psychoanalysis of unconscious motivation.

Freud's great discovery was not of *the* unconscious—this again is a reification of a function—but of the fact that our motivations are for the most part not conscious; "self" is not coextensive with consciousness. Consciousness of self is only a small part of self; much of self does not enter conscious recycling of perception, either because it is not problematic or because it is seen as threatening (conflicted) and must be defended against by being kept out of consciousness.

We must remember that the first few years of life are years of thought without symbolic transformation. Experiences are laid down in these first few years that are only symbolized later and then only in part. The unconscious script that you refer to is laid down by the affective communication, i.e., the communication between the autonomic nervous systems of the infant and his parents, the transformation of these experiences into associative ones in the neocortex and their eventual symbolic transformation during the preoperative phase (Piaget), and then their union with language in the concrete operational phase (Piaget).[5] So, for example, a hyperstimulated infant may lay down those reactive patterns which become translated into a search for excitement that underlies all other significant motivation as he grows older. Forgive the oversimplification. All I want to point out is that affective patterns and the reaction to them form the foundation for later symbolic thought development. An understanding of affect permits us to grasp how it is that the earliest interaction of parent and infant are of paramount importance even though reflective thought and verbal language are not yet possible.[6]

The concept of microdots seems valid. I would agree that we are all governed by a number of scenarios that are not conscious. How are such blueprints built up? In infancy the combination of sensorimotor schemata (Piaget)[7] with the attendant autonomic affective reaction lays down basic reaction patterns which determine how future experience will be perceived. Behavior is an attempt to control perception, to create situations that meet particular expectations or perceptual sets (Powers).[8] It is very important to remember, of course, that these early patterns are neurologically encoded action schemata; they are not capable of being recalled through imagery. Later, with the capacity for symbolization through imagination and imaginative recall, these basic patterns, or microdots, are imbued with the potential for pictorial representation; this phase is still unconscious but can become mobilized by psychoanalysis and reach awareness, albeit in always distorted and incomplete form. I doubt if these patterns can ever be changed in their essence; however, understanding their nature can promote further symbolic work and they can be given new meaning. If development is normal, the meaning these basic patterns have for the individual and the form of gratification he seeks mature with age and circumstances. Such an individual is "normal." More often than not, as we know, there is conflict between the demands of the culture and personal predilections. Given sufficient talent, an individual can manage to achieve gratification while seeming to bend to the dictates of his environment. These people compose the "successful" portion of the population who come to us for help. I think Sheldon Bach's recent article[9] beautifully illustrates how such individuals function, living out lives that look satisfying to others, while deeply disturbed by both failure and gratification in connection with their personal fantasies. Many people never achieve even this compromise; they simply resign themselves to much less than they unconsciously hoped for; they become depressed.

This leads to your problem with dreams. We can go along with Freud here and say that dream work proceeds all the time, but what we call "dreaming" is only a small part of that work that comes to consciousness. Remember that Freud said, correctly, insofar as we are dreaming we are not asleep. So when you are aware of dreaming, you are becoming aware of the brain's symbolic transformation of perceptions. Just as when you wake up at night and have to go to the washroom, you become aware of the fact that your kidneys have been functioning. (Forgive the repeated analogies to kidneys and urination; I find the comparison between kidney and brain apt because the kidney is in its own way as complex as the brain and performs functions of perception, discrimination, and selection that are every bit as marvelous as are the brain's. The difference between the two lies in the symbolic function. It is symbolic transformation that makes us human; the concept of an "I" is only one example of such a symbolic transformation.)

You are quite right in saying that dreaming is performed by someone you have never met, but are, I think, mistaken in personifying this function. As Karl Lashley said,[10] we are never aware of any mental processes—dreaming, thinking, perceiving, etc., are all processes that take place without the benefit of consciousness.

When you ask, "Do I get excited or does my brain as a communication network get me excited?" I think you limit your conceptualization unnecessarily. We may learn to label certain autonomic (affective) states "excitement" and associate them with various experiences, but that doesn't automatically happen. We have all seen patients who demonstrate every sign of excitement, but have never learned, owing either to arrested development or to conflict, to identify the feeling correctly.

Similarly, if we do learn to label and identify our emotions, whether we then go further and acknowledge them as part of the pattern of experience we call self is another matter. One can induce excited states chemically or through direct cortical stimulation (Wilder Penfield) which an individual will correctly identify but from which he will disassociate his self. Hysterics, of course, do this for different reasons.

By treating words like "I" and "mind" as substantive nouns, you will always find yourself in the blind alley of Cartesian dualism. Remember these are only words; we invented them and we can make them mean anything we need to make them mean. A functional outlook gives us the opportunity to see the process of mentation very differently. With such an outlook the problems that you pose cease to be concerns, at least for me. They are paradoxes created by an improper use of words foisted on us by the physical sciences, misconceptions which we must now change. When you get right down to it, the answer to most of the questions in psychology lies in an appreciation of the process of perception and the recognition that all reality is intrapsychic, created by our brain. What I shall call "I" is not a thing but an experience. Just as important, what we call "body," "table," "chair" are the same; they too are experiences. Our tendency to cling to concretism leads us to call some experiences "things" and then to attribute "reality" or "objectivity" to only those experiences and treat other experiences as "psychical" and somehow "unreal."   ·

"I" is a symbolic construct of the brain and has no existence apart from or over and above that organ. I quite agree with you that it would be an even bigger blow to admit this than was the recognition that we are not the center of the universe, that we are not a special creation of God, and that we are not the conscious masters of our fate but are determined unconsciously in much of our behavior. Nevertheless you, I am sure, would accept all these discoveries as demonstrably true; why not this last fact? No matter how distasteful the earlier blows to narcissism may have been, that didn't stop them from being so, did it? If life could come from inanimate matter as the universe evolved, why can't a self-aware being evolve as the brain becomes increasingly complex?

"I" does not exist at the beginning of infantile life any more than it existed at the beginning of the evolution of man. Just as language is a late development in man's history, so is the notion of an "I"—the latter being perhaps the latest step in our evolutionary development. "I" is the objectification of the symbolizing function of the brain. Who dreams? The brain. Upon awakening, the symbolizing function that has been exercised in dream formation becomes objectified and is expressed as "I dreamed." As you point out, in the ancient Greek days the explanation was different, the dream—i.e., the brain's symbolizing function—was externalized and attributed to the work of the gods. In times to come, perhaps other explanations than "I" will be given for the origin of dreams; it depends in what way we objectify brain activity. Similarly, we sleepwalk and get wherever we are going without being conscious of our actions, yet upon awakening we say "I walked in my sleep." "I" didn't walk anywhere; that is a *post facto* explanation; the muscles under the brain's direction functioned to move the organism.

A distinction should be made between the concept of "I" and the concept of "self." "I" is always linked to the experience of consciousness. As I have hypothesized, consciousness is an aspect of perception which permits past events to be subjected to further scrutiny through recall.[11] Consciousness is necessary for all higher animal life, but only with the aid of symbolism can the abovementioned objectification take place which designates the function of conscious replay as "I." Self is something else again. It antedates "I."

Recent studies on brain physiology give rise to interesting possibilities of localizing the various aforementioned functions described by Piaget. The sensorimotor and preoperational (symbolic) stage are, it would seem, right-brain functions. The concept of self is therefore a nonlinguistic right-brain activity. Already, however, there is selectivity. As I have discussed,[12] repression may be looked upon as the failure of symbolization of sensorimotor action memory. The sensorimotor body image, or self, may not become symbolized *in toto*. For example, the mother who avoids contact with her child's genitals when bathing, or gives them perfunctory cleaning while lingering lovingly over the other parts of his or her body, may transmit a prohibition to symbolization of those organs. We certainly find many adults in whom the genitals, though intellectually accepted, are not seen as part of the self. Indeed, many adults are quite ignorant of their genital anatomy; it is as if this is forbidden territory that may not be thought about, and isn't.

The right brain deals with events through what Heinz Werner has called "physiognomic perception," that is, it grasps totalities and their implications. With left-brain maturation and the development of language, the transfer of information to the left hemisphere takes place. The left brain seems to carry out those "logical" functions described by Piaget as fundamental to concrete and formal operations; it organizes events sequentially, treats them in terms of parts and wholes, and describes them with the aid of language or mathematics.

In the translation from preoperational to concrete, or from right-brain to left-brain organization, there is again opportunity for defense. Conflicted material, though it may be symbolically organized, is not translated into language, for example. This is the defense that Freud called disavowal.[13] (Disavowal explains how we can lie to ourselves, practice self-deception—a topic you deal with in your manuscript.) Literally, the left half of the brain doesn't know what the right half is doing. The right half of the brain is the seat of what Freud called the id—not that it is, as he suggested, a disorganized, seething cauldron; quite the contrary—which doesn't deal with life in terms of language. The failure to translate experience linguistically permits the right half of the brain to take into account what has happened without our being able to speak about it or "think" about it logically (sequentially, discursively).

You ask who does the dreaming. Let's change that to "What does the dreaming?" In all probability it is the right half of the brain. When we wake up, the left half deals with the symbolic material as best it can, and we call it "a dream." A dream, in my opinion, is a glimpse of how the brain actually deals with all messages. All messages are first organized by the right brain, and in a small number of instances, either because there is particular interest in the topic or because it is problematic and requires further processing for satisfactory ordering, the experience is translated into a left-brain one. In the process a lot is lost. The right brain is probably in closer contact with the limbic system and with affect, and this may represent a danger to the left hemisphere, which distorts and tones down the transaction. I believe that the dream work, so called, represents the distortion of a conflicted right-brain symbolic event by the left brain.

"Self" is a physiognomic totality and resides in the right hemisphere; it is a preoperational concept. "I" is that aspect of self-experience which the left brain acknowledges by admitting it to language and to consciousness. There is an awful lot of "self" that is disavowed and never becomes "I." But the process works in the other direction too, especially after formal operations become a possibility. Didactically perceived messages, having been registered, can ultimately become part of the right-brain experience. This is the difference between the novice and the expert; "expertise" is a right-brain achievement. For instance, our candidates learn psychoanalysis by rote, by imitation, and get frustrated by all they are asked to master that seems to make no sense until one day it becomes part of them. Then they are analysts, and "just know" what the right thing is to do. What was left-brain information has become the property of the right brain, a part of the self, and now feels as if it "belongs." So there can be information that belongs to "I," that is acknowledged intellectually as having been received and registered, without belonging yet to the "self"—and it may never belong. In analysis, resistance often maintains the gap between "I" and "self."

I think your microdots are right-brain schemata and they will only accept—i.e., make a part of the self—those messages that address the needs and fears laid down in infancy. When as analysts we threaten the microdots, or seem to be doing so, by implying that those early needs may be questioned or perhaps are not meant to be gratified, the right brain simply cuts off communication, and the analyst and the patient's left brain can talk from now till doomsday and there will always be that part of the patient's brain that says, "Let them talk, it makes no difference." However, the transference, that is, the meaning that the analyst has for the patient's right brain—where the analyst has significance in terms of the early sensorimotor patterns, microdots, or as Freud called them, wishes—permits the analysis to prevail, at least potentially. Love conquers all—sometimes! What it adds up to is that, as we know clinically already, the left-brain information becomes a right-brain concept if the transference love is properly interpreted and managed.

Dr. Colby writes:

I. Some Enigmas of Pronouns in Explanations of Human Behavior

To ask, "Who dreams my dreams?" "Who does the wishing?" or "Who digests my food?" and to answer with an "I" or an "it" raises some enigmas about how pronouns are used in providing explanations of human behavior. To explain is to make something intelligible to someone. Much depends on what beliefs the participants share in explanatory dialogues and what satisfies them as explanations.

Acceptable scientific explanations proceed as follows. A regularity or pattern of events is observed as characteristic of an individual or class of individuals, in this case humans. We first must agree on a description or characterization of what is happening. The described events are then considered to be the effects or result of underlying unobservable processes taking place in the individuals concerned. To understand these processes, we imagine the individual to be decomposable into parts and processes which are capable of generating the observed events of our agreed-on initial description. Empirical tests are then conducted to determine whether these imagined parts and processes are "real," i.e., are they believable existents. Since they cannot be observed directly, their effects must be detectable and demonstrable in order for us to accept them as real existents.

In this decomposition of a characterization, the individual as a whole is imagined to possess structures which are not just small-scale replicas of the whole but parts and processes possessed by the whole. Thus, the mind is not a group of homunculi but a structure of internally coded symbolic representations. When we speak of a human individual, we use pronouns like "she" and "who," but when we speak of parts, such as symbolic representations, we use the pronouns "it" and "what." When a person speaks of himself as "I," he is either referring to a whole individual or to a phenomenological, conscious, subjective "I." The first "I" can accurately be said, at a holistic level of description, to be doing things, but the second use of "I" as agent represents an illusion, since it itself is a description of a product or result of underlying processes and not an agency that does anything in its own right.

Phenomenologists and antiscientific humanists may abhor this strategy of decomposing wholes into parts, because to them it makes persons impersonal in that the mind's processes now seem to be sinister and inaccessible "it's" rather than personable "I's" or "she's." Many even prefer denizen views in which the inner demonic homunculi are warm little rascals like the psychoanalytic "id," mischievous but not beyond human taming. A magical view of the world sees nature as benevolent or malevolent toward humans and hence as liable to be influenced by them the way humans are influenced. A scientific picture of the world sees nature as neutral and indifferent to us, being composed of impersonal structures which can be influenced by us only through our understanding their causal laws.

Current models of the mind portray it as a set of symbolically coded representations (beliefs, affects, intentions, etc.) which are used computationally to fulfill the organism's purposes.[14] The behavior of the whole organism can be described with personal pronouns. But what generates that behavior is most accurately described by using inescapably impersonal pronouns referring to parts possessed by the whole. You (Observer I) can say, "I cannot remember his name," referring to yourself as a whole system. But to scientifically explain your lapse of recall, I (Observer II) would refer to a memory, an "it," possessed by you. In the long run, the scientific rather than the magical view is to be preferred because it is more effective in bringing about situations that humans desire. The relief of suffering from mental disorders will come about from better scientific explanations of how the mind really works, not from the populist posture that everything about the mind is already familiar and hence self-explanatory.

II. Consciousness of Self-Mentation

Assume a living organism possesses awareness and reactivity. It also possesses coded representations of its experience, which are used to react to what the organism becomes aware of. A simple organism is aware of itself and its world, but it lacks as awareness-contents a linguistically coded and auditorily displayed description of its own internal coded representations, a capacity provided by natural language. Human organisms possess, in addition to first-level coded representations, a second-level code, natural language, which allows them to construct, be aware of, and react to a description of some of their first-level representations. Such a two-level system allows humans not only to have a symbolic representation but also to understand that it is a symbolic representation.

Consciousness in humans contains, in addition to ordinary perceptions, an awareness of a running, self-referent, descriptive linguistic commentary which can be anticipatory, monitoring, or retrospective in nature. This second-order entity, a linguistic commentary, allows humans to "step back" and monitor other monitored performances. It provides them with a meta-level of self-regulation, since the internal commentary can be reacted to like any other inspectable element in awareness just as if its origin were an external, linguistic communication.

In these natural-language descriptions of the self's mentations appears the vertical pronoun "I." The term is ambiguous because it can refer to the person as a whole or to a part or process of a person under some decomposition. "I" can thus refer to an observed or an observer. (Naturally, an observer cannot observe itself but must be taken for granted by transcendental argument.) Introspection of what is referred to as "I" is a process of retrospection, i.e., inspection of something which has already been produced by a preceding cycle of mental activity. It can be reacted to in the next cycle like any other content of awareness.

A robot with awareness and reactivity can operate in a simple world without the property of generating linguistic commentary about what it is doing or plans to do. Then what is the computational advantage, if any, of possessing this sort of meta-system characteristic of humans? Is it an accidental consequence, a nonessential property like heart sounds? What is it used for?

One advantage is that a two-level system provides an ability to self-correct, modify, or reprogram the first-level coded representations in order to improve the performances or actions they govern. Given a description of an action, one can use it as a higher-level instruction to change an instruction in the lower-level code. Such a more complex system would have an adaptive advantage in a complex world because of the great flexibility of its first-level programs, which can be quickly modified to fit more optimally with a great variety of diverse situations. Thus the two-level system can continuously eliminate errors, remake and reconfigure itself at one level (within limits) to generate improved behavior. But is this why humans generate some awareness of their own mental productions? The question is quite baffling perhaps because it represents, next to the origin of the universe, and the nature of life, the deepest mystery we can think of.

Appendix B
Fixing

Speculations on mental functioning in the first months of life divide theorists into two camps. There are those who believe that from birth (or before) the infant is a psyche, a being that—even if as narcissistic as a black hole—is sentient and fantasizes. And there are those who think an "I" only gradually coalesces from originally uncoordinated ego functions that unfold as a result of a genetically controlled program plus postnatal external and internal stimuli. The insoluble problem with all questions of earliest mental life is that we can do nothing but guess at the infant's experience. That last idea would be disputed by many analysts, who would offer in rebuttal their observations of the transference in the analyses of adults, the observed fantasies (as in play) of small children, and the ordinary manifest behavior of infants. But it is beyond the power of each of these categories of information to penetrate into the infant's still wordless mind. Because children and adults speak and express themselves with a wide range of emotions, they can validate our interpretations of their experiences in ways infants cannot.

Suppose our theory of personality development requires that there be complex scripts in the infant from birth (or before). If it is announced, for instance, that an infant in its first weeks knows that there is out there, not part of itself, a creature who is to be categorized as a father, that this father has anatomy, that that anatomy includes a penis, and that he uses that penis to penetrate mother's body and thereby produce babies*—I can only shrug my shoulders. There is no scientific test for that theory or for its necessary, scientifically sensational claim that these intricate beliefs are inherited.

What evidence there is at present, however, makes me bet against the inherited-fantasies theory: studies of the anatomy and physiology of the infant brain, brain-dependent behavior showing that the central ner-

*A mighty complex and subtle fantasy system, fundamental to Kleinian theory, but one that taxes my understanding of the processes of evolution.

vous system only gradually matures into a more sophisticated organ, studies on neoteny (especially evidence that the human is at birth the least completely ready of all mammals). Example: You could say that infants do not speak for the first year or so because, having weighed the pros and cons, they have chosen to keep quiet. Or you could say that speech requires a certain amount of brain development, a theory that does not depend on those essences of the mental: choice and fantasy.

If the infant inherits fantasies, intrapsychic conflict is inherited. If not, there is a conflict-free phase of development. I would add that in humans, as in all other species of animal life, there is nonmental learning, such as conditioning and possibly—as in birds—imprinting. (Bowlby is essential here.[1] Too bad, though, that he does not consider fantasy more.) The capacity of cells, organs, and organisms to modify behavior in the absence of mental involvement, even in the absence of a central nervous system, is unquestioned. The human infant's tissues, like those of humans of all ages and those of any other species, are prone to such influences. Permanent behavioral styles, automatisms, call them what you will, are inserted by mothers from birth on into this congenital matrix, to form a foundation for behavior. These biologic ("instinctual") and biopsychic ("conditioned," "imprinted," what else?) anlagen will serve as vehicles for playing out the intrapsychic conflicts that in time arise. The point here is not that a behaviorist or ethologic model must be an alternative to a conflict model, but that both are at work.[2]

My theory of gender identity development says these biopsychic phenomena are present, shaping the infant's responses within its mother's embrace, becoming habitual, automatized fundamentals of later character structure. Not only are they not the product of intrapsychic conflict, but many of them are the result of *gratifying* experiences that the infant "learns" to repeat (the quotation marks are to indicate that we do not yet really know what the word "learn" means).

The term "conflict" needs to be clarified, for it refers to two different processes. The one that especially concerns analysts is intrapsychic conflict, wherein one part of oneself is fighting against another part of oneself, intersystemic or intrasystemic (antithetical scripts). There is another kind of conflict—more interesting to nonanalytic theorists—in which the conflict is between one person and another (as with a child fighting against its mother). After a few months, probably all conflict with the external world has its intrapsychic-conflict ramifications, but at the beginning of life, I do not think that is the case. At first there is just the mindless brain, vulnerable to external stimuli that permanently emplace—fix—some aspects of psychic life. After some of this earliest biopsychic experience is embedded in brain and psyche, fantasy begins, its task to modulate the impact of the outer world and inner stimuli, protecting us from—*giving us explanations for*—otherwise unmanageable forces that impinge from outside and from within.

These ideas are not, to put it mildly, revolutionary. By standing on the side of those who have long since written about such development, I am only adding, to their catalogue of fundamental defects and lacunae, a category of egosyntonic, strong, permanent, gratifying personality traits that may also from the start be the product of non-intrapsychic conflict.

In trying to make this theory less ragged, I have searched for already developed concepts to support my uncertain thoughts regarding earliest parental effects on the development of the infant's mind. For me, there is no more useful statement than the following, by Lichtenstein. Regarding his ideas, I would only recommend we not use the word "imprinting," since that process, as defined by ethologists, and as Lichtenstein recognizes, does not cover mother-infant relatedness and its outcomes in behavior with which we are familiar.

> I suggest the use of the well-known concept of "imprinting" for the description of certain aspects of early infant-mother interaction. Imprinting, in the definition of Lorenz, "is the name we have given the process by which the releaser of an innate reaction to a fellow member of the species is acquired." It is characterized by three observable facts. It is influenced by conspecific living material, it is restricted to critical phases of ontogenesis, and it is irreversible. The Innate Releaser Mechanism (IRM) is defined as "the innately determined readiness of an animal to respond with a certain action to a certain stimulus combination. It is an innate neurosensory correlate to a specific stimulus combination." Obviously, imprinting and innate releaser mechanisms, if applied to human development, are used as an analogy. What makes this analogy possible are two striking similarities in early phases of individuation. First, that certain responses on the part of the infant to the mother seem to be restricted to "critical phases of ontogenesis"; secondly, that the effect appears to be irreversible. But aside from these characteristics of timing and of irreversibility, what other analogy is there in the human situation to the "imprinting" stimulus combination, and what analogy could be found to an innate releaser mechanism in an infant? I believe that there are such analogies, that, in fact, they have been described by psychoanalytic observers of early infant-mother relations. The imprinting stimulus combination would be the individual and unique unconscious wishes, the unconscious needs of the mother with regard to her child. . . .
>
> The specific stimulus combination, conveyed to the infant by the mother, is "specific" in a more individual sense than the term implies

when used by the ethologists. It is a stimulus combination which is specific for the *individual* mother, and once the infant has been stimulated that way, the infant "recognizes" *his* mother by the specific individual combination of stimulations as well as frustrations long before there is a true perceptive recognition. . . . The primitive stimuli which cathect the apparatus of touch, smell, taste, etc., must be seen as "messages" conveying to the infant a great deal about the mother's unconscious wishes concerning the child. The way the mother is touching, holding, warming the child, the way in which some senses are stimulated, while others are not, forms a kind of "stimulus cast" of the mother's unconscious, just as a blind and deaf person may, by the sense of touch, "cast" the form and the personality of another person in his mind. . . .

These responses as well as the primitive stimuli that elicit them form a continuous interchange of need creation and need satisfaction between the two partners of the symbiotic world. While the mother satisfies the infant's needs, in fact creates certain specific needs, which she delights in satisfying, the infant is transformed into an organ or an instrument for the satisfaction of the mother's unconscious needs. It is at this point that I see a link between sexuality and the emergence of identity in man. An interaction between two partners where each partner experiences himself as uniquely and specifically capable of serving as the instrument of the other's sensory gratification—such a partnership can be called a partnership of sensual involvement. . . .

The mother does not convey a *sense* of identity to the infant but an *identity:* the child is the organ, the instrument for the fulfillment of the mother's unconscious needs. *Out of the infinite potentialities within the human infant, the specific stimulus combination emanating from the individual mother "releases" one, and only one, concrete way of being this organ, this instrument.* This "released" identity will be irreversible, and thus it will compel the child to find ways and means to realize this specific identity which the mother has imprinted upon it. The Innate Releaser Mechanism has, then, an analogy in the human infant in so far as there is an innately determined readiness in the human infant to react to the maternal stimulations with a "somatic obedience" experience. This "obedience" represents, however, fulfillment of the child's own needs: in being the instrument, the organ for the satisfaction of the maternal Otherness, the full symbiotic interaction of the two partners is realized for both of them. It would, however, be a mistake to see this "organ" or "instrumental" identity as too narrowly defined. The mother imprints upon the infant not *an* identity, but an *"identity theme."* This *theme* is irreversible, but it is capable of variations, variations that spell the difference between human creativity and "a destiny neurosis."[3]

These biopsychic phenomena emanating from the mother act on the infant to create permanent behavior patterns, probably (as in other species) by causing organized modifications of the brain: the external stimuli have been "fixed" in the brain.

So, to have a label on which to hang such data and theory, I suggest the term "fixing,"* which frees us from misusing the concept "imprinting."

"Fixing," then, is a hypothesized process by which stimuli—perceived and not perceived—from the external world and from within one's body cause permanent, structural central-nervous-system change, organizing habitual patterns of behavior not the result of the processes we call "thinking."

*To fix, say the dictionaries, is to fasten, secure, cement, anchor, set, harden; to organize; to found, ground; to establish, root, lodge, emplant, engraft, impress, embed; to form, shape, fashion, sculpt, cast; to solidify; to preserve; to make firm, fast, stable, or stationary, implant firmly, make permanent; to give a final or permanent form to, make definite and settled, crystallize; to give definite, visible, or fixed form to, capture, evoke; to make nonvolatile or solid; to treat so as to make some condition permanent; to attach, affix; to concentrate; to set or place definitely; to set or place in order or in a certain pattern, adjust or settle properly or for a desired end.

Abbreviations Used in the Notes

Am. J. Psychiatry	American Journal of Psychiatry
Am. J. Psychother.	American Journal of Psychotherapy
Arch. Gen. Psychiatry	Archives of General Psychiatry
Arch. Sex. Behav.	Archives of Sexual Behavior
Biol. Psychiatry	Biological Psychiatry
Biol. Reprod.	Biology of Reproduction
Br. J. Delinq.	British Journal of Delinquency
Br. J. Med. Psychol.	British Journal of Medical Psychology
Br. J. Psychiatry	British Journal of Psychiatry
Br. Med. J.	British Medical Journal
Bull. Johns Hopkins Hosp.	Bulletin of the Johns Hopkins Hospital
Bull. Menninger Clin.	Bulletin of the Menninger Clinic
Child Dev.	Child Development
Child Psychiatry Hum. Dev.	Child Psychiatry and Human Development
Int. J. Psychiatry	International Journal of Psychiatry
Int. J. Psychoanal.	International Journal of Psycho-analysis
Int. Rev. Psychoanal.	International Review of Psycho-analysis
J.A.M.A.	Journal of the American Medical Association
J. Am. Psychoanal. Assoc.	Journal of the American Psychoanalytic Association
J. Appl. Behav. Anal.	Journal of Applied Behavior Analysis
J. Endocrinol.	Journal of Endocrinology
J. Homosex.	Journal of Homosexuality
J. Nerv. Ment. Dis.	Journal of Nervous and Mental Disease
J. Pers.	Journal of Personality
J. Proj. Tech.	Journal of Projective Techniques
J. Psychol.	Journal of Psychology
J. Sex Res.	Journal of Sex Research
Math. Biosci.	Mathematical Biosciences
N. Engl. J. Med.	New England Journal of Medicine
Penn. Psychiat. Q.	Pennsylvania Psychiatric Quarterly
Psychoanal. Q.	Psychoanalytic Quarterly
Psychoanal. Study Child	The Psychoanalytic Study of the Child, ed. Ruth S. Eissler et al., vols. 1–25 (New York: International Universities Press, 1945–70); vols. 26–32 (New Haven, Conn.: Yale University Press, 1971–77).

Psychol. Issues	*Psychological Issues*
Psychol. Record	*Psychological Record*
Q. J. Exp. Psychol.	*Quarterly Journal of Experimental Psychology*
Sci. Am.	*Scientific American*
S.E.	*The Complete Psychological Works of Sigmund Freud (Standard Edition),* ed. and trans. James Strachey (London: Hogarth Press, 1953–66; distributed in the United States by W. W. Norton & Co., New York).

Notes

Introduction

1. "Each individual, through the combined operation of his innate disposition and the influences brought to bear on him during his early years, has acquired a specific method of his own in his conduct of his erotic life—that is, in the preconditions to falling in love which he lays down, in the instincts he satisfies and the aims he sets himself in the course of it." S. Freud, "The Dynamics of Transference" (1912), *S.E.* 12: 99.

2. J. Genet, *The Thief's Journal,* trans. B. Frechtman (New York: Grove Press, 1964), p. 7. Italics in original.

3. "a. Even where they can be summed up in a single sentence, phantasies are still scripts (scenarios) of organised scenes which are capable of dramatisation—usually in a visual form.

"b. The subject is invariably present in these scenes; even in the case of the 'primal scene,' from which it might appear that he was excluded, he does in fact have a part to play not only as an observer but also as a participant, when he interrupts the parents' coitus.

"c. It is not an *object* that the subject imagines and aims at, so to speak, but rather a *sequence* in which the subject has his own part to play and in which permutations of roles and attributions are possible.

"d. In so far as desire is articulated in this way through phantasy, phantasy is also the locus of defensive operations: it facilitates the most primitive of defence processes, such as turning round upon the subject's own self, reversal into the opposite, negation and projection.

"e. Such defences are themselves inseparably bound up with the primary function of phantasy, namely the *mise-en-scène* of desire—a *mise-en-scène* in which what is *prohibited (l'interdit)* is always present in the actual formation of the wish." J. LaPlanche and J.-B. Pontalis, *The Language of Psycho-Analysis,* trans. D. Nicholson-Smith (New York: W. W. Norton & Co., 1974), p. 318.

4. "It is thus possible to distinguish—although Freud himself never did so explicitly—between several levels at which phantasy is dealt with in Freud's work: conscious, subliminal and unconscious." Ibid., p. 316.

5. "The actual definition of fantasy is unclear in psychoanalytic literature; it is one of the many terms loosely used for a wide range of phenomena. In nonanalytic usage, Funk and Wagnall's *New Standard Dictionary* (1952) provides a definition that is adequate even if not completely acceptable in analytic thinking. The relevant part of the definition is as follows: '. . . 3: (Psychological) The form of representation that brings before the mind images as such, severed from their ordinary relations: in this sense very commonly spelled phantasy. (1) Any mental representation or image of a whimsical, bizarre, or grotesque character. Fantasy is particularly active (1) in wakefulness, in reverie, abstraction, intoxication, delirium, and insanity. And (2) in sleep, in dreaming, somnambulism, and hypnotism.'

"Actually, this definition applies to what are commonly known as daydreams. When dynamic functioning is considered, such a definition does not take into account all that is known and is, in fact, inaccurate since the images of a fantasy can be reconnected with their unconscious relations. Then their character is seen to be no longer grotesque or bizarre. Such a definition, however, points up another aspect of fantasy that is of great importance in psychoanalytic ego psychology, namely, that fantasy is a form of mental production and fantasying is the form of mental activity leading to the production of fantasy. There is a continuum of such mental productions ranging from unconscious fantasy, night dreams, daydreams, and imagination through thinking (problem solving) to abstract thinking. In ordinary analytic usage, fantasy is applied to the first part of this series, while thinking and abstract thinking are not in general classed with fantasies.

"Since the term fantasy is used to include such a range of mental phenomena, some means of clearly differentiating these phenomena is needed. It is not common usage to speak of daydreams or imaginations, but analysts reporting cases often speak of fantasies of a patient, meaning daydreams. We can distinguish different meanings of fantasy by differentiating between basic fantasies which are unconscious, pervade the whole character, and influence both the development and final form of the ego, and those more conscious daydreamlike products which are derivatives of the basic fantasy." E. D. Joseph, "An Unusual Fantasy in a Twin with an Inquiry into the Nature of Fantasy," *Psychoanal. Q.* 28 (1959): 189–90.

6. "The Freudian problematic of phantasy, far from justifying a distinction in kind between unconscious and conscious phantasies, is much more concerned with bringing forward the analogies between them, the close relationship which they share and the transitions which take place between one and the other: 'The contents of the clearly conscious phantasies of perverts (which in favourable circumstances can be transformed into manifest behaviour), of the delusional fears of paranoics (which are projected in a hostile sense on to other people) and of the unconscious phantasies of hysterics (which psycho-analysis reveals behind their symptoms)—all of these coincide with one another even down to their details.' In imaginary formations and psychopathological structures as diverse as those enumerated here by Freud, it is possible to meet with an identical content and an identical organisation irrespective of whether these are conscious or unconscious, acted out or imagined, assumed by the subject or projected on to other people.

"Consequently, the psycho-analyst must endeavour in the course of the treatment to unearth the phantasies which lie behind such products of the unconscious as dreams, symptoms, acting out, repetitive behaviour, etc. As the investigation progresses, even aspects of behaviour that are far removed from imaginative activity, and which appear at first glance to be governed solely by the demands of reality, emerge as emanations, as 'derivatives' of unconscious phantasy. In the light of this evidence, it is the subject's life as a whole which is seen to be shaped and ordered by what might be called, in order to stress this structuring action, 'a phantasmatic' *(une fantasmatique).* This should not be conceived of merely as a thematic—not even as one characterised by distinctly specific traits for each subject—for it has its own dynamic, in that the phantasy structures seek to express themselves, to find a way out into consciousness and action, and they are constantly drawing in new material." LaPlanche and Pontalis, *Language of Psycho-Analysis,* p. 317.

7. N. Leites, *The New Ego: Psychoanalytic Concepts* (New York: Science House, 1971).

8. "At this time the scientific life and the scientific imagination are not really accessible, for all that more is probably being written about science than at any time in its history. If it were accessible, we could demythologize it. When we had done this, we could incorporate it into public understanding. When it is incorporated into public understanding, then, and only then, will science be truly integrated into our culture." J.

Goodfield, "Humanity in Science: A Perspective and a Plea," *Science* 198 (1977): 585.

9. D. Shakow, quoted in A. Wolfson and H. Sampson, "A Comparison of Process Notes and Tape Recordings: Implications for Therapy Research," *Arch. Gen. Psychiatry* 33 (1976): 559.

PART 1. Hypotheses on Sexuality

Chapter 1. Sexual Excitement

1. "You see, I've decided that art is a habit-forming drug. That's all it is for the artist, for the collector, for anybody connected with it. Art has absolutely no existence as veracity, as truth. People always speak of it with great religious reverence, but why should it be so revered? It's a drug, that's all. The longer I go on, the more I'm convinced of it. The onlooker is as important as the artist. In spite of what the artist *thinks* he is doing, something stays on that is completely independent of what he intended, and that something is grabbed by society—if he's lucky. The artist himself doesn't count. Society just takes what it wants. The work of art is always positioned between the two poles of maker and onlooker, and the spark that comes from this bipolar action gives birth to something, like electricity. But the artist shouldn't concern himself with this, because it has nothing to do with him—it's the onlooker who has the last word. Fifty years later, there will be another generation and another critical language—an entirely different approach." Marcel Duchamp, quoted in C. Tomkins, "Not Seen and/or Less Seen," *The New Yorker,* February 6, 1965, p. 40.

2. "Experience is mastered by actively repeating what one has passively undergone. This is an extraordinary psychological principle, one that appears to be a unique discovery by Freud . . . : whatever someone has done to me, I must do to someone (or something) myself. . . . Before leaving the theme of doing what one has suffered, let us note its similarity to the primitive mechanism of undoing. More than similarity, what is involved is an evolution of more or less reflexive undoing in the direction of active and often constructive mastery of experience. A distinctive outcome of these impulses is a sense that accounts must be balanced. At first this takes the form of revenge and of the law of the talion. The part that the law of the talion plays in the development of conscience is acknowledged by few authors, two exceptions being John Stuart Mill and, among psychoanalysts, Odier." J. Loevinger, "Origins of Conscience," *Psychol. Issues* 9, monograph no. 36 (1976): 286, 282.

3. M. M. R. Khan, "The Function of Intimacy and Acting Out in Perversion," in *Sexual Behavior and the Law,* ed. R. Slovenko (Springfield, Ill.: Charles C Thomas, 1965), p. 402.

4. N. Friday, *My Secret Garden: Women's Sexual Fantasies* (New York: Trident Press, 1973), pp. 88–92.

5. Ibid., pp. 152–3.

6. K. Millett, *Sexual Politics* (New York: Doubleday & Co., 1970), p. 3, quoting Henry Miller, *Sexus* (New York: Grove Press, 1965), p. 180.

7. *Penthouse Forum*, August 1975, pp. 56–7.

8. S. Freud, "A Special Type of Choice of Object Made by Men" (1910), *S.E.* 11:-165–75.

9. S. Freud, "On the Universal Tendency to Debasement in the Sphere of Love" (1912), *S.E.* 11: 179–90.

10. S. Freud, "The Taboo of Virginity" (1917), *S.E.* 11: 193–208.

11. S. Freud, "A Child Is Being Beaten" (1919), *S.E.* 17: 179–204.

12. Freud, "On the Universal Tendency to Debasement in the Sphere of Love," p. 187.

13. "It must be understood that each individual, through the combined operation of his innate disposition and the influences brought to bear on him during his early years, has acquired a specific method of his own in his conduct of his erotic life—that is, in the preconditions to falling in love which he lays down, in the instincts he satisfies and the aims he sets himself in the course of it. This produces what might be described as a *stereotype plate* (or several such), which is constantly repeated—constantly reprinted afresh—in the course of the person's life, so far as external circumstances and the nature of the love-objects accessible to him permit, and which is certainly not entirely insusceptible to change in the face of recent experiences. Now, our observations have shown that only a portion of these impulses which determine the course of erotic life have passed through the full process of psychical development. That portion is directed towards reality, is at the disposal of the conscious personality, and forms a part of it. Another portion of the libidinal impulses has been held up in the course of development; it has been kept away from the conscious personality and from reality, and has either been prevented from further expansion except in phantasy or has remained wholly in the unconscious so that it is unknown to the personality's consciousness. If someone's need for love is not entirely satisfied by reality, he is bound to approach every new person whom he meets with libidinal anticipatory ideas; and it is highly probable that both portions of his libido, the portion that is capable of becoming conscious as well as the unconscious one, have a share in forming that attitude." S. Freud, "The Dynamics of Transference" (1912), *S.E.* 12: 99–100. Italics added.

14. S. Freud, "Fetishism" (1927), *S.E.* 21: 152–7; R. C. Bak, "The Phallic Woman: The Ubiquitous Fantasy in Perversion," *Psychoanal. Study Child* 23 (1968): 15–36; P. Greenacre, "Perversions: General Considerations Regarding Their Genetic and Dynamic Background," *Psychoanal. Study Child* 23 (1968): 47–62.

15. As is the case in Freud's description of fetishism. Although Freud says that the two ideas—that females are castrated and that they are not—must be kept apart, one does not find that adult fetishists consciously believe either that women have penises or that they are castrated. See R. J. Stoller, *Perversion: The Erotic Form of Hatred* (New York: Pantheon Books, 1975).

16. There is a theoretic issue of importance here, one that came to concern Freud: the meanings of the concepts "denial" and "splitting of the ego." It may be more useful to determine if an idea or fantasy is *in one's awareness* and in what form than to theorize where *in the ego* it resides. (For a psychic event can be observed as being in a state of consciousness, but to say that it is in the ego is to talk theory only.) As Freud describes splitting, he tries to account for events that seemingly cannot coexist in reality yet nonetheless do so in the ego. But another problem is in dealing with awareness: how can I succeed in not having to know what I know and yet still know it? Talking of "the ego" blurs our seeing the human need to create ignorance from knowledge in order to establish that one really is innocent.

It is just here that we need precise vocabulary. As can be seen from the Translator's Note in LaPlanche and Pontalis, *Language of Psycho-Analysis,* p. 120, the terminology is unclear; should we talk of "denial" or "disavowal," or are they synonymous? Although I hate to complicate the issue even further, I think we must also account for the mechanism that, I suggest, takes up so much of people's behavior, in a psychoanalytic hour or throughout the rest of the day: how does one keep *in consciousness* two or more incompatible thoughts, as one wants to do in daydreaming, lying, and secrecy? To me, the word "disavowal" seems best, with its connotation that one still retains awareness of what one wants to be rid of; while "denial" connotes that the denied is closer to becoming unconscious.

17. "Have we arrived at the simple proposition that splitting is little more than maintaining two or more incompatible attitudes and consciously defending each one, without seeing the logical traps? In that case, it is a thought disturbance—and an exceed-

ingly common one. The ego fails to be coherent about specific groups of ideas and their accompanying affects. If we focus on the ideas, we find them at variance with each other; if we center on the affects, we find in them the kind of incompatibility usually described as ambivalence. . . . In [Freud's] unfinished 'Splitting of the Ego in the Process of Defence,' he describes a fairly typical childhood problem situation: The child, being under the sway of a powerful instinctual impulse which it is accustomed to satisfy, is suddenly frightened by an experience which teaches it that continuing this satisfaction is a real danger. This presents a forced choice situation: The child must recognize the danger and renounce the satisfaction, or it must disavow reality (by make-believe) and retain the satisfaction. Freud's point is that some children take both courses at once. They reject the bit of reality imposing the prohibition and also accept the fear of the danger, experiencing the latter as a symptom. But then, in seeking to divest themselves of the fear, they can succeed only 'at the price of a rift in the ego which never heals but which increases as time goes on.' I find this a rather roundabout way of describing the essence of habitual lying." P. W. Pruyser, 'What Splits in 'Splitting'? A Scrutiny of the Concept of Splitting in Psychoanalysis and Psychiatry," *Bull. Menninger Clin.* 39 (1975): 18–19.

18. "The risk-taking nature of sexual action in public restrooms is one of the more important attractions they offer, at least to those participants with independent occupations.

"My interviews indicate that much of the effective value of the sexual release found in tearooms would be lost without the consequentiality that lies beyond the payoff phase of the game. Some of the older men said they were no longer able to reach orgasm outside the excitement of tearoom encounters. During the attack on the restroom by teen-age toughs that was recounted in Chapter 5, I observed three acts of fellatio within our besieged shelter. I find it impossible to understand how sexual acts could have occurred under those circumstances without recognizing the aphrodisiacal effect of danger.

"This, I suspect, is one factor that differentiates the sexual experience of tearoom action from that of masturbation. Autoerotic stimulation provides another common sort of sexual outlet free from personal involvement, but it is not an encounter, a game, a risk-taking adventure. Solitary masturbation involves neither conquest nor submission. [I say it does, but only as an element in the erotic script.] One does not leave it with the feeling of having played the game well or of having participated in a new experience. For those respondents with whom I have discussed the matter, masturbation is not considered a satisfactory alternative to tearoom contacts. They desire something more exciting, more stimulating—and that is available in the tearoom market place." L. Humphreys, *Tearoom Trade: Impersonal Sex in Public Places* (Chicago: Aldine Publishing Co., 1970), p. 151.

19. " 'We believe,' she said, sitting up seriously checking the cassette machine and holding it out, 'that a time will come when evil will be no more. She'll come again, and that will be the end of evil.'

" 'Who's *she?*'

" 'Jesus, of course.'

"Enderby breathed deeply several times. 'Look,' he said. 'If you get rid of evil you get rid of choice. You've got to have things to choose between and that means good *and* evil. If you don't choose, you're not human any more.

" 'You're something else. Or you're dead.'

" 'You're sweating just terribly,' she said. 'There's no need to wear all that. Don't you have swimming trunks?'

" 'I don't swim,' Enderby said.

" 'It *is* hot,' she said, and she began to remove her coke-and-hamburger-stained sweater. Enderby gulped and gulped. He said:

" 'This is, you must admit, somewhat irregular. I mean, the professor and student relationship and all that sort of thing.'

" 'You exhibited yourself. That's somewhat irregular too.' By now she had taken off the sweater. She was, he supposed, decently dressed by beach standards, but there was a curious erotic difference between the two kinds of top worn. This was austere enough —no frills or representations of black hands feeling for the nipples. Still, it was *undress.* Beach dress was not that. He said:

" 'An interesting question when you come to think of it. If somebody's lying naked on the beach it's not erotic. Naked on the bed is different. Even more different on the floor.'

" 'The first one's functional,' she said. 'Like for a surgical operation. Nakedness is only erotic when it's obviously not for anything else.' " A. Burgess, *The Clockwork Testament or Enderby's End* (New York: Alfred A. Knopf, 1975), pp. 41–2.)

20. "Wherever primitive man has set up a taboo he fears some danger and it cannot be disputed that a generalized dread of women is expressed in all these rules of avoidance. Perhaps this dread is based on the fact that woman is different from man, for ever incomprehensible and mysterious, strange and therefore apparently hostile. The man is afraid of being weakened by the woman, infected with her femininity and of then showing himself incapable. The effect which coitus has of discharging tensions and causing flaccidity may be the prototype of what the man fears; and realization of the influence which the woman gains over him through sexual intercourse, the consideration she thereby forces from him, may justify the extension of this fear. In all this there is nothing obsolete, nothing which is not still alive among ourselves." Freud, "The Taboo of Virginity," pp. 198–9.

21. G. Schmidt and V. Sigusch, "Women's Sexual Arousal," in *Contemporary Sexual Behavior,* ed. J. Zubin and J. Money (Baltimore: Johns Hopkins University Press, 1973), pp. 117–43; G. Schmidt, V. Sigusch, and S. Schafer, "Responses to Reading Erotic Stories: Male-Female Differences," *Arch. Sex. Behav.* 2 (1973): 181–99; G. Schmidt, "Male-Female Differences in Sexual Arousal and Behavior During and After Exposure to Sexually Explicit Stimuli," *Arch. Sex. Behav.* 4 (1975): 353–65.

22. *The Report of the Commission on Obscenity and Pornography* (New York: Bantam Books, 1970).

23. Stoller, *Perversion.*

24. M. de M'Uzan, "A Case of Masochistic Perversion and an Outline of a Theory," *Int. J. Psychoanal.* 54 (1973): 455–67; J. McDougall, "Primal Scene and Sexual Perversion," *Int. J. Psychoanal.* 53 (1972): 371–84; T. Reik, *Masochism in Modern Man,* trans. M. H. Beigel and G. H. Kurth (New York: Farrar, Straus & Rinehart, 1941); V. N. Smirnoff, "The Masochistic Contract," *Int. J. Psychoanal.* 50 (1970): 665–71.

25. For example, S. J. Morse, H. T. Reis, J. Gruzen, and E. Wolff, "The Eye of the Beholder: Determinants of Physical Attractiveness Judgements in the U.S. and South Africa," *J. Pers.* 42 (1974): 528–42.

26. R. G. Meyer and W. M. Freeman, "A Social Episode Model of Human Sexual Behavior," *J. Homosex.* 2 (1976–77): 123–31.

27. Although the following quotation is long, it is worth reading, for it illustrates why I think that, with the exceptions noted, the psychiatric-psychologic literature is not of much help: "The problem of accounting for the creation of a condition of mutual love between male and female, is at the same time one of accounting for their choosing each other and committing themselves to each other as mates. All of it is seen to be a phenomenon born of an interpersonal interaction process which we have already, in effect, characterized as one of *reciprocal instrumentality.* The concept is not wholly new, but neither is it so familiar that a few sentences describing it will not be useful, for it is in terms of it that the formulations constituting the entire theoretical framework are cast.

"It is proposed that reciprocal loving and conjugal pairing is a function, primarily, of a process of *reciprocally gratifying behavioral interchange.* It is said, 'primarily,' because it is recognized that an individual's transactions with others, external to the relationship, may be instrumental to the need gratification of the other and, hence, contribute to the individual's attractiveness. Reciprocally gratifying behavioral interchanges refers to an interaction wherein both the interacting parties engage in behaviors that are either satisfying in themselves to one or both parties, or are reciprocally gratified by the behavior of the other, or the products of it or the consequences of the behavior, or all of these. This assumes that some behaviors are gratified in the execution of them *per se*. For example, caressing a sex object could be pleasurable to the caressor without the caressee behaving in any way at all—he or she could be utterly passive or even dead. Such instances are not the rule, of course, but rather, the rare exception. The gratification is more often some particular response by the other. For instance, the caressor is rewarded by the expressions of pleasure and appreciation made by the caressee or gets caressed himself in return. The latter responses are themselves gratifying to both persons in the interchange.

"The central thesis of the instrumental theory of interpersonal relations as it applies to intersexual dyad formation may be formally stated as follows:

"*In intersexual dyad formation each person seeks, among his circle of acquaintances, within the compass of his self-acknowledged compeers, to form a relationship with that person or those persons whose behavioral and other resources provide (or are perceived to provide) maximum gratification and minimum punification for his needs.*

"Perhaps the phrase 'self-acknowledged compeers' is needful of some explication. It means, simply, all those included as acceptable associates in an intimate sex-love relationship, but it is variable with the goal of the association as the person himself defines it. He or she may be quite willing or even eager to date, go steady with, carry on an affair with, or even live with, someone he or she would not consider eligible for marriage because of racial or religious or other grounds for exclusion. It is common today on campuses of universities with a liberal climate of attitude and opinion for White and Black to engage in intimate social and sexual intercourse, but few of these liaisons will result in marriage. One or both partners will usually have reservations which effectively exclude the other from equal status, such as to preclude a marital union.

"The thesis as stated above is meant to apply, not to marital choice or mate selection alone, but to the formation of any and all intersexual relationships. Hence needs must be expected to vary somewhat in salience with the interaction goal, whether it be merely dating, going steady, living together or marriage. It does not require to be restated in its entirety for each of these kinds of relationships, but only to have inserted in it some words or a phrase to indicate the kind of dyadic relationship under scrutiny in a given case. Thus, 'In intersexual dyad formation, such as mate selection or marital choice, each person—'." R. Centers, *Sexual Attraction and Love* (Springfield, Ill.: Charles C Thomas, 1975), pp. 62–3.

28. F. A. Beach, "Behavioral Endocrinology and the Study of Reproduction," *Biol. Reprod.* 12 (1974): 2–18; R. R. Holt, "Drive or Wish? A Reconsideration of the Psychoanalytic Theory of Motivation," *Psychol. Issues* 9, monograph no. 36 (1976): 173–6; R. P. Michael and D. Zumpe, "Potency in Male Rhesus Monkeys: Effects on Continuously Receptive Females," *Science* 200 (1978): 451–3.

29. Freud, "The Taboo of Virginity," p. 196.

30. M. K. Opler, *Culture and Social Psychiatry* (New York: Atherton Press, 1967).

31. The following glimpse at their work can introduce the unfamiliar reader to their thesis: "Without the proper elements of a script that defines the situation, names the actors, and plots the behavior, nothing sexual is likely to happen. One can easily conceive of numerous social situations in which all or almost all of the ingredients of a sexual event are present but that remain nonsexual in that not even sexual arousal occurs. Thus, combining such elements as desire, privacy, and a physically attractive person of the appropriate sex, the probability of something sexual happening will, under

normal circumstances, remain exceedingly small until either one or both actors orga-
nize these behaviors into an appropriate script." J. H. Gagnon and W. Simon, eds.,
Sexual Conduct: The Social Sources of Human Sexuality (Chicago: Aldine Publishing
Co., 1973), p. 19.

32. "An example of this may be seen in Kosinski's novel, *Steps* (1968), where the
nameless hero finds himself looking down upon a fellow office worker (female) whom
he has long desired sexually and who is at the moment in a posture of unrestrained
sexual accessibility. Though it is a moment he has long desired, he finds himself unable
to become aroused. He then recalls the occasion of his initial sexual interest, a moment
in which, while watching her in the act of filing papers with uplifted arms, he caught
a fleeting glimpse of her bra. This trivial image, originally arousing, remains arousing,
and the hero goes on to complete the act. It is that image (and what it links to) that
both names her as an erotic object in terms of his sense of the erotic and also names
what it is about to do to her. Though the image need only be briefly suggested (both
in its original and subsequent utilization) and remains unknown to the behaviorist
observer, it becomes critical to the performance. Its meanings could be several. It could
mean, for example, that the sexual becomes erotically enriched when it is hidden, latent,
or denied, or when it is essentially violative (deriving from unintended exposure). It also
legitimates the appropriate name for the behavior. Consider the possible "labels" our
hero could have invoked that could have been applied to the behavior, each with its
own powerful and powerfully distinct associations: making love, making out, fucking,
screwing, humping, doing, raping. . . ." W. Simon, "The Social, the Erotic, and the
Sensual: The Complexities of Sexual Scripts," in *Nebraska Symposium on Motivation,*
ed. James K. Cole (Lincoln: University of Nebraska Press, 1973), pp. 71–2.

33. G. G. Abel, E. B. Blanchard, D. H. Barlow, and M. Mavissakalian, "Identifying
Specific Erotic Cues in Sexual Deviations by Audiotaped Descriptions," *J. Appl. Behav.
Anal.* 8 (1975): 247–60.

34. "The functioning of established pathological personality patterns is metaphorically
expressed in masturbation fantasies. The fantasy represents an optimal fulfillment of
the pathological goal. In the clinical material there is a high incidence of aggressive
interpersonal striving which, in fantasy, reflects a depersonalization of others. Aggression, in some form, is a nearly constant element in the literature on autoerotism.
. . ." W. Bonime, "Masturbatory Fantasies and Personality Functioning," in *Science
and Psychoanalysis* (New York: Grune & Stratton, 1969), 15: 45.

35. J. Nydes, "The Magical Experience of the Masturbation Fantasy," *Am. J. Psy-
chother.* 4 (1950): 303–10.

36. See Gagnon and Simon, *Sexual Conduct,* p. 25, for a fuller discussion of this failure.

37. "Not infrequently, in the course of analysis, a patient will report a recent episode
of masturbation and either state that the act was accompanied by no conscious fantasy,
or describe a rather nondescript fantasy, such as, 'I was having intercourse with a
woman.' When this occurs, leaving an unwelcome gap in our understanding, careful
questioning about the specific masturbatory technique and the subsequent associations
to it can lead to a surprising wealth of associations which may help to fill that gap. I
should stress that, more often than not, the patient will not volunteer such information,
unless trained to do so because . . . the silence about the technique can very effectively
serve the resistance. . . . When masturbation is accomplished by an unusual technique,
the analysis of the technique itself may open doors that lead to the uncovering of
complexes by revealing the nature of the unconscious fantasy involved. Technically,
this involves treating the technique of masturbation as a symptom, or even a dream
element, and encouraging relevant associations." I. Miller, "Fantasy and Masturbatory
Technique," *J. Am. Psychoanal. Assoc.* 17 (1969):828, 842.

38. See Simon, "The Social, the Erotic, and the Sensual," p. 75, for related thoughts.

39. Here is another description of these mechanisms at work in excitement: "Voyeurs are fixated on experiences that aroused their castration anxiety, either primal scenes or the sight of adult genitals. The patient attempts to deny the justification of his fright by repeating the frightening scenes with certain alterations; this type of voyeurism is based on the hunger for screen experiences, that is, for experiences sufficiently like the original to be substituted for it, but differing in the essential point and thereby giving reassurance that there is no danger. This tendency may be condensed with a tendency to repeat a traumatic scene for the purpose of achieving a belated mastery." O. Fenichel, *The Psychoanalytic Theory of Neurosis* (New York: W. W. Norton & Co., 1945), pp. 347–8.

40. "For whatever it is worth, we can note that males in all vertebrate species use their repertoire of threatening—not just 'aggressive'—behavior as a necessary part of their reproductive behavior. The shift from threat to sex does not dispense with the movements and postures of attack but simply introduces a variant, e.g., rather than attacking the female head on, the male shifts to a position parallel with the female." R. P. Michael, "The Relevance and Irrelevance of Primate Behavior for Man," paper presented at the annual meeting of the American Psychoanalytic Association, May 1978, Atlanta, Georgia.

41. In one classification, Freud divides jokes into "innocent" versus "tendentious" (hostile). What he says is similar to what I believe about sexual excitement (and excitement at large): "A non-tendentious joke scarcely ever achieves the sudden burst of laughter which makes tendentious ones so irresistible. Since the technique of both can be the same, a suspicion may be aroused in us that tendentious jokes, by virtue of their purpose, must have sources of pleasure at their disposal to which innocent jokes have no access. . . . We are now prepared to realize the part played by jokes in hostile aggressiveness. A joke will allow us to exploit something ridiculous in our enemy which we could not, on account of obstacles in the way, bring forward openly or consciously; once again, then, the joke *will evade restrictions and open sources of pleasure that have become inaccessible*. It will further bribe the hearer with its yield of pleasure into taking sides with us without any very close investigation. . . . Jokes, even if the thought contained in them is non-tendentious and thus only serves theoretical intellectual interests, are in fact never non-tendentious." S. Freud, *Jokes and Their Relation to the Unconscious* (1905), *S.E.* 8: 96, 103, 132. Italics in original.

42. In later years, Freud amplified his ideas on humor, and, as you can see, makes even easier my task of showing the similar dynamics in erotics and humor: "Humour has something liberating about it; but it also has something of grandeur and elevation . . . The grandeur in it clearly lies in the triumph of narcissism, the victorious assertion of the ego's invulnerability. The ego refuses to be distressed by the provocations of reality, to let itself be compelled to suffer. It insists that it cannot be affected by the traumas of the external world; it shows, in fact, that such traumas are no more than occasions for it to gain pleasure. This last feature is a quite essential element of humour. . . . Humour is not resigned; it is rebellious. It signifies not only the triumph of the ego but also of the pleasure principle, which is able here to assert itself against the unkindness of the real circumstances. . . . Its fending off of the possibility of suffering places it among the great series of methods which the human mind has constructed in order to evade the compulsion to suffer—a series which begins with neurosis and culminates in madness and which includes intoxication, self-absorption and ecstasy. . . . The main thing is the intention which humour carries out, whether it is acting in relation to the self or other people. It means: 'Look! here is the world, which seems so dangerous! It is nothing but a game for children—just worth making a jest about!' " S. Freud, "Humour" (1927), *S.E.* 21: 162, 163, 166.

In adding to Freud's remarks, I want to be peevish. The clowns, ashamed of their art, are so busy over the centuries publicly announcing their secret griefs. When will we learn that comedy is as profound, genuine, and worthy as—if not more than—tragedy? The content of each is the same, only the presentation is different. Certainly tragedy is no less contrived than comedy. And comedy is less pornographic; its problem in being accepted is that it carries insight about itself (not only about "the world" or "mankind") in its structure. Tragedy is the pornography of guilt, as war and gangster shows are of hatred, and supernatural tales are of horror: realistic fakes, cozy substitutes for the full experience.

In tragedy, the writer conspires with his audience in the illusion of catastrophe; we leave the theater inspired by our own wisdom. (Another fraud: calling the effects "catharsis.") The same insight done with humor would have shown us what idiots we are. Tragedy's wisdoms are more self-serving, convenient for melancholic philosophers: bitter truths about hunger elaborated over *gigot d'agneau en croûte*. But it doesn't work; instead—if you are dumb enough to want to experience the tragic—be the lamb led to slaughter.

43. E. Becker, *Angel in Armor* (New York: George Braziller, 1969), pp. 14–15.

44. G. Devereux, "Panel Report—Perversion: Theoretical and Therapeutic Aspects" (J. A. Arlow, reporter), *J. Am. Psychoanal. Assoc.* 2 (1954): 336.

45. O. Kernberg, "Barriers to Falling and Remaining in Love," *J. Am. Psychoanal. Assoc.* 22 (1974): 486–511; Kernberg, "Mature Love: Prerequisites and Characteristics," *J. Am. Psychoanal. Assoc.* 22 (1974): 743–68; Kernberg, "Boundaries and Structures in Love Relations," *J. Am. Psychoanal. Assoc.* 25 (1977): 81–114.

Chapter 2. Primary Femininity

1. See, e.g., H. Blum, ed., *Female Psychology,* a supplement to *J. Am. Psychoanal. Assoc.* 24 (1976): 1–350; Z. O. Fliegel, "Feminine Psychosexual Development in Freudian Theory: A Historical Reconstruction," *Psychoanal. Q.* 42 (1973): 385–408; R. Schafer, "Problems in Freud's Psychology of Women," *J. Am. Psychoanal. Assoc.* 22 (1974): 459–85; M. J. Winpfheimer and R. Schafer, "Psychoanalytic Methodology in Helene Deutsch's *The Psychology of Women,"* *Psychoanal. Q.* 46 (1977): 287–318.

2. Fliegel's review of this history, "Feminine Psychosexual Development in Freudian Theory," is essential background for this discussion.

3. S. Freud, "Female Sexuality" (1931), *S.E.* 21: 232. Italics added.

4. "As regards fundamental sense of self, boys believe themselves males awaiting castration and girls believe they are males who have been castrated: Freud's theory of sexual phallic monism." J. Chasseguet-Smirgel, "Freud and Female Sexuality: The Consideration of Some Blind Spots in the Exploration of the 'Dark Continent,' " *Int. J. Psychoanal.* 57 (1976): 275–86.

5. "Freud usually resisted being led by biological speculation, be it ever so plausible, when he could not confirm it by the findings of psychoanalytic introspective observation. An example of this empiricism is contained in his papers on female sexuality. Much has been said about Freud's supposed anti-feminine bias as evidenced by his stressing of the importance of the phallic strivings in the development of female sexuality. The obvious biological truth seems to be that the female must have primary feminine tendencies and that femaleness cannot possibly be explained as a retreat from disappointed maleness. It is yet improbable that Freud's opinion was due to a circumscribed blindspot that limited his powers of observation. His refusal to change his views on female sexuality was much more likely due to his reliance on clinical evidence—as it was then open to him—through psychoanalytic observation, and thus he refused to accept a plausible biological speculation as a psychological fact. Penetrating beyond the feminine attitudes and feelings of his patients he found regularly the struggle over phallic strivings and, *while he accepted biological bisexuality,* he rejected the postulate

of a preceding psychological phase of femininity without psychological evidence for it."
H. Kohut, "Introspection, Empathy, and Psychoanalysis," *J. Am. Psychoanal. Assoc.*
3 (1959): 479. Italics in original.

6. H. Roiphe and E. Galenson, "Early Genital Activity and the Castration Complex,"
Psychoanal. Q. 42 (1972): 334–47.

7. "In many crucial instances, the decision whether to speak of behavior or of aims or
attitudes as active or passive is like the decision whether to say of a certain glass of water
that it is half full or half empty. . . . Does the penis penetrate the vagina or does the
vagina receive the penis? . . . To designate is also to create and to enforce. By devising
and allocating words, which are names, people create entities and modes of experience
and enforce specific subjective experiences. Names render events, situations, and relationships available or unavailable for psychological life that might otherwise remain
cognitively indeterminate. Consequently, whether or not something will be an instance
of masculinity or femininity, activity or passivity, aggression or masochism, dominance
or submission, or something else altogether, or nothing at all, will depend on whether
or not we consistently call it this or that or consistently do not name it at all, hence
do not constitute and authorize its being. Similarly, to the extent that we link or equate
such names as, for example, femininity and passivity, we exert a profound and lasting
formative influence on what it is said to be like to be feminine or passive. Logically,
there is no right answer to the questions, what is masculine and what is feminine and
what is active and what is passive. There are no preconceptual facts to be discovered
and arrayed. There are only loose conventions governing the uses and groupings of the
words in question. And these conventions, like all others, must manifest values."
Schafer, "Problems in Freud's Psychology of Women," pp. 481, 478.

The inexactness of our language complicates the issue further. The same word
"passivity" can indicate inability to take responsibility, or desire for dependency, or
receptivity, gentleness, and acceptance.

8. K. Horney, "On the Genesis of the Castration Complex in Women," *Int. J. Psychoanal.* 5 (1924): 50–64; E. Jones, "The Early Development of Female Sexuality," *Int.
J. Psychoanal.* 8 (1927): 459–72; G. Zilboorg, "Masculine and Feminine," *Psychiatry*
7 (1944): 257–96.

9. R. J. Stoller, "A Contribution to the Study of Gender Identity," *Int. J. Psychoanal.*
45 (1964): 220–6.

10. For example, otherwise biologically normal females have been somewhat masculinized by progesterone given to their mothers to prevent abortion. See A. A. Ehrhardt
and J. Money, "Progestin-Induced Hermaphroditism: IQ and Psycho-Sexual Identity
in a Study of Ten Girls," *J. Sex Res.* 3 (1967): 83–100.

11. J. Money and A. A. Ehrhardt, *Man and Woman Boy and Girl* (Baltimore: Johns
Hopkins University Press, 1972).

12. J. Money, J. G. Hampson, and J. L. Hampson, "An Examination of Some Basic
Sexual Concepts: The Evidence of Human Hermaphroditism," *Bull. Johns Hopkins
Hosp.* 97 (1955): 301–19; R. J. Stoller, *Sex and Gender, Volume I: On the Development
of Masculinity and Femininity* (New York: Science House, 1968); A. Lev-Ran, "Gender Role Differentiation in Hermaphrodites," *Arch. Sex. Behav.* 3 (1974): 391–424.

13. Money, Hampson, and Hampson, "An Examination of Some Basic Sexual Concepts"; Stoller, *Sex and Gender, I;* Lev-Ran, "Gender Role Differentiation in Hermaphrodites."

14. Stoller, *Sex and Gender, I;* R. J. Stoller, *Sex and Gender, Volume II: The Transsexual Experiment* (New York: Jason Aronson, 1975).

15. E.g. P. Greenacre, "Early Physical Determinants in the Development of the Sense
of Identity," *J. Am. Psychoanal. Assoc.* 6 (1958): 612–27; M. S. Mahler, "Panel:
Problems of Identity" (D. L. Rubinfine, reporter), *J. Am. Psychoanal. Assoc.* 6 (1958):
136–8.

16. Money, Hampson, and Hampson, "An Examination of Some Basic Sexual Concepts"; Stoller, *Sex and Gender, I;* Lev-Ran, "Gender Role Differentiation in Hermaphrodites."

17. R. Edgecumbe and M. Burgner, "The Phallic-Narcissistic Phase," *Psychoanal. Study Child* 30 (1975): 165.

18. That girls and women suffer from penis envy is a matter of observation, not of theory or propaganda. It is still unclear, however, if that envy is an essential of the psychology of all girls and women, as Freud said. For instance, is it present in girls who have never seen a penis? The "yes" answer has been argued in two ways. First, that people have an inherited memory of penises, so that the actual experience of seeing one is not necessary for causing envy. Second, that baby girls always manage to see a penis— father's, a brother's, a friend's—even if they or the family deny they have. These explanations are weak in that they cannot be refuted experimentally or by observation. In addition, problems of testing are increased if one also interprets, as evidence of hidden envy, behavior in which there is no manifest envy (as by saying that absence of envy is evidence of reaction formation; it may be—and then, again, it may not). And certainly those who argue the importance of penis envy will have set up an untestable theory if they interpret *any* expression of envy in a girl or woman as being the direct derivative of *penis* envy.

In the theory that penis envy is a universal anlage of female psychology, there is also not enough slack to allow for differing intensities of the envy. Some girls have more reason to be envious than others. For instance, a little girl whose brothers are favored by the parents is likely to have a greater problem than one who has no brothers, or than a little girl who is the object of her parents' great joy. Or, penis envy could at times simply be a later version of a more fundamental state of envy; girls without the primordial envy would be less inflamed on first seeing what they do not have.

As others have suggested, some of these hunches could be clarified (though not proved, of course) by studies of other cultures. In places where genitals are not hidden, how do little girls, from earliest life on, respond to penises; and are there, in those societies, differences in femininity that can be traced back to viewing penises? Or, if no penis envy (or its derivatives) is visible, why not?

To return to our world, there is still the question crucial to Freud's theory: Why should the view of a penis traumatize a girl? The obvious answer is that it is so visible, so usable, and therefore apparently superior to the girl's anatomic state. That seems likely enough; certainly, if she is a year and a half or older, she has had enough experience with her own body that her response is more likely to be envy (or some other form of anger) than if she were to observe, say, a creature with two heads.

But another factor may be at work, too: in a family where everyone feels genitals must be hidden, may not the resulting atmosphere of mystery, danger, and excitement potentiate the trauma? It would not be so much the penis, then, as the family's exaggeration of the importance of not seeing genitals that would lay the groundwork for trauma. This would be so even in families that make a big show of being "liberated," for that kind of display would also alert a child.

19. And if you grant yourself the right to play that game, our side demands the same (Chasseguet-Smirgel, "Freud and Female Sexuality," p. 277): how about an inherited memory of vaginae and uteri in females, which Freud ignores; or, how about an inherited memory of vaginae and uteri in males? It is hard to lose an argument if you are allowed to postulate inherited memories, the wild joker of analytic theory.

20. Cf. Jones, who describes a protophallic state, in which neither boys nor girls yet know about castration, nor girls about penises. E. Jones, "The Phallic Phase," *Int. J. Psychoanal.* 14 (1933): 1–33.

21. Freud, "Female Sexuality," p. 233. Italics added.

22. R. Green, "Human Sexuality: Research and Treatment Frontiers," in *American*

Handbook of Psychiatry, ed. S. Arieti, 2nd ed. (New York: Basic Books, 1976), pp. 665–91.

23. W. Young, R. Goy, and C. Phoenix, "Hormones and Sexual Behavior," *Science* 143 (1964): 212–18.

24. Green, "Human Sexuality," p. 666.

25. J. A. Kleeman, "The Establishment of Core Gender Identity in Normal Girls: I. (a) Introduction; (b) Development of the Ego Capacity to Differentiate," *Arch. Sex. Behav.* 1 (1971): 103–16; Kleeman, "The Establishment of Core Gender Identity in Normal Girls: II. How Meanings Are Conveyed Between Parent and Child in the First Three Years," *Arch. Sex. Behav.* 1 (1971): 117–29.

26. And psychologic tests of the transsexuals seen by our research team are scored like those of (and do not distinguish the patients from) females with hysteric personality. See also J. C. Finney, J. M. Brandsma, M. Tondow, and G. LaMaistre, "A Study of Transsexuals Seeking Gender Reassignment," *Am. J. Psychiatry* 132 (1975): 962–64.

27. Stoller, *Sex and Gender, I and II.*

28. Stoller, *Sex and Gender, II.*

29. R. J. Stoller, "Etiological Factors in Female Transsexualism: A First Approximation," *Arch. Sex. Behav.* 2 (1972): 47–64.

30. R. J. Stoller, *Splitting: A Case of Female Masculinity* (New York: Quadrangle Books, 1973).

31. Stoller, "Etiological Factors in Female Transsexualism."

32. The one exception always permitted (exemplified in two different forms by Freud and Hartmann) has been that biologic givens contribute to personality development. More recently, others have also supported the idea that nonconflictual forces can influence personality development. For instance: "In our categorization of infantile disorders, we have learned to distinguish between two types, intermingled though they are with each other. One belongs to the infantile neurosis and its forerunners, its earliest appearances caused by conflicts between drive activity and environmental forces, its later stages due to purely internal conflicts between contrasting tendencies within the personality structure, both accompanied by fear, anxiety, guilt, inhibition, loss of pleasure or function and by symptom formation. Experience has proved that psychoanalysis is the method of choice for treating these disorders since interpretation of the repressed, of transference and resistances enables the child's ego to undo the damage it has done to itself by adopting pathological conflict solutions and to replace these faulty structures by more adaptive ones.

"The second type of disturbance is of a different nature. It arises during the child's early period of growth and maturation and has to be ascribed to direct interference with the course of normal development. Instead of being born with the average expectable physical and mental equipment, reared in an average environment and developing its internal structure at the usual rate, a child can be subjected to deviations in any or all of these respects and consequently develop deviant, atypical or borderline features. There is no question here of the child's ego having done harm to itself; on the contrary, harm has been inflicted on it by circumstances entirely beyond its control.

"Developmental pathology, no less than the neurotic one, is open to psychoanalytic exploration, explanation and understanding. In spite of this, it does not answer to psychoanalytic therapy in the same manner. Even the most correct uncovering of past and forgotten circumstances and events (such as physical or mental handicap, neglect, rejection, lack of security and maternal care, precocious or delayed ego or superego functioning) does not blot out their impact on the shaping of the child's personality or eradicate their roots, i.e. does not act as a radical therapy. At best, it helps the child to cope better with the after-effects of what has happened to him." A. Freud, "Changes in Psychoanalytic Practice and Experience," *Int. J. Psychoanal.* 57 (1976): 258–9. See

also A. P. Weil, "The Basic Core," *Psychoanal. Study Child* 25 (1970): 442–60; M. Balint, *The Basic Fault: Therapeutic Aspects of Regression* (London: Tavistock, 1968); and A. Freud, "The Infantile Neurosis," *Psychoanal. Study Child* 26 (1971): 79–90.
33. Fliegel, "Feminine Psychosexual Development in Freudian Theory."

PART 2. Data: Belle

Chapter 3. Case Summary

1. "Before I continue the account, I must confess that I have altered the *milieu* of the case in order to preserve the incognito of the people concerned, but that I have altered nothing else. I consider it a wrong practice, however excellent the motive may be, to alter any detail in the presentation of a case. One can never tell what aspect of a case may be picked out by a reader of independent judgement, and one runs the risk of leading him astray." S. Freud, "A Case of Paranoia Running Counter to the Psychoanalytic Theory of the Disease" (1915), *S.E.* 14: 263.
2. H. Lichtenstein, "Identity and Sexuality," *J. Am. Psychoanal. Assoc.* 9 (1961): 179–260.
3. E. L. Abelin, "Some Further Observations and Comments on the Earliest Role of the Father," *Int. J. Psychoanal.* 56 (1975): 293–302.
4. R. J. Stoller, *Splitting: A Case of Female Masculinity* (New York: Quadrangle Books, 1973).

Chapter 4. The Erotic Daydream

1. This is not to imply that penis envy develops only at this rather advanced state of the socialization of children; the work of Galenson and Roiphe shows us much earlier roots. See, e.g., E. Galenson and H. Roiphe, "Some Suggested Revisions Concerning Early Female Development," *J. Am. Psychoanal. Assoc.* 24 (1976): 29–58. See also A. Freud, "Observations in Child Development," *Psychoanal. Study Child* 6 (1951): 18–30.
2. Cf. G. Zavitzianos, "The Object in Fetishism, Homeovestism and Transvestism," *Int. J. Psychoanal.* 58 (1977): 487–95. Zavitzianos has coined the term "homeovestism" for the practice of putting on the clothes of one's own sex to produce sexual excitement. He says (and I agree) that such an act should not be considered fetishism. He also says: "The basic trend in 'homeovestism' in women is 'the denial of the female genitals to prevent castration anxiety.' " I did not find evidence for that in Belle.
3. The following remark about orgasm applies as well to the "truths" of erotic excitement: "Orgasm is endowed with the power to confirm, create, and affirm conviction." K. Eissler, "Notes on Problems of Technique in the Psychoanalytic Treatment of Adolescents," *Psychoanal. Study Child* 13 (1958): 242.
4. "The resolution of the oedipus complex fixes what can best be described as the 'central masturbation fantasy'—the fantasy whose content contains the various regressive satisfactions and the main sexual identifications." M. Laufer, "The Central Masturbation Fantasy, the Final Sexual Organization, and Adolescence," *Psychoanal. Study Child* 31 (1976): 300.
5. R. C. Bak, "The Phallic Woman: The Ubiquitous Fantasy in Perversion" *Psychoanal. Study Child* 23 (1968): 30.
6. For some people intercourse is foreplay, while the main act—the real pleasure—is masturbation. See S. Freud, " 'Civilized' Sexual Morality and Modern Nervous Illness" (1908), *S.E.* 9: 200: "A witty writer (Karl Kraus in the Vienna paper *Die Fackel*)

. . .: 'Copulation is no more than an unsatisfying substitute for masturbation.' " Or S. Freud, " 'Wild' Psycho-analysis" (1910), *S.E.* 11: 223: "We have long known, too, that mental absence of satisfaction with all its consequences can exist where there is no lack of normal sexual intercourse; and as therapists we always bear in mind that the unsatisfied sexual trends (whose substitutive satisfactions in the form of nervous symptoms we combat) can often find only very inadequate outlet in coitus or other sexual acts."

7. Cf. hallucinated imaginary companions in Stoller, *Splitting.*

Chapter 7. Sadomasochism

1. S. Freud, "Analysis Terminable and Interminable" (1937), *S.E.* 23: 216–53.

2. Cf. M. de M'Uzan, "A Case of Masochistic Perversion and an Outline of a Theory," *Int. J. Psychoanal.* 54 (1973): 455–67.

3. R. C. Bak, "The Phallic Woman: The Ubiquitous Fantasy in Perversion," *Psychoanal. Study Child* 23 (1968): 29–30.

4. C. Brenner has reviewed the issues from the classical analytic position in "The Masochistic Character," *J. Am. Psychoanal. Assoc.* 7 (1959): 197–226. Berliner, in three papers, reviews and revises classical analytic theories. Like Reik and others (e.g., Smirnoff, myself) he stresses the interpersonal-become-intrapsychic more than the instinctual-become-intrapsychic. See B. Berliner, "Libido and Reality in Masochism," *Psychoanal. Q.* 9 (1940): 322–33; Berliner, "On Some Psychodynamics of Masochism," *Psychoanal. Q.* 16 (1947): 459–71; Berliner, "The Role of Object Relations in Moral Masochism," *Psychoanal. Q.* 27 (1958): 38–56.

5. Kardiner and others present an extensive criticism that emphasizes interpersonal rather than instinctual forces in masochism. See A. Kardiner, A. Karush, and L. Ovesey, "A Methodological Study of Freudian Theory: III. Narcissism, Bisexuality and the Dual Instinct Theory," *J. Nerv. Ment. Dis.* 129 (1959): 215–20.

6. P. Ricoeur, *Freud and Philosophy: An Essay on Interpretation,* trans. D. Savage (New Haven, Conn.: Yale University Press, 1970), pp. 286–7.

7. "A sense of guilt is invariably the fact that transforms sadism into masochism." S. Freud, "A Child Is Being Beaten" (1919), *S.E.* 17: 189. Cf. R. M. Loewenstein, "A Contribution to the Psychoanalytic Theory of Masochism," *J. Am. Psychoanal. Assoc.* 5 (1957): 213–14: "Psychoanalytic experience invariably confirms Freud's view that masochistic perversions in men, as well as the moral masochism, result from a turning of sadism against the self under the influence of guilt feelings."

8. "Moral masochism and hypocrisy have in common that a kind of morality is being used in them for the gratification of deneutralized drives. The difference between the two is clear, however. In moral masochism proper, the masochistic gratification is unconscious and the moral motivation may be conscious or not. In hypocrisy the moralistic motivation is consciously stressed in order to hide more or less preconscious gratifications of ego interests or of sadism. Thus to some extent sadism of the superego is close to hypocrisy. The difference between them is that in sadism of the superego and in masochism of the ego, the self is the victim; in hypocrisy, the gratification is derived at the expense of others." Loewenstein, "A Contribution to the Psychoanalytic Theory of Masochism," pp. 212–13. The philosophic problem revolves around whether one can be unconsciously sly.

9. Cf. L. A. Spiegel, "Moral Masochism," *Psychoanal. Q.* 47 (1978): 209–36.

10. V. N. Smirnoff, "The Masochistic Contract," *Int. J. Psychoanal.* 50 (1970): 666–7.

11. Ibid., pp. 668, 670.

12. Berliner, "Libido and Reality in Masochism," p. 331. See also Loewenstein, "A Contribution to the Psychoanalytic Theory of Masochism."

13. T. Reik, *Masochism in Modern Man,* trans. M. H. Beigel and G. M. Kurth (New York: Farrar, Straus & Rinehart, 1941), p. 49. I disagree with Reik's last sentence and also with his repeated statements that the dynamics he has found belong only, or almost only, to masochism.

14. Ibid., p. 58.

15. Ibid., pp. 252, 254, 419, 429.

16. See E. Markovitz, "Aggression in Human Adaptation," *Psychoanal. Q.* 42 (1973): 226–33, for a welcome discussion of these distinctions.

17. Webster's *Third New International Dictionary,* 1961.

Chapter 8. Exhibitionism

1. The following will sound naïve, but it is not: I do not see how a therapist—whether an analyst practicing analysis or a physician doing a physical examination—can be enticed by a patient if he really wants to understand the area, anatomic or psychologic, he is investigating. One would expect just that lack of excitement if, as my theory says, the desire to examine does not contain a desire to harm; only if he is fetishizing the patient into parts, indulging in the victim-victor, simulated-risk, mystery, peeking routine, will he get caught by sexual excitement. But if he is truly interested in what he is doing—physical or psychologic examination—there is no space inside him at that time for sexual excitement. It is inappropriate, not forbidden or renounced in a fit of obstinate frustration, but simply not a part of his present psychodynamic state. "The patient, whose sexual repression is of course not yet removed but merely pushed into the background, will then feel safe enough to allow all her preconditions for loving, all the phantasies springing from her sexual desires, all the detailed characteristics of her state of being in love, to come to light; and from these she will herself open the way to the infantile roots of her love." S. Freud, "Observations on Transference Love" (1914), *S.E.* 12: 166.

It is not so simple, however. An essential tool for analytic work is the way we respond to our patients. We must vibrate as sensitively as a musical instrument, or we will not know, except intellectually, what the patient is experiencing and what the patient does to provoke responses in others. To do our work, we must receive the messages our patients send, but we cannot do this if there are cultural, language, neurotic, or personality chasms between us and the patient. (If a tribeswoman scarred for beauty shows me her scars, I will not sense her meaning, nor will she, on meeting my blankness, fathom my failure to respond.) When Belle tries to buy me off with a bit of thigh, I have to know—empathically, not just theoretically—what other men in our culture also know about flashing thighs. But my response is minimal, a signal; it has behind it no pressure toward action. The transducer would register no change.

2. Cf. D. G. Brown, "Drowsiness in the Countertransference," *Int. Rev. Psychoanal.* 4 (1977): 481–92. How are empathy and resonance related to countertransference?

3. "An exactly analogous state of affairs occurs in the same field when a person who is masturbating tries in his conscious phantasies to have the feelings both of the man and of the woman in the situation which he is picturing. Further counterparts are to be found in certain hysterical attacks in which the patient simultaneously plays both parts in the underlying sexual phantasy. In one case which I observed, for instance, the patient pressed her dress up against her body with one hand (as the woman), while she tried to tear it off with the other (as the man). This simultaneity of contradictory actions serves to a large extent to obscure the situation, which is otherwise so plastically portrayed in the attack, and it is thus well suited to conceal the unconscious phantasy that is at work." S. Freud, "Hysterical Phantasies and Their Relation to Bisexuality" (1908), *S.E.* 9: 166.

4. "Characterized by excitability, emotional instability, over-reactivity, and self-

dramatization. This self-dramatization is always attention-seeking and often seductive, whether or not the patient is aware of its purpose. These personalities are also immature, self-centered, often vain, and usually dependent on others." *Diagnostic and Statistical Manual of Mental Disorders,* 2nd ed. (Washington, D.C.: American Psychiatric Association, 1968), p. 43.

5. "I think that the undoubted intellectual inferiority of so many women can . . . be traced back to the inhibition of thought necessitated by sexual repression. . . . I do not believe that women's 'physiological feeble-mindedness' is to be explained by a biological opposition between intellectual work and sexual activity." S. Freud, " 'Civilized' Sexual Morality and Modern Nervous Illness" (1908), *S.E.* 9: 199.

6. For a review of the literature and discussion of cases in children, see M. Berger and H. Kennedy, "Pseudobackwardness in Children: Maternal Attitudes as an Etiological Factor," *Psychoanal. Study Child* 30 (1975): 280; bibliography of pseudo-stupidity, p. 281; see also 302 ff.

7. "By focal *symbiosis* I mean a condition in which a symbiotic relationship exists in respect to the functioning of a special organ or body area. Usually the individuals participating in this symbiotic relationship are of uneven development: parent and child, older and younger sibling, or even stronger and weaker twins. The focal symbiosis represents the special site of emotional disturbance in both members of the symbiotic pair. But it is ordinarily manifest in the weaker or smaller partner, who remains functionally dependent in this specific area on the active response of the other partner, far beyond the maturational period at which the special function would ordinarily become autonomous. I would conceive of a focal symbiosis as being an intensely strong interdependence (usually between mother and child, but sometimes, as in my cases, with people other than the mother) which is limited to a special and rather circumscribed relationship rather than a nearly total enveloping one. Probably it represents most frequently an area of pathology of the adult member of the symbiotic pair which is then projected onto the child with focussed anxiety or conviction of a corresponding disturbance in the infant." P. Greenacre, "On Focal Symbiosis," in *Dynamic Psychopathology in Childhood,* ed. L. Jessner and E. Pavenstedt (New York: Grune & Stratton, 1959), p. 244.

8. R. D. Stolorow, "Toward a Functional Definition of Narcissism," *Int. J. Psychoanal.* 56 (1975):181: *"Narcissism as a sexual perversion.* Narcissism as a sexual perversion refers to the taking of one's own body, or more specifically the mirror image of one's own body, as a sexual object. In modern clinical thinking it is insufficient to interpret a sexual perversion solely in drive theory terms as a libidinal fixation (in this case, a libidinal fixation on the self as sexual object). It is also necessary to understand the function served by perverse activity within the personality. With regard to the narcissistic perversion, Elkisch (1957) and Lichtenstein (1964) have noted that patients become preoccupied with their mirror image in order to restore and stabilize a crumbling self-representation. A narcissistically disordered patient of my own would gaze lovingly at his mirror image (with or without masturbatory activity) as a reparative device following injurious experiences which threatened his self-representation with fragmentation. Reich (1960) and Kohut (1971) have both observed that a wide variety of sexual perversions may function as sexualized attempts to ward off self-depletion and self-fragmentation, to revive the sense of having a cohesive self, and to restore self-esteem. Hence, it would seem that a functional conception of narcissism in terms of the maintenance of the self-representation contributes significantly to our understanding of the narcissistic perversion and perverse activity in general."

9. S. E. Pulver, "Narcissism," *J. Am. Psychoanal. Assoc.* 18 (1970): 319–419; Stolorow, "Toward a Functional Definition of Narcissism," pp. 179–85.

Chapter 9. Lovely

1. R. J. Stoller, *Sex and Gender, Volume II* (New York: Jacob Aronson, 1975).
2. R. J. Stoller, *Sex and Gender, Volume I* (New York: Science House, 1968).

Part III. Theories of the Mind

Chapter 10. Microdots

1. E.g., in *The Interpretation of Dreams* (1900), *S.E.* 5: 595, Freud describes a similar process at work in dreaming: "The intensity of a whole train of thought may eventually be concentrated in a single ideational element. Here we have the fact of 'compression' or 'condensation.' " And later, in "Revision of the Theory of Dreams" (1932), *S.E.* 22: 20: "It is as though a force were at work in dreaming which was subjecting the material to compression and concentration." See also P. Ricoeur, *Freud and Philosophy: An Essay on Interpretation,* trans. D. Savage (New Haven, Conn.: Yale University Press, 1970), p. 93, on Freud's concept of condensation.

2. "Among the derivatives of the *Ucs.* instinctual impulses, of the sort we have described, there are some which unite in themselves characters of an opposite kind. On the one hand, they are highly organized, free from self-contradiction, have made use of every acquisition of the system *Cs.* and would hardly be distinguished in our judgement from the formations of that system. On the other hand they are unconscious and are incapable of becoming conscious. Thus *qualitatively* they belong to the system *Pcs.,* but *factually* to the *Ucs.* Their origin is what decides their fate. . . . Of such a nature are those phantasies of normal people as well as of neurotics which we have recognized as preliminary stages in the formation both of dreams and of symptoms and which, in spite of their high degree of organization, remain repressed and therefore cannot become conscious. They draw near to consciousness and remain undisturbed so long as they do not have an intense cathexis, but as soon as they exceed a certain height of cathexis they are thrust back. Substitutive formations, too, are highly organized derivatives of the *Ucs.* of this kind; but these succeed in breaking through into consciousness, when circumstances are favourable—for example, if they happen to join forces with an anticathexis from the *Pcs.* " S. Freud, "Communication Between the Two Systems" (1915), *S.E.* 14: 190–1.

3. "Not only memories, as Freud assumed, but also the perception of immediate experience, far from being a passive camera-like registration, is selectively organized and given meaning by schemata, motives, and past experience. It is the factual, objective, impersonal description of reality that is the product of a lengthy construction, one that involves an interpersonal abstracting and conceptualizing process, and is not merely the result of the inhibition of the distorting effect of drive discharge. The dichotomy between factual reality and fantasy, despite its reassuring simplicity, may lead us into hopeless dead ends. . . . even the remote past—whether factual or psychical in origin—remains preserved essentially intact in the present and therefore can act as an immediate causal agent of present behavior. Infantile experiences have been preserved by repression and thus function as a direct cause of present symptoms. This implies a kind of short-circuiting of what would otherwise be a lengthy time sequence where all the causal links would have to be filled in. Unconscious wishes and cathected memories of past events are synonymous for Freud." J. G. Schimek, "The Interpretations of the Past: Childhood Trauma, Psychical Reality, and Historical Truth," *J. Am. Psychoanal. Assoc.* 23 (1975): 860.

4. A. D. Rosenblatt and J. T. Thickstun, "Modern Psychoanalytic Concepts in a General Psychology," *Psychol. Issues* 10, monograph no. 42/43 (1977): 71.

5. S. Isaacs, "The Nature and Function of Phantasy," in *Developments in Psycho-*

Analysis, ed. J. Riviere (London: Hogarth Press, 1952), pp. 83–5.

6. See R. S. Wallerstein, "Psychoanalysis as Science: Its Present Status and Its Future Tasks," *Psychol. Issues* 9, monograph no. 36 (1976): 198–228. See also J. G. Schimek, "A Critical Re-examination of Freud's Concept of Unconscious Mental Representation," *Int. Rev. Psychoanal.* 2 (1975): 171–87, for a review and discussion of the concept "unconscious mental representation."

7. Cf. S. I. Greenspan, "A Consideration of Some Learning Variables in the Context of Psychoanalytic Theory," *Psychol. Issues* 9, monograph no. 33 (1976).

8. Schimek, "Interpretations of the Past," pp. 854–8, reviews the history of Freud's struggle with this question. J. LaPlanche and J.-B. Pontalis, "Fantasy and the Origins of Sexuality," *Int. J. Psychoanal.* 49 (1968): 1–18, give us a scholarly discussion of these so far insoluble issues.

9. "We will examine as an example how an individual teaches himself to remember a telephone number. We conceive of this as a process of informational compression in which the individual produces more and more miniaturized copies of the original information. This he does by using the original to produce a more miniature copy, and then using this compressed copy to produce a still more miniaturized copy, which in turn is miniatured in a series which, for example, may begin 5 —— 9 —— 2 —— 3 as it is first read from the telephone book, and then is speeded up in the first internal reproduction to 5 — 9 — 2 — 3, which is then reverberated in immediate memory and further speeded up on the second internal reproduction to 5 - 9 - 2 - 3, which on the next repetition is said still more quickly as 5923, until finally it is so abbreviated that it is unconscious, but one knows that one knows it and can reproduce it from within. This miniaturization, however, involves more than simply speeding up the performance, since the sounds of the digits had to be clipped and abbreviated without destroying their essential message. Otherwise such a series of increasingly compressed equivalents might be like the blurred features of a person seen from an increasing distance. They would be of no use unless they were recognizable as compressions of the original model rather than equivalents of the just preceding miniature. It must be possible not only to recognize the original from the miniature, but also to reproduce the original exactly from the miniature. The compression relationship must be reversible and expandable. This is achieved in teaching oneself to remember by applying the inverse of the compression transformation—for example, using the operator "decreased speed" on the miniature, which had been produced from the original by the operator 'increased speed.' In this way one can learn to reverse what one has just done." S. W. Tomkins and S. Messick, *Computer Simulation of Personality* (New York: John Wiley & Sons, 1963), pp. 42–3.

10. Zangwill, in reviewing F. C. Bartlett's fundamental work on remembering, confirms the analyst's belief that memories are not pure reproductions of past events but that rather, as Bartlett believed, "Remembering can in no sense be regarded as the mere revival of earlier experience; it is a process of active reconstruction, much of it based on factors of general impression and attitude, together with the reinstatement of a small amount of critical detail. In his [Bartlett's] own words, recall is far more decisively an affair of construction than one of mere reproduction. . . . Bartlett regarded his experimental findings as incompatible with any notion of what, following Philippe, he called 'fixed, lifeless traces,' that is to say, *simulacra* of past events in some way preserved in their original form and whose re-excitation constitutes recall." O. L. Zangwill, "Remembering Revisited," *Q. J. Exper. Psychol.* 24 (1972): 126–7.

11. P. W. Pruyser, in his aforementioned article, asks, "What splits in 'splitting'?" My answer: A knot of discrete scripts—a microdot—unravels a bit. One example: ambivalence—I hate you/I love you—with both stories manifest at the same time. An awesome example: psychosis, a state in which fantasies break out of their cages. See P. W. Pruyser, "What Splits in 'Splitting'? A Scrutiny of the Concept of Splitting in Psychoa-

nalysis and Psychiatry," *Bull. Menninger Clin.* 39 (1975): 1–46.

12. Rosenblatt and Thickstun, "Modern Psychoanalytic Concepts in a General Psychology," p. 71.

13. Cf. J. Sandler and W. G. Jaffe, "Towards a Basic Psychoanalytic Model," *Int. J. Psychoanal.* 50 (1969): 81–3.

14. Cf. R. P. Abelson, "Computer Simulation of Social Behavior," in *Computer Models of Thought and Language,* ed. C. Schank and K. M. Colby (San Francisco: W. H. Freeman & Co., 1973), pp. 294–5.

15. R. R. Greenson, "On Moods and Introjects," *Bull. Menninger Clin.* 18 (1954): 10.

Chapter 11. Who Is Belle?

1. Our geniuses have more access to the process, via inspiration and intuition, than the rest of us; at least, they can harness it enough to deliver a product in the real world more consistently than we can. We must stumble along, inefficiently slower, undependable, and with a lesser product, having to rely on effort, experience, and practice. "Although Einstein is on the one hand an 'apostle of rationality,' he steadily warns us not to 'look in vain for logical bridges,' but to make, when necessary, the great 'leap' to basic principles: 'To these elementary laws there leads no logical path, but only intuition supported by being sympathetically in touch with experience.' " (M. Brenman-Gibson, "Notes on the Study of the Creative Process," *Psychol. Issues* 9, monograph no. 36 [1976]: 330.) True, but nothing to brag about, for I think "intuition" is no more than a microdot of a number of logical, though not yet conscious, thoughts. Discovery, obviously, does not occur at the moment of "inspiration"; rather, that moment is the end product (arrival at consciousness) of a longer, unconscious, highly logical process that puts the pieces together.

　　Cf. E. Beres and J. Arlow, "Fantasy and Identification in Empathy," *Psychoanal. Q.* 43 (1974): 46: "When the therapist appears to arrive intuitively at an understanding of his patient he is actually becoming aware of the end product of a series of mental operations carried on outside the scope of consciousness."

2. S. Freud, "The Ego and the Id" (1923), *S.E.* 19: 46.

3. P. Ricoeur, *Freud and Philosophy: An Essay on Interpretation,* trans. D. Savage (New Haven, Conn.: Yale University Press, 1970), p. 378.

4. "No activity of the mind is ever conscious." K. S. Lashley, "Cerebral Organization and Behavior," in *The Brain and Human Behavior: Proceeds of the Association for Research in Nervous and Mental Disease,* ed. H. C. Solomon, S. Cobb, and W. Penfield (Baltimore: Williams & Wilkins Co., 1958), 36: 4.

5. Ricoeur, *Freud and Philosophy,* p. 60.

6. Lashley, "Cerebral Organization and Behavior."

7. "One feels the presence of an invisible *spiritus rector,* a central manager who arranges the stage for the different figures in an almost rational way, often in the form of a more or less sentimental drama." (C. G. Jung, "On the Psychogenesis of Schizophrenia," in *The Collected Works of C. G. Jung,* Bollingen Series XX, ed. G. Adler et al., trans. R. F. Hull [Princeton, N.J.: Princeton University Press, 1960], 3: 235.) But the philosophers warn us that this fancy demands a rector who runs the rector who runs the rector —an infinite regression.

8. "The phenomenon of subliminal perception calls attention to the absence in psychoanalytic theory of an adequate set of hypotheses dealing with the perception of external reality (sensory perception) and its vicissitudes." M. F. Basch, "Perception, Consciousness, and Freud's 'Project,' " in *The Annual of Psychoanalysis,* ed. Chicago Institute of Psychoanalysis (New York: International Universities Press, 1975), 3: 5.

9. See W. James, *Principles of Psychology* (New York: Henry Holt & Co., 1890), 2: 241, on "ignored sensation." On hypnosis, see L. Chertok, D. Michaux, and M. C. Droin, "Dynamics of Hypnotic Analgesias: Some New Data," *J. Nerv. Ment. Dis.* 164 (1977): 88–96. See J. LaPlanche and J.-B. Pontalis, "Fantasy and the Origins of Sexuality," *Int. J. Psychoanal.* 49 (1968): 1–18, on levels of unconscious fantasy. See D. C. Dennett, *Content and Consciousness: An Analysis of Mental Phenomena* (New York: Humanities Press, 1970), on classes of awareness. On habituation, see D. R. Aleksandrowicz, "Are There Precursors to Repression?" *J. Nerv. Ment. Dis.* 164 (1977): 191–7. On free will, see A. Grünbaum, "Free Will and Laws of Human Behavior," in *Psychoanalysis and Contemporary Science,* ed. L. Goldberger and V. H. Rosen (New York: International Universities Press, 1975), pp. 3–39.

10. *"Perceptual defense: Is it repression?* Probably no topic in the recent history of experimental psychology has led to as bitter and sustained controversy as the area of perceptual defense. 'Perceptual defense' refers, of course, to the purported tendency of subjects to resist perceiving anxiety-provoking stimuli. (With certain identifiable subjects, at certain levels of stimulus emotionality, an opposite, sensitization phenomenon may be observed, termed 'perceptual vigilance.' The exceptional attention lavished upon the topic by a generation of psychologists has produced what is perhaps the most profound and wide-ranging analysis of the issues confronting the study of repression-like phenomena in the laboratory. Probably every question to have arisen in other laboratory literatures on repression has cropped up in the perceptual defense area, where it is likely to have been subjected to deeper and more articulated analysis than elsewhere. The contested issues have ranged from the most technical methodological matters to questions of logic and philosophy.

"For example, it was thought initially by some critics that the very notion of perceptual defense rested on a logical absurdity, for it seemed altogether paradoxical to conceive of a subject defensively *not perceiving* a stimulus without first *perceiving* the stimulus to be defended against. This issue, as Sackeim and Gur have pointed out, is analogous to certain philosophic objections to the general notion of repression and the unconscious. Even a psychological version of Zeno's paradox arose, wherein it was argued that perceptual defense implied a censoring homunculus, which in turn had to imply a homunculus within the homunculus, and thus an infinite (and therefore impossible) regress of homunculi. Such arguments were a natural consequence of the now abandoned behavioristic Weltanschauung of experimental psychology of those days (which now dominates personality and clinical psychology a generation later)." M. H. Erdelyi and B. Goldberg, *Let's Not Sweep Repression Under the Rug: Towards a Cognitive Psychology of Repression* (in press).

11. J.-P. Sartre, *Being and Nothingness: An Essay on Phenomenological Ontology,* trans. H. E. Barnes (New York: Philosophical Library, 1956).

12. For the idea that dreams are a different language rather than a *disguising* language, see R. Greenberg and C. Perlman, "A Psychoanalytic-Dream Continuum: The Source and Function of Dreams," *Int. Rev. Psychoanal.* 2 (1975): 441–8.

13. Cf. H. Hartmann, "Psychoanalysis as a Scientific Theory," in *Essays on Ego Psychology* (New York: International Universities Press, 1964), p. 35: "Analysis can be termed a systematic study of self-deception and its motivations."

14. Sartre, *Being and Nothingness,* pp. 49–50.

15. Ibid., pp. 52–3.

16. R. J. Stoller, *Splitting: A Case of Female Masculinity* (New York: Quadrangle Books, 1973).

17. Ricoeur, *Freud and Philosophy,* p. 181.

18. S. Freud, "A Difficulty in the Path of Psycho-analysis" (1917), *S.E.* 17: 143.

19. Cf. P. Noy, "Metapsychology as Multimodel System," *Int. Rev. Psychoanal.* 4 (1977): 9.

20. By something, I do not mean a reified thing, for this something is no *thing*. "Unfortunately, Freud never realized he was investigating behavior and disposition to behavior only, but thought he was examining the vicissitudes of some entity called 'thought' or 'psychical process,' which, being reified, had to be given both a location and a force. He believed he had escaped the error of concretizing the psychological by locating it in a 'mental' apparatus and powering it with 'psychic' energy; what escaped him is that the psychological is not the antithesis of the physical. A thought is no more 'nonphysical' than it is 'physical,' it is 'not nothing,' it is 'no-thing.' The problem that Freud attempted to resolve here was a general one then and today in science at large. We insist that, nouns like 'thought,' 'idea,' and 'psychical structure,' must have an existence apart from their surround, because we are raised to believe that what is 'real' has spatial extension and is tangible. Obviously, if thoughts and other psychological events are not material entities, they must be nonmaterial entities, and if they are not neuronal impulses in the brain alone, they must be nonmaterial entities in a nonmaterial apparatus. As Susanne Langer points out—such words are verbal nouns; there is no such entity as a 'thought,' there is only thinking, an activity of the brain. At best, unconscious thought and conscious thought are terms describing phases of brain functioning. 'Thinking' and 'running' are activities inseparable from their underlying organic substrate; to describe thoughts as existing between neurons, as Freud does . . . is equivalent to claiming that running is made up of 'runs' that exist between the muscle spindles." M. F. Basch, "Theory Formation in Chapter VII: A Critique," *J. Am. Psychoanal. Assoc.* 24 (1976): 90.

21. Ricoeur, *Freud and Philosophy,* p. 428.

22. "The nucleus of the *Ucs.* consists of instinctual representatives which seek to discharge their cathexis. . . . There are in this system no negation, no doubt, no degrees of uncertainty: all this is only introduced by the work of the censorship between the *Ucs.* and the *Pcs.* . . . The processes of the system *Ucs.* are *timeless;* i.e. they are not ordered temporally, are not altered by the passage of time; they have no reference to time at all. Reference to time is bound up, once again, with the work of the system *Cs.* . . . The *Ucs.* processes pay just as little regard to *reality.* They are subject to the pleasure principle. . . . [The characteristics of the *Ucs.* are] *exemption from mutual contradiction, primary process . . . timelessness,* and *replacement of external by psychical reality.* " S. Freud, "The Unconscious" (1915), *S.E.* 14: 186–7. (These attributes will later be given to the id, the newer agency described to make up for deficiencies in the theory content of the *Ucs.*)

But; but; but: "[Freud's] main reason for refusing to extend the analogy with other minds to the attribution of consciousness to the Unconscious is that: 'a consciousness of which its own possessor knows nothing is something very different from a consciousness belonging to another person, and it is questionable whether such a consciousness, lacking, as it does, its most important characteristic, deserves any discussion at all.'

"But of course if the Unconscious were conscious of *itself,* then it would have a 'possessor' distinct from the subject of ordinary consciousness in the same person, and it would be only the latter who was unconscious of these conscious states of the Unconscious. However, Freud also offers other reasons against their consciousness, namely problems of inconsistency, peculiarity and incoherence, as well as indeterminateness in the number of subjects required to accommodate all other states consciously in more or less unified fashion." T. Nagel, "Freud's Anthropomorphism," in *Freud: A Collection of Critical Essays,* ed. R. Wollheim (New York: Anchor Books, 1974), p. 16.

23. "Among the derivatives of the *Ucs.* instinctual impulses, of the sort we have

described, there are some which unite in themselves characters of an opposite kind. On the one hand, they are highly organized, free from self-contradiction, have made use of every acquisition of the system *Cs.* and would hardly be distinguished in our judgement from the formations of that system. On the other hand they are unconscious and are incapable of becoming conscious. Thus *qualitatively* they belong to the system *Pcs.,* but *factually* to the *Ucs.* Their origin is what decides their fate." S. Freud, "Communication Between the Two Systems" (1915), *S.E.* 14: 190–1.

24. Not all. For instance, Dr. W. W. Meissner wrote to me: "Your question 'Who is the dreamer' touches on a very sensitive and difficult point. The issue is the one that Gilbert Ryle raised in regard to the 'ghost in the machine.' Putting it in other terms, the problem is one that psychoanalytic theorists have assiduously avoided namely, the question where is the 'person' in the psychoanalytic account of psychic functioning. The ego psychologists have stood on both sides of the question, at one point insisting on the conceptualization of the ego as an organization of psychic functions (the more or less structural account of the ego) and the opposite account, which appoints the ego as the personal agent who would stand in as the respondent to your inquiry. For them it is the ego, then, who is the dreamer, who makes the dreams, or who makes the sexual excitement. There is an obvious tension, if not contradiction, in this approach which has been focused and I think characterized perhaps somewhat extremely by Guntrip in his addressing the question of the 'personal ego.'

"The problem has also been side-stepped by our too easy resort to anthropomorphizing as a vehicle of conceptualizing. While one can readily admit that this is a highly metaphorical and intermediary step in the evolution of the theory, one also tends to bypass certain critical questions such as the one you raise. We end up with a substitute formulation in terms of multiple agencies carrying out differential functions and lose sight in the process that we are in fact talking about theoretical constructions which are a way of articulating and understanding the activity of an integral and unitary personality. My own thoughts about this problem have led in the direction of settling for the structural view of the ego as a theoretical construct concerned with the organization of functions and correspondingly displacing the problem of the theoretical status of the person or personalized agent into the realm of the self. It has occurred to me, for example, that over and above preoccupations with narcissism it is precisely the inability of analytic theory to conceptualize the person that has in effect called forth an increasingly elaborate account of the self. If one follows Kohut's account it becomes quite clear that the reassessment of narcissism requires a different set of concepts to account for intrapsychic experience than is provided by merely the structural (tripartite) theory, but it is not clear that this added dimension plays into the problem. The object-relations theorists have come much closer to focusing the issues related to the concept of self, particularly in terms of the personalizing of experience and action. Having said that, it becomes quite apparent that, if one follows through on that line of thinking, it opens up a very difficult and very problematical realm of discourse where a considerable amount of thinking and refocusing of clinical material and formulating of it in terms which articulate it with our pre-existent concepts about the operations and interrelations of psychic agencies. The interesting thing about Schafer's work is that in focusing on the language of action he in fact steps back from the structural account and reintroduces the aspects of a personal agency which in fact gives rise both to the structural construction and to the demand for an articulated and developed concept of the self and its functions and capacities. Schafer would like to say that one need not go into that dark forest, but I think the theoretical demands cannot be so easily avoided."

25. R. Schafer, *A New Language for Psychoanalysis* (New Haven, Conn.: Yale University Press, 1976), p. 86.

26. Ibid., p. 133.

27. Ibid.

28. Ibid., p. 318.

29. W. W. Meissner, "New Horizons in Metapsychology," *J. Am. Psychoanal. Assoc.* 24 (1976): 177, reports on a paper given by Schafer.

30. W. I. Grossman and B. Simon, "Anthropomorphism: Motive, Meaning, and Causality," *Psychoanal. Study Child* 24 (1969): 78–111; A. Sugarman, "Object-Relations Theory: A Reconciliation of Phenomenology and Ego Psychology," *Bull. Menninger Clin.* 41 (1977): 113–30.

31. As E. Peterfreund warns in "Information Systems and Psychoanalysis," *Psychol. Issues* 7, monograph no. 25/26 (1971): 70–4.

32. A. M. Mendez and H. J. Fine, "A Short History of the British School of Object Relations and Ego Psychology," *Bull. Menninger Clin.* 40 (1976): 358.

33. W. R. D. Fairbairn, *An Object-Relations Theory of the Personality* (New York: Basic Books, 1952), p. 98.

34. Ibid., p. 85.

35. See also Winnicott: real self, false self, conformist ego, false self on a conformity basis, thinking self, central self, incommunicado self. Anyone can invent his own system. The present enthusiasm is for the total self, the nuclear self, the under-stimulated self, the overstimulated self, the fragmentary self, the body self, the mind self, the overburdened self. Yet in some ways my position is like that of such object-relations theorists as Fairbairn and Guntrip, who see all mental activity as, by definition, structured and therefore believe that, as Sugarman puts it: "All is ego [I would say, with Schafer, "All is I," or "All is self"], and the ego is a dynamic structure from which the dynamic substructures of personality originate. The concept of dynamic structure means that no separation exists between energy and structure. Psychological structure implicitly contains its own motivational source, in this case, internal objects" ("Object-Relations Theory," p. 123). This means that any psychologic activity we shall ever observe, in others or ourselves—except in earliest infancy—is already modified ("structured") or it would not be "mental."

36. Here is Fairbairn, in honorable agony: "I myself feel convinced that the basic endopsychic situation above described is the situation underlying Freud's description of the mental apparatus in terms of ego, id, and super-ego. It is certainly the endopsychic situation upon which I deliberately base the revised theory of mental structure which I now submit, and which is couched in terms of central ego, libidinal ego, and internal saboteur. As it would, of course, be natural to expect, there is a general correspondence between Freud's concepts and those which I have now come to adopt. In the case of 'the central ego' the correspondence to Freud's 'ego' is fairly close from a functional standpoint; but there are important differences between the two concepts. Unlike Freud's 'ego,' the 'central ego' is not conceived as originating out of something else (the 'id'), or as constituting a passive structure dependent for its activity upon impulses proceeding from the matrix out of which it originated, and on the surface of which it rests. On the contrary, the 'central ego' is conceived as a primary and dynamic structure, from which, as we shall shortly see, the other mental structures are subsequently derived. The 'libidinal ego' corresponds, of course, to Freud's 'id'; but, whereas according to Freud's view the 'ego' is a derivative of the 'id,' according to my view the 'libidinal ego' (which corresponds to the 'id') is a derivative of the 'central ego' (which corresponds to the 'ego'). The 'libidinal ego' also differs from the 'id' in that it is conceived, not as a mere reservoir of instinctive impulses, but as a dynamic structure comparable to the 'central ego,' although differing from the latter in various respects, e.g. in its more infantile character, in a lesser degree of organization, in a smaller measure of adaptation to reality and in a greater devotion to internalized objects. The 'internal saboteur' differs from the 'super-ego' in a number of respects. For one thing

it is in no sense conceived as an internal object. It is wholly an ego structure, although, as we have seen, it is very closely associated with an internal object. Actually, the 'super-ego' corresponds not so much to the 'internal saboteur' as to a compound of this structure and its associated object. . . . At the same time, the 'internal saboteur' is unlike the 'super-ego' in that it is conceived as, in itself, devoid of all moral significance. Thus I do not attribute the affect of guilt to its activity, although this activity is unquestionably a prolific source of anxiety. Such anxiety may, of course, merge with guilt; but the two affects are theoretically distinct. Here it should be noted that, whilst introducing the conception of internal saboteur, I am not prepared to abandon the conception of the super-ego as I have now come to abandon that of the id. On the contrary, it seems to me impossible to offer any satisfactory psychological explanation of guilt in the absence of the super-ego; but the super-ego must be regarded as originating at a higher level of mental organization than that at which the internal saboteur operates. Exactly how the activities of the two structures are related must in the meantime remain an open question." *An Object-Relations Theory of the Personality,* pp. 106–7.

37. Reik speaks of "the abuse of the analytical terminology . . . where a technical term is inserted because either the concept or the conceiving is lacking. This passionate preference for analytical technical terms recalls the behavior of the comedian Karl Valentin of Munich, who appeared on the stage with spectacles without lenses. Asked for the reason, he replied: 'They're better than nothing at all!' " T. Reik, *Masochism in Modern Man,* trans. M. H. Beigel and G. M. Kurth (New York: Farrar, Straus & Rinehart, 1941), p. 406.

38. M. M. Gill, "Psychic Energy Reconsidered: Discussion," *J. Am. Psychoanal. Assoc.* 25 (1977): 595.

39. S. Freud, "On the Universal Tendency to Debasement in the Sphere of Love" (1912), *S.E.* 11: 181.

40. See, for example, Gill, "Psychic Energy Reconsidered."

41. Ricoeur, *Freud and Philosophy,* p. 66.

42. L. S. Kubie, "Problems and Techniques of Psychoanalytic Validation and Progress," in *Psychoanalysis as Science,* ed. E. Pumpian-Mindlin (Stanford, Calif.: Stanford University Press, 1952), pp. 46–124.

43. "The close association in our literature between the concepts of peremptoriness, instinctual drives, and psychic energy apparently leads many to believe that the abandonment of the concept of psychic energy amounts to giving up the idea of instinctual drives. That is simply not true. What is true is that the biological phenomena related to instinctual drives cannot be directly translated into the realm of psychoanalytic psychology, but become relevant there only in terms of their meaningfulness, in terms of motivational systems as exemplified in Rosenblatt and Thickstun's discussion" (Gill, "Psychic Energy Reconsidered," p. 593). The discussions by Klein, Gill, and Holzman in *Psychol. Issues* 9, monograph no. 36 (1976) are invaluable here. So are those by Schafer, Rosenblatt and Thickstun, Kubie, Rubinstein, Holt, Gardner, Klein, and Peterfreund; for references, see M. F. Basch, "Psychoanalysis and Communication Science," in *The Annual of Psychoanalysis,* ed. Chicago Institute of Psychoanalysis (New York: International Universities Press, 1976), 4: 420–1. A good review of the pros and cons is in R. S. Wallerstein, "Psychoanalysis as Science: Its Present Status and Its Future Tasks," *Psychol. Issues* 9, monograph no. 36 (1976): 211–13 n.

Here are quotations from Basch that emphasize our responsibility to focus on meaning:

"The blips and squiggles on an EEG, no matter how refined that instrument will become, will never be memory, fantasy, or anything resembling either. Freud went too far when he attempted to divorce mentation from the neurological. Neurological activity is the necessary condition for thought processes in the human being—necessary, but not sufficient. In other animals attraction, avoidance, or inactivity is determined by the effect of stimuli on inherited reaction patterns. In man, reaction patterns are for the most part culturally determined and it is the *symbolic* significance of stimuli that is important. The power of activity in the brain does not lie in the energy expended in the transmission, but in the meaning of the message it conveys. We are so used to equating force with energy that we do not stop to consider that most of the time when we speak of 'energy' we are referring to the power of signals. A traffic light enforces behavior, not through the energy it transmits to the driver, but through the message it delivers. A psychoanalyst's interpretation may make a patient feel more 'energetic,' but that is only a manner of speaking, for no measurement will reveal any significant energy alteration in the patient. What has happened is that a correctly timed and accurate interpretation has conveyed a novel perspective to the patient which presents him with a degree of choice he has not had before—the freedom to choose between previously unavailable alternatives creates an emotional state misnamed 'energetic.' " "Theory Formation in Chapter VII," p. 91.

"Behavior is not determined by energy transformations within the brain but by the selective effect that signals have in activating and forming neural connections. This function is studied by communication theory, which quantifies in terms of information, not energy." M. F. Basch, "Toward a Theory That Encompasses Depression: A Revision of Existing Causal Hypotheses in Psychoanalysis," in *Depression and Human Existence,* ed. E. J. Anthony and T. Benedek (Boston: Little, Brown & Co., 1975), p. 495.

"It is incorrect in principle to derive a theory of cognition (perception, learning, memory, conception, etc.) from a clinical method that is avowedly limited to investigating the significance or *meaning* of conflict in thought or deed. . . . The concept of a psychic apparatus does not represent an inference *from* psychoanalytic data, but rather, speculations *about* psychoanalytic data." Basch, "Theory Formation in Chapter VII," pp. 61, 62.

On the other hand, Galatzer-Levy reminds us that the centuries-long elaboration of the concept of physical energy took the same course as the present controversies on the existence of psychic energy. See R. M. Galatzer-Levy, "Psychic Energy: A Historical Perspective," in *The Annual of Psychoanalysis,* ed. Chicago Institute of Psychoanalysis (New York: International Universities Press, 1976), 4: 41–61.

Holt is also worth quoting: "Meanings still have no recognized place in metapsychology; 'drive-derivative' and equivalent expressions are merely a back door by which they are smuggled in despite their lack of proper scientific credentials. For the odd paradox of metapsychology is that despite its apparent reliance on 'psychical' concepts, these are modeled after the concepts of physics (energy, force, structure) and physiology (excitation, pathway), and the mere addition of the adjective does not convert them into units or dimensions of semantic, phenomenal, or other meaningful realms. . . .

"Let me remind you that Freud worked productively for his first fifteen years as a psychoanalyst without the concept of *Trieb,* relying primarily on wish as his motivational term. The main dynamic concept in *Studies on Hysteria*—affect-charged, repressed memories—has the major defining properties of wish: it is a cognitive-affective concept, framed in terms of meanings and potentially pleasant or unpleasant outcomes of possible courses of action. The principal motivational concept used in the brilliant case history of Dora and in Freud's masterpiece of combined clinical insight and theoretical elaboration, *The Interpretation of Dreams,* is wish. With it, he was able to do almost everything that an analyst needs to be able to do with a motivational concept, and even after introducing *Trieb,* he did not cease to make frequent use of wish. Therefore, substituting wish for drive means coming back to clinical home ground, while abandoning a largely redundant part of metapsychology that has failed to work, despite its popularity among analysts who have the mistaken impression that drive has the better scientific footing.

"One of the advantages of wish is that it does not easily lend itself to the reifying and personifying (anthropomorphic) fallacies with which drive is so rife. A wish implies a person doing the wishing, and we are unaccustomed to speaking of a wish as if it had a life and mind of its own, as the Freudian *Triebe* so often seem to. A wish can be conscious or unconscious; it can conflict with another one; it can be countered, blocked, or modified by defenses and controls. Wishes are plainly near cousins to *plans* on one side (secondary process) and to fantasies on the other (primary process); they are concrete, often immediately available to introspection, not lofty or vague abstractions.

"With the concept of wish, we can reassert, in answer to the behaviorists and other mechanistically inclined theorists, that behavior *is* purposive, that fears, longings, plans, fantasies, and other mental processes are not epiphenomena, but must be central to any adequate psychology of human behavior, and that the person is often not conscious of what his purposes are. Those who find it hard to shake off reductionistic habits of thought may find these ideas more acceptable if they think of wishes and plans as strictly analogous to the programs of computers.

"To those who object that wishes are not biological enough, that they do not readily lend themselves to the explanation of psychosomatic problems, I would say that they can express our limited understanding just as well as the metapsychological language of instincts or drives, and have the advantage of not committing us to a great deal of pseudoexplanatory mythology that does not have satisfactory grounding in fact. Before we can begin to make any more progress in this complicated area, we have to agree to stop pretending that we have answers to insoluble philosophical problems. No matter what metaphysical position you take, there remains an impenetrable mystery in the fact that subjective experience exists in a physiochemical world. Perhaps we shall someday learn what are the sufficient conditions for a physiochemical system and take on attributes we call mental; at present, we just do not know." R. R. Holt, "Drive or Wish? A Reconsideration of the Psychoanalytic Theory of Motivation," *Psychol. Issues* 9, monograph no. 36 (1976): 168 n., 179–81.

Good. But who does the wishing?

44. Ricoeur, *Freud and Philosophy,* p. 70.

45. S. Freud, "Anxiety and Instinctual Life" (1933), *S.E.* 22:85.

46. G. Ryle, *The Concept of Mind* (New York: Grove Press, 1949), p. 186.

47. Peterfreund, "Information Systems and Psychoanalysis," p. 228.

48. Ibid., p. 266. Cf. Erdelyi and Goldberg: "The 'censors' in the model necessarily imply a complex semantically-tuned control mechanism, capable of making decisions based on expected consequences. This mechanism formally emerged as the 'Ego' in Freud's late writings, and was specifically attributed the control of defense processes. The actual processes themselves were again formulated through a multiplicity of analogic devices. Direct inhibition, i.e., blocking of information—what many would conceive of as repression in the narrow sense—and displacement, were typically formulated in terms of vector dynamics involving 'forces' or neurological 'excitations' ('cathexes' and 'counter-cathexes'). In other cases, as we have seen, 'attentional' mechanisms were imported. In still other cases, as in projection and reversal, transformational notions were introduced. Political concepts, obviously, such as 'compromise,' 'censorship,' 'suppression-repression' were also frequently invoked, as were analogies from the arts ('symbolism,' 'deep meanings,' 'interpretation,' 'displacement of accent,' 'condensations,' 'plastic word representation,' etc.). This wild sprawl of incompatible metaphor sketches indicates to us that Freud had pushed too far ahead of his time and had outrun —and run out of—sensible linguistic vehicles through which to give coherent expression of his theory. In support of this contention we offer the fact that so many of the apparently intractable problems and contradictions besetting Freud's patchwork system dissolve, with not the slightest effort, with the application of the computer analogy. . . .

"While it would be ingenuous to suppose that the computer analogy provides a conceptual panacea for the theoretical problems in the field, it nevertheless yields a momentous breakthrough. First, as we have already indicated, it makes possible a grand unification, into a single coherent scheme, of the hitherto unwieldly patchwork of component theories, which are often redundant, sometimes contradictory, and invariably expressed in incompatible metaphor languages. The computer, then, provides a theoretical *lingua franca*. There is probably no defense process discussed by Freud which does not naturally lend itself to a computer artification. Moreover, the postulated mechanisms supporting such defense processes, such as control processes, perceptual systems, memory buffers, censors (filters, decision nodes), and so forth, are not only not bizarre, but obvious and essential features of any of today's 'compound instruments.' " *Let's Not Sweep Repression Under the Rug* (in press).

49. Gill, "Psychic Energy Reconsidered," p. 591.

PART 4. Conclusions

Chapter 12. Treatment and Research

1. "I have strongly emphasized the value of constructions. We cannot do without them in the analysis of the neurotic patient. They form the foundation for his improvement. To point out the value of constructions is perhaps the most important task in our supervisory analyses. . . . The construction, instead of being a cerebral endeavor—an opinion held frequently by those who try to cook their meal on the analytic stove— is essential for the entire field of analysis. Through his constructions, the analyst reveals himself to be in the service of helping the patient as well as in the service of furthering science." M. Katan, "Childhood Memories as Contents of Schizophrenic Hallucinations and Delusions," *Psychoanal. Study Child* 30 (1975): 373.

2. M. Viederman, "The Influence of the Person of the Analyst on Structural Change: A Case Report," *Psychoanal. Q.* 45 (1976): 231–49, and A. Namnum, "Activity and Personal Involvement in Psychoanalytic Technique," *Bull. Menninger Clin.* 40 (1976): 105–17, have most helpful reviews and discussions of these issues; and of course there is R. R. Greenson's classic work *The Technique and Practice of Psychoanalysis* (New York: International Universities Press, 1967).

3. S. Freud, *An Outline of Psycho-analysis* (1938), *S.E.* 23: 202.

4. "Unless we are careful, any interpretation of the transference: 'You are treating me as if I . . .' will imply the underlying '. . . and you know very well that I am not really what you think I am.' [How fundamentally different, then, is my analytic technique, for I believe that if we are careful—i.e., in touch with the psychic reality inside all but certain psychotic or brain-damaged patients—any interpretation of the transference in some way implies: "You are treating me as if I . . . and yet you know very well that I am not really what you think I am."] Fortunately we are saved by the technique: we do not actually make this underlying comment. Speaking more fundamentally, the analytical rule should be understood as . . . an absolute suspension of all reality judgements. This places us on the same level as the unconscious, which knows no such judgements. [I think "the unconscious" knows such judgments very well indeed]." J. LaPlanche and J.-B. Pontalis, "Fantasy and the Origins of Sexuality," *Int. J. Psychoanal.* 49 (1968): 2.

5. Perhaps the form all analysts take with their patients has in it a touch of Belle's Director. L. Friedman, "The Therapeutic Alliance," *Int. J. Psychoanal.* 50 (1969): 139–53, alerts us to the paradox inherent in the therapeutic alliance: that the patient's "necessary deep attachment to the physician"—the transference—must serve both the patient's primitive libidinal needs and the reality-bound desire for freedom from the tyranny of those needs. Can a patient use the first to accomplish the second? If Belle

had put that into words, she might have asked, "How can you expect me to analyze my dread of being abandoned, if the end result of my analysis will be an abandonment: the ending of analysis?"

With Belle, I had to dig out (it did not occur simply with quiet interpretation) her intention to be "cured" by remaining forever attached to me, even if analysis formally ended. What in innumerable ways was a good working alliance—a sensible part of herself had the same goals for treatment that I had—was nonetheless underlain by the understanding, for a long time unspoken and in part unconscious, that by being a cooperative patient she could guarantee that I would never let her go. At the heart of the positive transference with all patients may be the belief "I shall never be abandoned." See also M. Schmideberg, "After the Analysis . . . ," *Psychoanal. Q.* 7 (1938): 122–42.

6. E. Becker, *Angel in Armor* (New York: George Braziller, 1969), p. 29.

7. L. Rangell, "A Psychoanalytic Perspective Leading Currently to the Syndrome of the Compromise of Integrity," *Int. J. Psychoanal.* 55 (1974): 3–12; Rangell, "Lessons from Watergate: A Derivative for Psychoanalysis," *Psychoanal. Q.* 45 (1976): 37–61.

Recall Orwell's "doublethink": "To know and not to know, to be conscious of complete truthfulness while telling carefully constructed lies, to hold simultaneously two opinions which cancelled out, knowing them to be contradictory and believing in both of them, to use logic against logic, to repudiate morality while laying claim to it, to believe that democracy was impossible and that the Party was the guardian of democracy, to forget whatever it was necessary to forget, then to draw it back into memory again at the moment when it was needed, and then promptly to forget it again, and above all, to apply the same process to the process itself—that was the ultimate subtlety: consciously to induce unconsciousness, and then, once again, to become unconscious of the act of hypnosis you had just performed. Even to understand the word 'doublethink' involved the use of doublethink." G. Orwell, *1984* (New York: New American Library, 1950), pp. 32–3.

8. Rangell, "Lessons from Watergate," pp. 53, 55.

Appendix A

1. G. Ryle, *The Concept of Mind* (New York: Grove Press, 1949).

2. L. A. White, *The Science of Culture: A Study of Man and Civilization* (New York: Grove Press, 1949).

3. M. F. Basch, "Psychoanalysis and Communication Science," *The Annual of Psychoanalysis,* ed. Chicago Institute of Psychoanalysis (New York: International Universities Press, 1976), 4: 385–421.

4. J. Bronowski, *The Identity of Man* (Garden City, N.Y.: Doubleday & Co., 1949).

5. M. F. Basch, "Developmental Psychology and Explanatory Theory in Psychoanalysis," *The Annual of Psychoanalysis,* ed. Chicago Institute of Psychoanalysis (New York: International Universities Press, 1977), 5: 229–63.

6. M. F. Basch, "The Concept of Affect: A Re-examination," *J. Am. Psychoanal. Assoc.* 24 (1976): 759–77.

7. J. Piaget and B. Inhelder, *The Psychology of the Child,* trans. H. Weaver (New York: Basic Books, 1969).

8. W. T. Powers, *Behavior: The Control of Perception* (Chicago: Aldine Publishing Co., 1973).

9. S. Bach, "On the Narcissistic State of Consciousness," *Int. J. Psychoanal.* 58 (1977): 209–33.

10. K. S. Lashley, "Cerebral Organization and Behavior," in *The Brain and Human*

Behavior: Proceeds of the Association for Research in Nervous and Mental Disease, ed. H. C. Solomon, S. Cobb, and W. Penfield (Baltimore: Williams & Wilkins Co., 1958), pp. 1–18.

11. M. F. Basch, "Toward a Theory That Encompasses Depression: A Revision of Existing Causal Hypotheses in Psychoanalysis," in *Depression and Human Existence,* ed. E. J. Anthony and T. Benedek (Boston: Little, Brown & Co., 1975), pp. 485–534.

12. Basch, "Developmental Psychology and Explanatory Theory in Psychoanalysis."

13. M. F. Basch, "Interference with Perceptual Transformation in the Service of Defense," in *The Annual of Psychoanalysis,* ed. Chicago Institute of Psychoanalysis (New York: International Universities Press, 1974), 2: 89–97.

14. K. M. Colby, "Mind Models," *Math. Biosci.* (1978): 159–85.

Appendix B. Fixing

1. J. Bowlby, *Attachment* (New York: Basic Books, 1969).

2. Kubie recognized these issues twenty-five years ago: "In essence, my thesis is that in all forms of adult human psychopathology, distortions of symbolic functions occur which cannot occur in the human infant before symbolic functioning begins, nor in animal forms which are not capable of a high degree of symbolic thinking, feeling, and behavior.

"This thesis raises two important subsidiary issues: can the concepts of neurosis and psychosis be applied to subhuman forms without introducing anthropomorphic fallacies? Secondly, can these concepts, derived as they are primarily from the clinical study of adults, be applied to infants at an age before they are capable of at least a rudimentary form of symbolic thinking, feeling, and behavior? This, in turn, calls into question the entire structure of Klein's theory of infantile psychopathology, which implicitly and explicitly adultomorphizes the infant. Klein invests the infant's unmyelinated cerebrum and his partially myelinated afferent and efferent pathways with adult conscious and unconscious symbolic perceptions, conceptions, and fantasy formations; in short, with the full complement of adult psychic equipment. . . . For the time being . . . there remains one basic reason for making a clear-cut distinction between psychopathological processes the essence of which consists in the distortion of symbolic functions, and on the other hand those psychopathological processes which arise through the distorting impact of highly charged emotional experiences occurring at an early age, before symbolic processes are established. These latter can be induced experimentally in preverbal animal species, which are capable of a limited degree of symbolic function at most. They can also occur as a response to primitive emotional stresses, when these occur in preverbal stages of human life, while the capacity for symbolic function still remains similarly limited. Such presymbolic changes leave residual emotional disturbances, which in turn influence the symbolic aspects of all later responses to injury. Furthermore, as Spitz and others have shown, they may influence the later acquisition of symbolic functions. But it is the disturbance in the symbolic function itself which characterizes adult human psychopathology in a pathognomonic fashion. Ultimately it will be necessary to work out in detail the interrelations of these two fundamental aspects of psychopathology." L. S. Kubie, "The Distortion of the Symbolic Process in Neurosis and Psychosis," *J. Am. Psychoanal. Assoc.* 1 (1953): 64, 66.

3. H. Lichtenstein, "Identity and Sexuality," *J. Am. Psychoanal. Assoc.* 9 (1961): 204–8. Italics in original.

Index

About the Author

Robert J. Stoller, M.D., is a psychoanalyst and professor of psychiatry at the School of Medicine of the University of California at Los Angeles, where he teaches medical students and psychiatric residents. He is a member of the American Psychoanalytic Association and received his psychoanalytic training at the Los Angeles Psychoanalytic Institute. Professor Stoller is the author of numerous papers on the development of gender identity. He has previously published four books on the subject: *Sex and Gender, Volume I: On the Development of Masculinity and Femininity; Splitting: A Case of Female Masculinity;* and *Sex and Gender, Volume II: The Transsexual Experiment.* His most recent book, *Perversion: The Erotic Form of Hatred,* was published by Pantheon in 1975. In addition to his research in gender identity, Professor Stoller has a continuing interest and involvement in research in medical education.